GOD,
COUNTRY,
NOTRE DAME

GOD, COUNTRY, NOTRE DAME

Theodore M. Hesburgh, C.S.C.

WITH

Jerry Reedy

DOUBLEDAY

New York   London   Toronto   Sydney   Auckland

PUBLISHED BY DOUBLEDAY
a division of Bantam Doubleday Dell Publishing Group, Inc.
666 Fifth Avenue, New York, New York 10103

DOUBLEDAY and the portrayal of an anchor with a dolphin
are trademarks of Doubleday,
a division of Bantam Doubleday Dell Publishing Group, Inc.

Photographs without credits appear
courtesy of the University of Notre Dame.

Library of Congress Cataloging-in-Publication Data
Hesburgh, Theodore Martin, 1917–
God, country, Notre Dame: the autobiography of Theodore M. Hesburgh /
Theodore M. Hesburgh with Jerry Reedy.
1. Hesburgh, Theodore Martin, 1917–   . 2. University of Notre Dame—Presidents—
Biography. 3. College presidents—Indiana—Biography. 4. Catholic Church—United
States—Clergy—Biography. 5. Social reformers—United States—Biography.
I. Reedy, Jerry. II. Title.
LD4112.7 1952.A3   1990
378.1'11'—dc20
[B]   90-33371
CIP
ISBN 0-385-26680-4

To my mother and father for the early years, and to my colleague and friend Father Ned Joyce and my secretary, Helen Hosinski, for all the years since.

CONTENTS

PREFACE

Someone once asked me what I would want engraved on my tombstone if I were allowed only one word.

"Priest," I answered.

From the age of six I knew what I wanted to be: "Priest." It was an integral part of my being. I just knew it. Having been a Catholic priest now for more than forty-seven years, I am happy in my choice. I want nothing else, have never wanted anything else, never *been* anything else but a priest. I say this now so that you, the reader, will know where I am coming from as you read the thoughts and events of my life.

I have traveled far and wide, far beyond the simple parish I envisioned as a young man. My obligation of service has led me into diverse yet interrelated roles: college teacher, theologian, president of a great university, counselor to four popes and six presidents. Excuse the list, but once called to public service, I have held fourteen presidential appointments over the years, dealing with the social issues of our times, including civil rights, peaceful uses of atomic energy, campus unrest, amnesty for Vietnam offenders, Third World development, and immigration reform.

But deep beneath it all, wherever I have been, whatever I have done, I have always and everywhere considered myself essentially a priest.

I prostrated myself before the main altar at Notre Dame and was ordained in 1943. Since then I have offered Mass every day, save one, and I have prayed the breviary each day, too. Even so, as I get older, it is increasingly clear to me that I know God all too little. I believe in Him profoundly, I pray to Him often, and I am grateful that He revealed Himself to us as Jesus Christ, Our Lord and Savior, Who became one of us and gave His life for love of us.

What is a priest? St. Thomas Aquinas said that a priest is a mediator; that he stands as a kind of bridge between God and humankind. The priest tries to bring God's word and grace to humankind and strives as well to bring humankind to God, in faith, hope, and love. I have tried to be that kind of priest.

Jesus said that when we feed the hungry, give drink to the thirsty, clothe the naked, visit the sick and the prisoner, open our hearts to the stranger, we are really loving and caring for Him, especially as He is found in the poor and abandoned. Thus does God become a living and visible reality all around us. All human beings are our brothers and sisters, all are our neighbors, especially when in need. It matters not whether they are white or black, red or yellow, men or women, Eastern or Western, Northern or Southern, young or old, intelligent or dull, good or bad, attractive or repulsive. I believe that since we all are created in the image of God, I cannot love God without loving and serving them as best I can.

"What you did for one of these, My least brethren, you did it for Me," said Christ. If one believes this, it becomes a way of life. I think it was easier for me than for most others because I had the grace to be accepted into a religious order: the Congregation of Holy Cross. That meant, besides living in a great community of my peers, taking the vows of poverty, chastity, and obedience.

Poverty in the religious sense is a great blessing. I was freed to proclaim the primacy of the spiritual in life, not to be bound to the search for material possessions. I always had enough to eat, clothes to wear, a simple room in which to sleep, and money when it was needed for books or travel or incidentals. Actually, I came to deal with billions of dollars, but not for myself, not to have and to hold, but only to use for others in need. I always felt wonderfully free in a world too often shackled to material possessions: bank accounts, houses, cars, clothes, whatever. I had what I needed and needed nothing more. I raised and spent gobs of money, but always for good causes, for the good of those in material or spiritual need.

The vow of celibacy probably seems inhibiting or even unnatural to many, and it certainly is not a common calling. But for me, it has been, again, a liberating experience. Since I didn't belong to anyone, I belonged to everyone. Each time I am called "Father," I know that the caller owns me, as a child does a parent, and that he or she has a call on me for anything needed, especially compassion and understanding in the spirit of Christian love: loving and serving Jesus Christ by loving and serving all those in need, anywhere and everywhere.

When Christmas cards arrive each year, I am always reminded that so many of my lifelong friends and closest collaborators in good works are not Catholics or even believers. I have been inspired by all of them. I continue to love them and hope they love me. We have been comrades-in-arms in many difficult and trying crusades for justice and peace, for human rights, for economic, social, and political development in the Third World, for ecology, and for ecumenism.

In all these endeavors, especially those for His least brethren wherever they are, God knows that I am trying to love Him. In some mysterious way, I believe that these friends of mine who do not share my religious beliefs will also be seen by God as loving and serving Him, even though they may not realize it. I don't worry about their salvation. They know why I am doing these things, and I am sure that God recognizes and will eternally reward their goodness, as St. Paul put it, *in caritate non ficta*, in unalloyed love.

The vow of obedience is the hardest in that one gives up that most precious of divine gifts, freedom. In obedience, one does what one is assigned to do. My whole life as a priest would have been vastly different, and probably less productive, had I been able to do what I wanted to do, instead of what I was assigned to do. On three occasions early in my priestly life, I was asked my preference in possible alternate assignments. I voiced my wish and each time I was assigned to the alternative. Somehow, it worked out for the best.

In a curious, almost contradictory way, I have always felt unusually free. As long as I performed my primary assignment, the Congregation of Holy Cross allowed me extraordinary freedom to accept nonclerical opportunities to serve in a wide variety of national and international tasks. During my presidency of Notre Dame, I served (albeit part-time and concurrently) for forty-five years in the public sector and over sixty years in the private sector. That would not have happened if I had gone my own way in the beginning.

Again, in a curious and mysterious way which I attribute to the providence of God, although one seems to be giving up the familiar things that others enjoy—material goods, the wonderful pleasure of marriage and family, and one's precious freedom— somehow one still has an enormously challenging and satisfying life, which is to say, a happy one. I am under no delusion about being as holy as I should be—far from it—but at least I keep trying, and each day there is that palpable grace of God that somehow keeps me from going overboard, from taking myself too seriously, from losing hope. Through the years of learning and personal experience I believe I have become as much a realist as an optimist, and as such I do believe today with all my heart that within God's providence we can make this a better world.

As a priest, my faith and hope and love are in an eternal and not a temporal, terrestrial context. Even so, I am not about to default or give up on this globe we call earth. I still intend to spread faith, hope, and love as widely as I can during whatever time I am given to live here on earth. These three virtues are the keys to peace and justice and to a better and more equitable world.

GOD,
COUNTRY,
NOTRE DAME

ONE

GROWING UP
CATHOLIC

EVERY FAMILY should have an Aunt Mary, or better still, a Great-Aunt Mary, someone who cherishes and keeps the stories and relationships of the important people in your life before you were born. My Great-Aunt Mary Hesburgh lived in a big, open, airy house on Staten Island in New York City, where she worked as a matron in a jail, and when I visited with her she, being a genuine storyteller, loved to "pile it on" for me.

According to Aunt Mary, the Hesburghs came to America from the Grand Duchy of Luxembourg in 1848 during a big wave of immigration of young men fleeing the wars which tended to engulf the Low Countries of Luxembourg and Belgium. My great-grandfather, not wanting to be part of any of those conflicts, packed up his wife, two sons, and daughter, Mary, and came to America. One of those sons was my Great-Uncle Nick, who had gone blind in his late seventies and was living with Aunt Mary on Staten Island. The other was my grandfather, Theodore Bernard

Hesburgh, my namesake except that my middle name is Martin, after my Irish maternal grandfather.

Grandfather Hesburgh was quite a remarkable man. He worked his way through college selling patent medicines door-to-door in New York. In order to do that he learned Yiddish, Russian, German, French, Italian, and Spanish, as well as English, and he would fascinate me with demonstrations of how you could say the same thing in so many different languages. His facility with languages delighted me and I am sure that's one of the reasons I got interested in languages later on.

For most of his life my grandfather taught school. Somewhere along the line he started writing literary criticism and articles on economics and labor affairs for newspapers in New York. Despite his many gifts, my Grandfather Theodore had a lot of hard luck in life. His wife died at the age of twenty-one while giving birth to their third son. The baby died, too. Then, about two weeks later, a pharmacist botched a prescription for my grandfather's two-year-old son, and the boy died of poisoning. So, within a period of two weeks my grandfather had lost his wife and two of their three sons. Undoubtedly these tragedies caused something within him to snap. He abandoned his faith in God, quit his job, left New York City, and took his remaining son, my father at age three, and went to live with Hesburgh relatives on a corn farm in Iowa.

In Iowa my grandfather resumed teaching—in a one-room rural school—and continued writing for newspapers. But he was not the same man. The joy of life had gone out of him. It was not long before my Great-Aunt Mary journeyed out to Iowa to fetch her motherless nephew, my father, back to Staten Island, where she could mother him properly. My grandfather gave his consent but stayed on in Iowa himself. Aunt Mary was living with the widow of her brother and the widow's son, Lonnie, who was the same age as my father. The two boys grew up together like brothers. My father finished high school by going to classes at night. That's where he learned to write the old Gregg shorthand, a kind of squared-off business shorthand that was popular back then. My mother wrote it, too, and come to think of it, so did

Father John Cavanaugh, who was president of Notre Dame just before me.

I'm not sure exactly when my grandfather left Iowa, but I know it must have been several years after Aunt Mary came to collect my father. I know, also, that when he did move back to New York and took a small one-room apartment in Brooklyn, his luck didn't get any better. After enduring many years of failing eyesight, he went completely blind. This would be tough enough for anyone, but Grandfather was a voracious reader and blindness really devastated him. I never heard him complain. Not to be completely undone, he turned to the radio and I think he listened to it just about every waking moment in that little room.

When I was in my teens, my grandfather and I used to correspond. When his eyesight failed, of course, he couldn't write anymore, but he'd have his landlady read my letters to him. Occasionally I'd take that long trip from Staten Island to Brooklyn to visit with him. The last time I saw him was when I was in New York on my way to enroll at the Gregorian University in Rome. I was twenty years old, so that would have been in 1937. I got there about nine o'clock at night and found him sitting all by himself in total darkness. I asked him where the light switch was. He said he didn't know, because a light switch couldn't do you any good if you were blind.

I groped around for a chair, found one, and sat down. Then I told him how bad I felt that he had given up his faith. I think I said something like "Here I am giving my whole life to God and you don't even believe in Him."

"I didn't say I didn't believe in Him," he then said. Given what I knew about my grandfather, that statement made no sense to me at all. We got into a pretty fierce argument, with neither of us giving an inch.

Finally, I blurted out with an excess of youthful zeal, "I think the only way I'm going to get you back to God is to pray and sacrifice a lot for you." When I got to Rome, I did just that: praying and making personal sacrifices for him.

Before long I received word that he had phoned my cousin Elizabeth Keuthen and asked her to take him to the rectory of the local parish. There he asked the priest to hear his confession and then he started going to Mass regularly.

When my grandfather grew ill, Elizabeth put him in a Catholic hospital, where, she told me later, he said the rosary and received communion every day. "He died like a saint," the nuns told Elizabeth. Nuns who work in hospitals tend to say things like that, but it was a nice way for Grandfather Theodore to go, given his general outlook on life and everything that had happened to him. And I don't mind saying that the manner of his death was also a great consolation to me at the time.

I can cover my mother's side of the family much more briefly, because I don't know as much about it. My maternal grandfather was Martin Murphy, an utterly delightful Irishman whose parents brought him to this country when he was seven weeks old. He was about as different from my Grandfather Theodore as anyone I can imagine. There's a story about Grandfather Murphy's going to a county fair when he was a young man and drinking too much cider. According to this oft-told story, Grandfather Murphy in his cups got up in front of a large group of people, danced an exuberant jig, made a fool of himself by falling down on his backside, and then, feeling so embarrassed about it, swore off liquor for life.

Grandfather Murphy was a plumber who specialized in hot-water heating systems and lived with his wife on Franklin Avenue at 167th Street in the Bronx. He was a genial, lovable, fun-loving man who was also very religious and a daily communicant at six o'clock Mass. Tragedy struck when some obstetrical mishap resulted in his beloved wife's being confined to a wheelchair after she gave birth to their first and only child, my mother. When his wife died ten years later, Grandfather Murphy then married a rather sour spinster named Kilkenny, hoping that she would make a good mother for his only daughter. It did not work out that way. According to my mother, her stepmother rarely had a kind word for anyone and succeeded in making both my grandfather and her pretty miserable. She must have resented the close relationship between my mother and my grandfather, I think, because they doted on each other. Despite her stepmother, my mother managed to get through her growing-up years in pretty good shape.

After taking business courses in high school, Mother became the secretary to an executive at AT&T and, with the rapid growth of the telephone company at that time, believed she had a promising career ahead of her. Then, however, she met this tall, good-looking salesman who cared deeply for her. He turned her head and she changed her plans. Just about that time my mother, who had a lovely soprano singing voice, entered the Metropolitan Opera Auditions contest, and lo and behold, she won a four-year scholarship to study at La Scala in Italy. She gave that up, too, in order to marry my father.

I'm not sure how my mother and father first met, but I do remember my mother telling stories of parties in New York City and picnics on the Hudson. I got the idea they used to pal around together in a large group of young people, and so I suppose their relationship just grew naturally out of their social life. During their courtship my dad was sent to upstate New York by the Pittsburgh Plate Glass Company, the youngest salesman the company had ever sent out to develop a new territory. That did not stop him, however, from coming down to the Bronx regularly to see her. My mother's stepmother disliked my father intensely and did everything she could to break their engagement. She even accused my mother of wanting to marry my father solely to spite her. But my parents were obviously very much in love, and they went ahead and got married anyway. The wedding took place on February 2, 1913, at St. Augustine's Church in the Bronx, the parish my mother had grown up in, and then they moved to Syracuse, where my father worked.

Sometime during the earlier years of their marriage my dad switched from horse and buggy to a Model T, one of the first, and he was on the road in the Model T five days a week; but every Friday, of course, he'd come home for the weekend.

I grew up with three sisters. The firstborn was Mary Monica, who arrived nineteen months before I did. After me came Elizabeth Anne, whom we always called Betty, then Anne Marie. All the time that the girls and I grew up together I prayed for a brother. At age sixteen I finally got one. My parents named him James, and naturally we all called him Jimmy. While we did not grow up together, because I left home when he was only nine months old, we did become close later on.

My parents' first home was a second-floor apartment on Midland Avenue in Syracuse. I was baptized in St. Anthony's Church, close by, and my first year of school was at the public school kindergarten, which was just across the street from our apartment. We then moved to an apartment on Arthur Street in Most Holy Rosary parish. All five of us started school there and, except for kindergarten, I got all of my precollege schooling at Most Holy Rosary School.

My dad moved steadily up the ladder at Pittsburgh Plate Glass, opening up new branch operations for the company in Rochester, Albany, and Binghamton, and becoming manager of the Syracuse branch. Like most couples tasting the first fruits of success, my parents bought a house in a brand-new development called Strathmore. I remember vividly the excitement I felt the first time I walked into our new home, the smell of fresh timbers, the freedom that came with not having someone living over us or under us. It was 1925 and I was eight years old. That was home for me, the house in which I grew up until I went away to college and the seminary. My parents and Jimmy lived there for a long time after that.

My parents complemented each other very well. My mother, Irish on both sides of her family, was easily the romantic one of the pair. An aura of joy and merriment seemed to surround her all the time. She loved being with people; she laughed and sang even when she thought no one was around. My father by temperament was much more serious and sober about life. Maybe it was because of the hardships he knew as a boy and the influence of his father, but whatever the reason, he just wasn't a demonstrative, touchy-feely kind of person. Nor was he given to much gaiety. But he enjoyed life in his own way, taking a lot of satisfaction in his family and his work. He was steady as a rock, and when goodies where handed out, my father always took last place: We all came first.

Both my parents were very religious, though in ways that

reflected their disparate personalities. While my father practiced his religion very quietly, my mother was much more vocal, open, and even flamboyant about church matters. They had their share of differences, as all families do, but there never was any doubt that they loved each other deeply and that a sense of love and faith filled our home at all times. My mother loved to travel, to go out and do things, and she spoke often of wanting to live in New York City for its theater, opera, music, and culture. My father, on the other hand, thought New York City was a miserable place of smoke, noise, and dirt, and he hated travel. After all, he was on the road five days a week and heaven to him was sitting in front of the blazing fireplace for hours doing crossword puzzles, or puttering around the yard, or strolling through the woods looking for ferns or bushes he could transplant into our yard. Summers were special, though, and my father enjoyed as much as everyone our ritual of driving up to a cottage on Lake Ontario for our annual two-week summer vacation.

Ours was a typical Catholic household of the period. My sisters and I all went to Catholic schools. Encouraged to be "religious," we never missed Mass; some of us went every day. We never ate meat on Friday. We never lied, stole, or cheated—at least we never got away with any such sins. And we never, never talked about sex—in any way, shape, or form. For me the highest calling in life was to become a priest. When I was an eighth grader and an altar boy, I found out about the Congregation of Holy Cross when four of its missionaries came to our church to preach fire and brimstone sermons about sinners dying in whorehouses and spending eternity in hell. Because the altar boys were considered too young to hear such stories, one of the priests would take us into the sacristy, with the doors closed, to tell us about life as a Holy Cross priest. One of them, Father Tom Duffy, made a great impression upon me and before long he was urging my mother and father to enroll me in the Holy Cross high school seminary at Notre Dame the following year.

Though my mother approved of my wanting to be a priest, she felt I was too young to leave home. "No dice, Father Duffy," she would tell him over and over. And I remember to this day her reply to his warning, "If he doesn't come and he goes to high school here, he may lose his vocation." She looked Duffy straight in the eye and said, "It can't be much of a vocation if he's going to lose it by living in a Christian family." Mother had spoken, and that was that.

I enjoyed a wonderful time in Most Holy Rosary parochial high school. In the depths of the Depression, I scrounged like every kid my age to make pocket money. I mowed lawns, hauled coal ashes, sold newspapers, sold watercress and nuts I found in the woods, and in my senior year I worked forty hours a week at a gas station. Still, I had time for sports and play with my neighborhood friends, and, yes, lots of dancing and dating with girls at the high school. But even though I dated and partied as much as anyone in high school, I never wavered in my desire to be a priest. There were many nights when I'd roll in at 2 A.M. after having a good time and I'd just sit on my bed and say to myself, "This isn't enough for me. There's something more that I need out of life." It was God's way, I think, of letting me know that my vocation was more important than my high school social life.

Despite all these activities, my primary full-time job was school-work. My friends and I had four years each of English, Latin, and religion; three years each of French and history; and one year each of algebra, geometry, and chemistry. And I will never forget those devoted nuns who ran the school, taught us discipline, rapped our knuckles, and hammered the lessons into our heads—Sister Augusta, Sister Justita, Sister Q, Sister Delphina, and Sister Mary Veronica. Superbly prepared for teaching and all with master's degrees, they received about $30 a month in return for teaching full-time, overseeing many of the extracurricular activities, and keeping the church clean. I wonder how many high schools today are providing an education that is any better than the one I received between 1930 and 1934.

Equally important as any of our academic studies were the sense of morals and the personal values we learned throughout the twelve years of our primary and secondary school education. In those days all schools, public and private, sought to instill in children a long list of homespun values which were taught philosophically, if needed, to avoid overtones of religion: It is better to be honest than dishonest, better to be kind than cruel, better to help than to hurt someone, better to be patriotic than not . . . Where are those values being taught today in our public schools? And if children do not absorb those fundamental values from their teachers or their parents, is it any wonder that they turn to the street smarts of the ghettos?

Throughout my high school years, Father Duffy and I kept in touch regularly, and when the day arrived for me to make up my mind about the seminary, Father Duffy gave me a choice. I could join the Eastern Province of Holy Cross in a brand new seminary at Stonehill College in Massachusetts or I could join the western province and enroll at the University of Notre Dame. It took me about one third of a second to choose the dream of practically every Catholic schoolboy in the country, and the following fall, off I went to Notre Dame.

One of the things that I'll always remember about my father was his deftness with words. He took great pains with words and always had a well-thumbed dictionary close by. Later on in his life he became addicted to crossword puzzles and developed a killer instinct at Scrabble, at which he beat me regularly and with great glee. I remember very clearly when he beat me after I had become president of Notre Dame. He turned to my mother and said, "They just don't make college presidents the way they used to."

When we were growing up, I was always closest to my sister Mary because we were the closest in age. We did a lot of our schoolwork together, and I remember that she was bright and very good in school. She also had artistic talent. When we'd do our homework together at the kitchen table, she'd work for about five minutes and then start drawing. She sketched well enough to earn a fine arts degree at Syracuse University. After that, she taught art for a couple of years; then right after World War II ended, she married a dentist by the name of Al Lyons. Our affection for each other grew stronger as we got older. From the time I left home for the seminary in 1934 to when I was ordained some nine years later, I think Mary wrote me just about every week, although, understandably, her letters slowed down a little after she and her husband started their family: two boys who graduated from Notre Dame and two girls who graduated from St. Mary's and Maramount colleges.

My dad had his own pet names for all my sisters. His name for Mary was Sarah, I suppose because she was steady and the oldest. Betty he called Greta because she was the liveliest one of the three. She also had a great voice, like my mother, and sang in the glee club at New Rochelle College. After she graduated from there, she earned master's degrees in sociology and psychology. When she was left alone with six kids, the youngest being only three at the time, her advanced degrees enabled her to get a job as a high school counselor and gave her the financial wherewithal to keep her family together. All six graduated from Notre Dame.

I don't remember my dad's name for Anne—I think Agnes—but I always called her Tom because she was clearly the tomboy and athlete of the family. She did not care much for school, but she loved to bowl, to play golf, and to be outdoors running or jumping or doing something. She also had an incredible memory and could always beat the rest of us playing cards or in any game that involved remembering facts. Anne married a war hero named Jack Jackson, who was shot so many times that I think he spent half of his World War II service in military hospitals.

Anne was the only one in the family who did not go on to college, but among the rest of us there were four B.A.s, four master's degrees, and one doctorate. Considering the fact that neither of our parents had gone to college, the Hesburgh kids managed in one generation to bring the family well along in terms of its educational level. After the war ended, all three of my sisters were married within a year. I know their leaving home so close together was quite a blow to my mother, because she was very close to them, almost like an older sister; they would borrow one another's clothes and nylons and jewelry and things.

So all of a sudden my mom and dad had no one left—except Jimmy, who provided them with a kind of renewed parenthood involving school, scouts, summer camp, and all the rest. Without

Jimmy I think they would have been pretty lonely. During those years Jimmy developed a closeness to my dad that I never had.

Jim graduated from Notre Dame and later Harvard Business School after a stint as an officer in the Navy. The most intelligent decision he ever made was to marry his high school sweetheart, Mary Kelly. All of their six children attended Notre Dame. Five have graduated; Christopher is a sophomore. All four girls are married to Notre Dame grads.

Years later, when Mary had a mastectomy, the odds were five to one in her favor that she'd recover completely, but those odds weren't good enough in her case and the cancer either returned or came out from wherever it had been hiding. I knew she had always wanted to see Europe, so I suggested that she accompany me on a trip I had to make that summer. I made time for her to see places that would appeal to her artistic sensibilities, like the cathedral of Notre-Dame de Paris and Chartres. I was in Mexico on another trip when I found out that Mary had only a short time to live. Naturally, I went to her as fast as I could. When I walked into her room in Oneida, New York, where she lived, I offered to say Mass for her then and there, saying, "But first I'll anoint you, if you want me to."

Mary knew her death was imminent and she was tough about it. "Why the heck do you think I sent for you, just for the fun of it?" she quipped.

"I have to ask you something before I anoint you," I said. "Do you want to go to confession?"

"I went to confession just before Christmas and it's now the third of January and I've been lying here sick in bed ever since," she replied with a glint in her eye. "I couldn't have done anything wrong if I'd wanted to." It was clear she neither needed nor wanted to go to confession, so I anointed her and said Mass. About a week later I was with her when she died.

Mary was only in her early forties when she died, and she had four young children. The oldest was eight and the youngest two. As she was dying, she made me promise that I'd keep an eye on her kids and see to it that her husband married again as soon as possible. She even named the woman he should marry. The woman was the widow of a dentist to whom she had been married only three months. It took Mary's husband five years to get over her death and to marry the woman she had picked out for him.

A virulent form of liver cancer took my dad very quickly in 1960. Near the end he fell out of bed a lot. My mother, not strong enough to get him back in, would just spend the rest of the night sitting on the floor next to him. Just a few days before he died I went to Syracuse for his seventy-third birthday and was there to say Mass in his room and to anoint him. When he died, I remember that Jimmy broke down and cried. I kept in close touch with my mother after that, mostly by telephone, and I made it a point to visit or to take her on a trip every summer. She was always ready to take off to somewhere with me. I could call her from New York at noon and tell her to be ready to go to Canada at three and she'd be packed and waiting when I got there. She spent the last part of her life, needing twenty-four-hour care, at a place called Loretta Rest, run by the Franciscan Sisters in the Syracuse diocese. When she got old, my mother always told me, "I don't care if you go tooting all over the world, I want you here when I'm dying." I did not let her down. Jimmy, Betty, Anne, and I were with her during her final forty-eight hours, and when she died in her seventy-ninth year, we were gathered around her bedside.

T W O

LEARNING

M Y F A T H E R , mother, sister Mary, and I drove in a borrowed car from Syracuse, New York, to South Bend, Indiana. We did not stop off at the 1933 world's fair in nearby Chicago, famous as it was, because my father said he could not afford the price of admission. It was mid-September 1934, in the depths of the Depression, and I was seventeen. A world apart from what I had known before, the campus of Notre Dame was shaded by giant oaks, quiet, lovely, and awe-inspiring in a medieval sort of way.

I was instructed to check into Holy Cross Seminary on St. Mary's Lake the next day, which gave us time to walk around the seminary grounds and make our way to the south side of the lake to the Notre Dame campus. My family and I spent the night at a bed-and-breakfast tourist house, and the next day they came with me as I checked into Holy Cross Seminary. Those were poignant moments together as we parted and they waved goodbye. Soon after they left, I suffered my first wave of unequivocal homesickness. It hung on for a month or so, then faded slowly away as I settled into the routine of classes and seminary life.

In the beginning we wore street clothes and did not look any different from other students on campus. We did live by a different rule book, however. We were in training for the priesthood and so, of course, we could not date, nor could we correspond with old girlfriends, and campus clubs were off limits, too. So while you could say we were at Notre Dame, socially we were strictly Holy Cross seminarians. The dichotomy was particularly painful during my first Christmas at Notre Dame, when the regular university students cheerfully left to spend the holidays with their families, and we seminarians were left behind, lonely and cold.

Naturally, I saw Father Tom Duffy from time to time at the seminary. Having inspired me to sign up, he must have felt it was his duty to check up on me every now and then. But the only Holy Cross priests I saw with any regularity were the ones I had for classes. We lived and took most of our classes at the seminary. For special classes like Doc Hinton's chemistry lab and Father Wenninger's life sciences, we walked over to the Notre Dame campus. Most of our courses were prescribed and required, but I did choose Latin and Greek and, when I could, I gravitated toward any course that smacked even remotely of philosophy. At the time, I was entertaining the notion of becoming a philosopher-priest. I did particularly well in English—or at least I thought I did—until my final exam was returned to me. My grade was 95 but my instructor, Father Leo Ward, wrote a comment on my paper which I have never forgotten: "If you don't learn to simplify your style with simple words, you will wind up being a pompous ass." His own style was simple and clear, I noted.

Between my first year as a postulant at Holy Cross Seminary on St. Mary's Lake and my sophomore year as a "professed religious," or one who had taken his vows, at Moreau Seminary on St. Joseph's Lake, the other lake on the Notre Dame campus, I spent a year at Rolling Prairie, along with twenty-nine other novice Notre Dame seminarians and twenty other brother postulants who came from elsewhere to be Holy Cross brothers. Rolling Prairie is a hamlet of six hundred population about thirty miles west of

Notre Dame. It is also the name of a farm that the Holy Cross order owns nearby. Most Notre Dame graduates have probably never heard of the place, but if you were a Holy Cross seminarian of my era, you got to know it very well. It was where you discovered that there was more to becoming a Holy Cross priest than tending to your religious and intellectual development. In many ways, Rolling Prairie was our boot camp (not unlike the Marines' Parris Island, perhaps), complete with rigorous physical training and a hard-nosed drill instructor. Its purpose, we learned much later, was to indoctrinate the incoming class of seminarians to the discipline and rigors of priesthood by exposing them to hard physical labor. It was a test and a challenge, designed to weed out at the beginning those young men who thought they wanted to be priests but did not have the stamina and will to stay the course. Incidentally, no doubt the Holy Cross brothers wanted to make Rolling Prairie into a working, productive farm, capable of supporting those who lived there.

The order had purchased the dilapidated six-hundred-acre farm just a few years before, and ours was only the second class to take up residence there. The seminarians who came the year before us had hardly made a dent in the place. The singular improvement on the farm was a large, spanking-new building which housed all of us and, luxury of all luxuries, provided each of us with a private room. It was to be our only luxury there.

After an eight-day retreat, prior to receiving our black serge habits, we were turned over to the two men in immediate charge of us, Brother Seraphim and Father Kerndt Healy. Seraphim, a former German soldier who had immigrated to the United States after World War I and spoke a dramatic, accented English, was the taskmaster. He seemed to delight in finding ways to make hard work even more difficult. Father Healy was a different sort— Harvard graduate, subtle, distinguished, and every inch a gentleman. But tough, too. It bothered him that a priest might leave the community after ordination, and so he considered it his sacred duty to bear down hard during the novitiate. If someone was going to leave, Healy wanted him to leave sooner rather than later.

And many did. At the end of our year at Rolling Prairie, of the original twenty-nine, only nine of us remained.

The first workday on the farm, Seraphim lined us up outside and handed each of us a bucket. "You will now proceed in line at right angles to the building," he said, "and you will go around the whole building and pick up every stone—in silence." As we filled our buckets, we would dump them in designated places and fill them up again. In about an hour and a half, we had heaped the stones up in huge piles, each about six or seven feet high. Elsewhere, there wasn't a stone to be found. I was impressed at how much work could get done with everyone working in silence.

We also built a barn. Then near the barn we poured a circular cement foundation eighteen feet in diameter and two feet deep. We had no idea what it was for, until one morning they rolled us out of bed at 4 A.M. and took us in trucks to an old silo about a mile away from the barn. We were going to move the silo to the barn, we were told. Cement block by cement block, about fifty-five pounds apiece, we unraveled that silo, which stood forty or fifty feet high. Standing on a kind of shaky circular scaffold on the inside that could be raised and lowered, we took the blocks off from the top down, one by one, row by row, lowering them to the ground with ropes and pulleys. Then we loaded the blocks onto trucks, took them to the new site, and built the silo anew.

About the middle of the afternoon when we had just about finished, I paused to think what a long, hard day it had been and how relieved I was to be near the end of it. As we completed the job and sat down to rest, Seraphim said, "Now we paint it."

What he meant was, "Now *you* paint it."

I asked him how we were going to do that, and he said, "You start at the top with a rope."

"You start at the top with a rope?" I repeated in bewilderment. "I've never done this before, Brother."

To which he replied, "You will learn."

The next thing I knew I was sitting on a kind of swing, a board suspended by a rope on either end, and I was hanging there on the outside of the silo about fifty feet off the ground. On each end of the board hanging from a hook was a bucket of whitewash and

LEARNING

a bucket of water. My instructions were simple. I was to dip my brush in the water first, then in the whitewash, then apply the whitewash to the silo. Inside the silo Seraphim manipulated the ropes so that I was pulled somehow around the silo, painting as I went, and then lowered and rotated on the next level down. All this time I was worrying what would happen to me if a rope broke or a hook gave way. But I finished in a couple of hours and the worst thing that happened was that I was covered with whitewash. That evening I ran into Father Healy, who commented with a smile, "You looked very dashing up there today."

The central building at Rolling Prairie was heated by a wood-burning furnace. Actually, the furnace could have burned coal, but wood was cheaper. All we had to do was cut down enormous beech trees, saw the wood into three-foot lengths, and then split the logs with wedges and sledgehammers. It seemed that was all we did in the spare time we had. Brother Seraphim added his touch of increased difficulty. Rather than waste any of the wood, he required us to saw the trees down at ground, rather than waist-high, level. Wielding a huge two-handled crosscut saw at just inches off the ground is near backbreaking work. I have a scar just above my right knee, a reminder of when I got too close to the saw. We also cleared sumac and brush, six of us wielding brush axes on some twenty or thirty acres of that tangled, disagreeable stuff.

As hard on us as he was, Seraphim never hesitated to pitch right in himself when it came to really hard and sometimes dangerous work. When there was honey to be collected, for example, he would often go to the bee hives himself, arriving back at the house covered with stings and welts. One day, right out of the blue, though, he told me to go and get the honey. The hives were on top of a hill, about a hundred yards from the barn and some fifty yards from a small lake, stored in racks covered with a tarp, and with some barbed wire around the perimeter to keep the animals out. To get the honey you had to climb under the barbed wire, take off the tarp, grab a case of honey, set it down, put the tarp back on, carry the rack to the barbed-wire fence, set it down, crawl under the fence, pull the rack under the fence, then pick the rack up again and run like hell.

The bees knew why you were there, and so even before you got the tarp off, they were in your hair and ears and down your neck and up your pants. By the time I had the case of honey on the other side of the fence, I was covered with bees. Streaking off down the hill faster than I'd ever run in my life, I burst into the barn and found Seraphim, practically threw the honey at him, and raced off for the lake and dove in. Bees aren't much for water, so I escaped with my hide still mostly intact, but just barely.

We all thought Brother Seraphim was fiendishly inventive. One time we were putting in a road and a sewer line, working very hard beneath a boiling summer sun, when a thunderstorm came up, complete with lightning and hail. I dropped my pickax and made a dash with all the others for the barn. There we sat down, drenched, and grinned at one another in silence: We were safe from the storm and from work. Some of us, no doubt, grinned at Seraphim: What could he possibly find for us to do here? Ah, his eye roamed the barn, and off at the far end he spied a stall with fifty sheep in it. His eyes suddenly lit up. "I want each of you to go get a sheep and bring it back and pick the lice off it."

"What?" we all cried out in unison.

"I want each of you to go get a sheep and bring it back and pick the lice off it," he patiently repeated. Then with a great air of resignation, he said, "OK, you dumbkopfs, come here, I'll show you." He went over and picked up a sheep, cradled it on his lap, and started going through the wool with his hands. When he found a louse, he'd kill it by squeezing it between his thumb and fingernail. "Now," he said, "I want you to do that for all the sheep." For the next two hours we sat there with sheep on our laps, picking out lice. The sheep stank, and pretty soon we did, too. On top of that, we also became infested with their lice, and had to bathe that night in Lysol.

By fall, we thought we had done every dirty job imaginable, but once again we had underestimated Brother Seraphim. One brisk November day when he had us all lined up and was handing out work assignments, he reached near the end of the line and said,

"And now we will have the butchering crew—you, you, you, and you. The last "you" was me. Seraphim turned us over to Brother Marinus, an older novice and former farmhand who knew all about butchering. Brother Marinus proceeded to teach us everything anybody would ever want to know about butchering pigs. He went through the actual deed with us the first time around. After that, we were on our own. Lest the technique ever be lost or forgotten, I pass it along now, as I still remember it vividly over these past fifty years. If you are queasy, however, I suggest you skip this part.

First we had to catch the pig, which meant trapping him in a kind of slotted box—head in, tail out—so we could deal with him. When ready to administer the coup de grace, we grabbed the pig by the hind legs and pulled him out of the box. That made the pig scream; he probably had some sense of what was coming. With one of us at each of his four legs, we pulled and stretched him. This enabled Marinus to clunk the pig over the head with the broad side of an ax. He then slit its jugular with a knife. The pig, five feet long and weighing at least two hundred pounds, was screaming and trying to get away during the clunking and slitting, so it was all we could do to hang on. At the same time, one of us was supposed to catch the blood in a pan so the chickens could have it.

Next we rubbed wood ashes all over the carcass and lowered it into a barrel of extremely hot water to remove all the hair. We dunked the pig in the hot water about three times to make sure that the hair would come off easily. The way you test whether or not it will is by pulling on the pig's tail. If the tail hair comes off easily, you know that the rest of the hair will, too. When Marinus demonstrated for us, the hair came off so fast it flew out of his hand and hit me square in the face. Yuk! You then proceed to scrape off the rest of the hair, and when you're done, you have this glistening, hairless animal that stinks.

Next we cut off the head. How? First we sliced all the way around the neck, then grabbed the pig's ears and twisted the head off. If the end product is to be sausages, as it was in this case, you have to shave the head at this point. That done, we cut the tendons on its back feet and hung the carcass on a hook, head down. Below it we placed a large basket to catch the entrails and then proceeded to disembowel the animal. With the belly facing toward us, we made a long vertical cut, starting at the bung hole and running all the way down to the chest area. Everything fell neatly into the basket. After reserving the heart, liver, and kidneys, we threw the viscera over the fence to the victim's brother pigs. They devoured them in minutes.

We sloshed the abdominal cavity with several buckets of hot water, which gave us an animal that was clean inside and out. That reduced the stench somewhat. With the carcass spread-eagled nice and flat with the open side down on a board, we cut the pig in half by sawing lengthwise along the backbone. Two of us then each grabbed a half and took it up to the storage cooler in the house.

The assault upon our sensibilities was now over, but the real work had just begun. The next day we cut off the two hams, then big slabs of fat about an inch thick, which we cut into squares to be made into lard. We built a wood fire under a big steel kettle in the barnyard and threw in the squares of fat and cooked them until they foamed up. When the foam had settled back again, we ladled the stuff into a special press, which squeezed the clear lard into a fifty-gallon drum. We then cranked the bits and pieces of skin and fat through the press, which gave us something that tasted just like crisp bacon. We developed a liking for it and snacked on it as we worked.

The hams we soaked in a big barrel of brine. The meat just beneath the layer of fat we put into another barrel of brine. That would be made into bacon. We sliced up the ribs to be barbecued later. Everything left over—the ears, nose, lips, you name it—we put through the grinder and mixed with herbs for sausage. Not surprisingly, once you've made sausage, you can easily lose your taste for it. But the hams and bacon, smoked over a hickory fire, were delicious and were served often to us hardworking, hungry young men with hearty appetites. On Thursday, the heaviest workday of the week, for some reason I could never fathom, we often had ham and beans for breakfast.

LEARNING

In the spring we learned to plant corn. We used a corn drill that put four kernels of corn into each little mound of earth, evenly spaced out. When the corn had come up about a foot, we "suckered" it, meaning we went down the rows and pulled out the weakest of the four little plants, so that the others would grow better. We did about a hundred acres this way, which represented about one sixth of the entire farm. The corn came up beautifully, a joy to behold, but then a terrible drought set in and the corn began to dry up. All was not lost, however. While the corn still had some juice left in it, we went out into the field with corn knives and cut it down to within an inch of the ground, the whole one hundred acres, stalk by stalk. It was depressing work, because we had been looking forward to eating fresh corn. Instead, we ground up the stalks and made a rich, sweet-smelling feed for the chickens. We did harvest one surviving field of corn, cutting and husking enough to feed the livestock through the winter. They ate well and we all learned something of farming.

The bulk of the acreage was planted in wheat and rye. When it was time to harvest the grain, we did it communal style along with all the surrounding neighbors. On the morning of the big day, we got up at 4 A.M. and worked hard until it was almost dark. We must have filled several thousand two-hundred-pound sacks with wheat and rye. I don't know how much grain we harvested, but it was an awful lot. The most memorable part of that harvest day was the enormous lunch provided by all our farmer neighbors. I think they must have vied with one another as to who could put out the most extravagant feed. There were enormous flagons of milk and steaks as big around as tennis racquets. Corn, potatoes, and other vegetables were served in huge bowls. We seminarians stuffed ourselves with abandon and topped it off with apple pie à la mode.

Classes at Rolling Prairie were less strenuous, of course, than the farm work, but not by much. We rose at 5 A.M., spent half an hour in meditation, went to Mass, made our thanksgiving, and listened to a reading from a religious book. The tome they were using at the time, and had been using for many years, must have been written about 1400. It was so outdated you would crack up laughing if you read it today. But then we took it seriously because both the Church and community life were very structured and disciplined. It certainly never occurred to any of us to challenge anything.

There were also our regular household chores. We cleaned our rooms, policed the corridors, and washed the breakfast dishes before lining up for farm work at 9 A.M.. That was in addition to our "work" assignments inside the house: waiting tables, preparing meals, cleaning up the dining room and kitchen. I washed an awful lot of dishes in my time and learned that the best way to handle a disagreeable job was to do it just as fast as you could. Two other young men and I learned to wash the dinnerware and cutlery of some sixty diners before they finished their meal and left the dining room. As bad as that was, the most dreaded job was waiting on the head table. There Father Healy sat and used mealtimes to test us and try our patience. It was a kind of hazing. You'd bring him toast and it would be too hot. You'd take it away and let it cool and then bring it back and it would be too cold. Or it would be too light or too dark. It was a game, of course, and if you played it right, you did not let it get to you. You just kept your mouth shut and went along with it.

There were only two hours a day when we were allowed to break silence: the hour after lunch and the hour after dinner. That was it. At mealtimes we used sign language to communicate. If you wanted bread, for example, you held up four fingers. For potatoes, you held up a closed fist. If you wanted someone to pass the milk, you had to go through the motions of milking a cow. To an outsider dropping by, the refectory at Rolling Prairie would have presented quite an amusing sight: sixty presumably normal young men sitting at tables jabbing fists and fingers in the air and pretending to be milking cows. But that's the way it was in the seminary in the mid-thirties.

Despite what I had to endure from Father Healy at the head table, he and I became friends, and every once in a while he would do something nice for me, but always very subtly. Once he stopped me in a hallway and asked me to go out on the porch with him. There he asked me to take his picture in his new cape, which he had just received from Rome. I snapped his photo with an old box camera he had handed me, and he casually remarked, "Well, as long as you're here I might as well get a picture of you." After he took my picture he said, "Oh, I forgot, we're not supposed to take pictures of novices." That rule was new to me, if there really was one, so I assumed Healy was just having one of his little jokes and I forgot all about it. About a month later I got a letter from my mother saying how nice it had been of Father Healy to photograph me in my cassock and send the picture to her. I think Healy felt sorry for me because my parents lived too far away to visit every couple of months, as other parents were allowed to do.

Despite all the farm work and house duties, I did a lot of reading that year. I would guess I read over a hundred books in this period, most of which were on spiritual subjects, including a lot of Cardinal Newman and other classics. And I enjoyed them, too, far more than I did the ancient Latin texts assigned to us and, for that matter, most of the daily lectures on the spiritual life, which I found less than exciting.

In the spring I was given the great honor of doing the reading of the three-hour service for Good Friday. My text was "The Royal Road of the Holy Cross," which was a chapter from the *Imitation of Christ* by Thomas à Kempis. That didn't mean, however, that I was excused from my other duties, which at the time happened to be shoveling manure away from the little pig houses, where the manure had been stacked all winter to keep the piglets warm. I was not quite finished when it was time for me to do my reading. I had to rush back to the house, run upstairs, take a shower, put on my cassock, and read "The Royal Road of the Holy Cross." When the service was over, I put my work clothes back on and finished spreading the manure.

During our last month at Rolling Prairie, we broke in the new class arriving for the next year. I was selected to give the traditional one-hour *daily* lecture to them, and that was more than an honor; it was a blessing to be able to talk for so long at one time after a year of near-total silence. I felt pretty good about myself at the end of that year at Rolling Prairie. I was in the best physical shape of my life, weighing 145 pounds without an ounce of fat on me.

And I had learned one thing for sure: Whatever life held for me, I would never be a farmer.

On August 16 we took our temporary vows of poverty, chastity, and obedience for three years. We then began preparing for our sophomore year at Notre Dame, where we would be living and studying at Moreau Seminary on St. Joseph's Lake. Nine of the original twenty-nine novices who left Notre Dame for Rolling Prairie a year before returned for their sophomore year. Living and studying at Moreau Seminary on St. Joseph's Lake was almost cozy and homelike after a year at Rolling Prairie. But by no means did we just pray, study, and sing at Moreau. Most of our time was devoted to our spiritual and intellectual development, but we also had a substantial amount of grunt work to do. In my case, it usually was waiting on tables. I waited on priests and seminarians. I waited tables at layman's retreats. I waited tables so much during my three years at Moreau that I developed a healthy respect for the job and an abiding tolerance for restaurant waiters no matter how surly or slow they might be. To this day I become upset if anyone is impolite to a waiter or waitress.

I also washed thousands and thousands of dishes at Moreau. For one year I was part of a four-man crew washing dishes for about a hundred diners. We hated the job with a passion, but we decided that the best way to make it bearable was to do it very well and very fast. It became a contest for us to get our technique down pat so that we finished washing and got every last dish dried and back on the shelf by the time the bell rang at the end of the meal. Sometimes we won and most of the time we finished just a few minutes after the bell rang. A word about bells. I rather like church bells and altar bells and musical bells of any kind. But at Moreau Seminary there were bells for starting class and ending class, bells for calling you to choir practice and to work details, bells for the recreation periods, different bells for different activities from study periods to playing baseball. I grew to hate those bells as much as I disliked the amount of time we had to put in waiting tables and washing dishes, time that I thought then (and now) could have been better used for our intellectual studies. I never gave voice to those thoughts, you can be sure, because I had taken a vow of obedience, and mine was not to question my superiors.

My most memorable day at Moreau, perhaps, was one of my last as a sophomore, a hot day in July, when I was studying in my room on the top floor of the seminary and thinking about removing my heavy cassock and stripping down to my shorts. That was against the rules. As if someone could read my thoughts, I was summoned forthwith "to the boss's office," which was that of the seminary's superior. In the office was Father Ted Mehling, the assistant superior at the time. He was the calmest, most unflappable clergyman I had ever met, always neatly dressed and immaculately groomed. When I walked into his office, he looked up with that deadpan expression of his and handed me a piece of paper. Then he said, "This is for you. You're going to Rome to study next year."

"I am?" I looked at the paper. It began, "The obedient man shall speak of victory." Then there was a line where my name had been written in, followed by "has been assigned next year," and then another line filled in with the words, "to study in Rome." The paper was signed by Father Burns, the provincial of the order.

As I finished reading, Mehling said, "Oh, McDonagh is going, too. Would you send him in for his paper?" Too stunned to say anything, I just turned around and walked out in a kind of semitrance. Tom McDonagh was one of my best friends at Rolling Prairie and Moreau and I did not want to ruin his surprise, and so I simply told him that Mehling wanted to see him. When he came out, he was just as stunned as I had been. That night after dinner we both went back to Mehling's office and asked him what? how? when? why? but all he would tell us was that school in Rome did not start until November and that we would be spending the rest of summer at the order's summer camp up in Lawton, Michigan. Not a word about Rome at the summer camp. Mac and I worried about all sorts of things, especially whether or not we would see our families before we left. I had not seen mine for two years.

With special permission, we returned to Moreau, and with fear in our hearts we telephoned for appointments to see Father Burns, the provincial of the Holy Cross order at Notre Dame. To our surprise, he told us to come by at 3 P.M. When we got there, he said his office was too hot and suggested we take a walk instead.

Walking back and forth behind Sacred Heart Church and the Main Building, he succinctly answered our questions. Father Burns was a tall, stately, intellectual man in his sixties, and getting answers from him was like pulling teeth. We were leaving September 25 on the S.S. *Champlain,* a French ship. We would be allowed two weeks at home with our families, no more, and the order would pay for our travel from our homes to the ship in New York. We would have to pay our way home. That struck me as grossly unfair. Crazy. McDonagh lived in East Chicago, only a hundred miles away; the school would pay his way to New York City. But I would have to pay for four hundred miles to get home to Syracuse, which was so much closer to New York, and besides I did not think I had the money, even if I could get a superior's permission to withdraw my gas station money. We went on like this for quite a while, McDonagh and I asking questions and Father Burns answering them. All the while as we walked back and forth, he had not answered the most important question of all: What were we going to be doing after we got to Rome?

When he told us ever so casually, he never broke stride: "Oh, you're going to get a doctorate in philosophy and a doctorate in theology."

"Both philosophy and theology?" McDonagh and I asked.

"Yes," he said. "It will take some time, but you'll be able to do it because you're going to be there for eight years."

When you're twenty years old, eight years is almost half your life. The thought of being away from our families that long gave both of us considerable pause. Some of our excitement about going to Rome began to fade. But there was nothing we could do. We had taken the vow of obedience.

Back in his office, Father Burns began figuring our expense money for the trip. "Well, Mr. Hesburgh, you're going to Syracuse on your own, so all I have to do is get you from Syracuse to New York. That's about ten dollars," he said. "Then you'll have to spend three dollars at Leo House in New York, and that includes breakfast, so that's thirteen dollars, and there'll be five dollars for the steward for the seven days you're on the boat." He continued in this vein for several more minutes. Somehow he figured it would cost so little to stay at the Canadian Hotel in Paris and the excursion rate on the train from Paris to Rome would be so cheap as to be hardly worth mentioning. When he was all done adding everything up, he looked up at me and said, "I make it that I owe you about nineteen dollars to get you from Syracuse to Rome."

I remember thinking to myself that Burns must have been the chintziest guy that God had ever created, but I kept my mouth shut. He then went through the same routine with McDonagh. He wrote out two checks, folded them in half, and handed them to us. I wasn't sure I should thank him, but I did anyway, and so did Tom. When we got outside we unfolded the checks and discovered that each of them was for one hundred dollars. Then we heard someone laughing behind us. It was Father Burns. "Don't forget to send anything back that you don't spend," he said. "I don't want Father Sauvage in Rome to get his hands on it."

Rome was a new world—vast, different, somewhat frightening—for Tom McDonagh and me, as it would be for any young American so far away from home for the first time. Father Georges Sauvage, the superior of our new home, was strikingly brusque in demeanor and decidedly Gallic in outlook. Tall and ramrod straight, he was a man of strong opinions and certitude on every subject far beyond religion and church matters. He had no hesitancy whatever in instructing us how we were to live every hour of the day while we were under his care and responsibility. One thing became clear soon after our arrival: We were there to study and learn and to grow spiritually. In contrast to life at Moreau Seminary, there were great gobs of time here that we spent alone in our Spartan rooms with our books.

We arrived there on a Friday with four other seminarians who came from the Eastern Province of the Holy Cross order, all us exhausted and very very hungry. We had endured seasickness on the voyage, sleepless nights on makeshift cots in Paris, and then we had sat up some twenty-four hours on a train that rattled us all the way to Rome. We had gone some thirty-six hours eating nothing more than a few snacks we could buy from the window of the train. Our first meal in Rome was an omelet, Italian flat beans, Bel Paese cheese, and those wonderful little loaves of bread pointed at the ends called *sfilatini*. Every two places or so all the way around the table stood a bottle of wine, and Father Sauvage soon noticed that we were not touching the wine.

"Pour yourself a glass," he invited us in French.

"We can't," I explained. "We've taken the pledge." I had to explain that many of us had promised just prior to confirmation not to drink anything alcoholic until age twenty-one. I thought that would satisfy him.

"Ho, ho, ho, that's a typical Irish approach to life," he cried out across the table. "You Americans have one bad fault that you got from the Irish. You think the reason for drinking is to get the strongest stuff you can find and drink as much as you can as fast as you can. While you're in this house, you will drink wine twice a day at meals and sometimes between meals if we have a party. Over the next several years you will drink a good deal of wine while you are in this house. But you will never get drunk, I promise you! You will learn to drink rationally. Now take some wine." End of lecture. End of pledge.

But not the end of Sauvage's opinion seminar. As much as he loved wine, he hated smoking. At the suggestion of one of the Notre Dame priests, I brought a carton of Camels all the way from Syracuse and presented them as a gift to Sauvage. American cigarettes were considered a luxury in Europe, I was told. He merely raised his eyebrows and, if I remember correctly, he did not say thank you. I thought he would put them in a place where we could help ourselves after meals, the only time the two or three smokers among us could indulge. Instead, he took them up to a little-used parlor on the second floor and left them there to gather dust. Sauvage, we learned, was a reformed smoker.

Father Sauvage's interest in our journey to Rome centered on what class we had traveled from Paris and how much it had cost. We told him second class, which meant that instead of sitting on a hard wooden bench for twenty-four hours we had a little cushion under our derrieres. "You gentlemen don't know what the vow of poverty is about," he exclaimed. "I always travel third class when I go to Paris."

By the time he got through with us that first night it was about ten-thirty. We were looking forward eagerly (or sleepily) for a good night's rest because nothing was scheduled for the following day. Innocent seminarians that we were, we assumed that our superior would recommend that we sleep late. "You will get up at 5 A.M.," Sauvage ordered. We would be getting up at 5 A.M. every morning, including Christmas, work or no work, holiday or no holiday.

Fourteen of us lived in the house: Father Sauvage, two priests studying for doctorates, two theology students who were a year away from ordination, two seminarians a year ahead of us, a French Holy Cross Brother who was the tight-fisted house manager, and we six new seminarians from America. It was a three-story house in a good section of Rome on the Via dei Cappuccini, a two-block street that comes down from the Capuchin church between Via Veneto and Via Sistina, two of Rome's most famous thoroughfares. We were only a block away from the Piazza Barberini and about a fifteen-minute walk to the Gregorian University, where we took our classes. All the floors in the house were marble (in Rome, if you have a wood floor, you pay a luxury tax), which helped keep the house cool in summer but made the place bone-chillingly cold in the winter. Each of us had a basin and a pitcher of water in our room for washing up. I shaved with cold water in my room. With five of us sharing one bathroom on each floor, there was always a line waiting and, of course, there was one fellow who seemed to want to spend eternity there each morning. (The long wait for the bathroom reminded me a little, just a little, of sharing a bathroom with my three sisters back home in Syracuse.) We were allowed one hot bath a week because there was only one small hot-water heater for all of us. We were allowed as many cold baths as we liked. In January it was so cold in my room my fingers were always too numb for me to do any typing. The marble floors were so cold that we used little wooden platforms under our desks to put our feet on. I don't remember ever being warm during those Roman winters.

Our routine was rigid. Up at five, meditation and morning prayer, Mass, breakfast (bread, cheese, coffee), classes, noon chapel, lunch, classes, an afternoon walk, study, chapel, a light supper, half-hour recreation (Ping-Pong or bridge) in the front room, and then (at about nine) to bed or to study in your room for as late as you liked, just so long as you were up and at 'em at 5 A.M.

Our lives in Rome and at the Gregorian University were truly international, a substantial change from my fairly provincial existence in Syracuse and at Notre Dame. At the Gregorian I was sitting in classes with students from every nation on earth— literally. There were forty-seven countries in the world at that time, and there was at least one student from each country at the university. Every single Catholic rite was represented.

At the house, Father Sauvage required us to converse in French, read our lessons in French, even pray in French. With the help of my old high school classes, I quickly became fluent in French, although to this day my accent remains American. At the university, our classes were in Latin: chemistry, calculus, anthropology, philosophy—you name it. I even studied Hebrew in Latin (which is something I don't recommend to anyone). Not only were the lectures in Latin, but all the exams and the textbooks, too. I took all my notes in Latin, and typed them up in Latin at the end of the day. To increase our fluency, we always spoke Latin as we walked to and from the university. Hearing Latin four hours a day and reading it another six hours, it was not too long before I could write it as easily as I wrote English, pluperfect subjunctives and all. During my first free month in Rome, before classes began, I read the *Confessions* of St. Augustine in Latin, as well as his commentary on St. Matthew's Gospel. I also studied Italian intensely, buttonholing any unsuspecting Italian student at the university who did not speak English. I made it a point never to speak English if I could avoid it.

On our daily afternoon walks, the moment we stepped out of the house we were in Italy and we had to speak Italian. Italian came fairly easy to me because I had studied Latin as far back as high school. I learned Spanish from a Mexican student at the Gregorian. Between classes for all the time I was in Rome, we met and talked, I in Italian and he in Spanish; and besides teaching each other a foreign language, we became friends. In addition to strong-arming native speakers, I set myself a goal of learning ten new words in French, Italian, and German every day. For just fifteen minutes each day in my room I would review the ten words I had learned the day before, practice ten now ones, and take a peek at the ten I would learn the next day. Ten words a day may not seem much, but in my first year I learned more than thirty-six hundred words in each of three languages and that made me close to fluent in them. I grew to love languages and I have no doubt that the fluency I acquired in Rome helped me enormously in all the work I was to do the rest of my life.

Our daily walks at 3 P.M. were a marvelous, welcomed relief from the rigidity and routine of our studies. Rome is a diverse and fascinating city. On our walks we always wore our cassocks and the traditional round black Roman hat with a wide brim. If it was chilly, we would also wear a long black coat called a *douillette*. There was even a certain formality to the afternoon stroll. At the front door we would form two lines, one facing the other, and the fellow across from you was your partner for that day's walk. The door would be flung open, and off we would go, striding down the street in black, wide-brimmed pairs. Nobody was exempt, not even the priests who lived in the house. It struck me as a little crazy at the time, and still does, but I suppose the exercise was good for all of us, and we did visit every corner of Rome.

Aside from the afternoon jaunts, the most enjoyable aspect of my Roman education was leaving Rome in the summer for two months in the Alps near the Austrian border, just below the Brenner Pass. In the little town of Sarnes, up the mountainside above Bressanone, we stayed in a house called The Place of the Spoiled Priests, which, as the name suggests, had once been a rehabilitation center for priests in trouble. It was a sprawling Tyrolean guest house where we lived two to a room and were allowed to sleep until 6 A.M., a whole extra hour! We had Mass every morning and night prayers before retiring, but the rest of the time we were on our own to say the expected prayers and to expand our intellectual horizons.

Before leaving for the Tyrol, each of us had to inform Father Sauvage of our self-directed program for intellectual development while there. Having given this a lot of thought, I was able to rattle off my plans rather quickly: I intended to do all the exercises in a high school German textbook I had found that covered two years of German. Then I would learn to conjugate all the irregular German verbs, and find some German-speaking locals to talk with. After that, I would read the New Testament in German. To reinforce what I was learning about philosophy, I would read half of a French textbook by a French Jesuit that coincided with what I had studied so far at the Gregorian, namely logic, metaphysics, ethics, and psychology. Then, because metaphysics was so fundamental, I would read a six-hundred-page metaphysics book that an Italian scholar had written. I would also read what I had been told was the best novel ever written in Italian, *I Promessi Sposi (The Betrothed),* which was about seven hundred pages long and was written during the time of Charles Borromeo and the plague in northern Italy. Lastly, because we were going to spend a week visiting museums and art galleries in Florence, I intended to read a history of Italian art in Italian.

"Isn't that a bit much for two months?" Father Sauvage asked. I did not think so, I replied, because I planned to take everything in stride.

At the end of the summer I was able to report to him that I had said all my required prayers each day, and that I had completed everything on my intellectual development list. He just looked at me in that inscrutable way he had, and said, "Well, then, I have nothing else to say to you."

There were two reasons I was able to get so much done over that summer. One, I had acquired discipline over the years of my Catholic education, and Rolling Prairie taught me in particular just how much can be accomplished if one focuses on the task at hand without interruptions and without distractions. The free time between morning and evening prayers at The Place of the Spoiled Priests had given me that opportunity to focus and to concentrate.

My education at the Gregorian, I have to confess, left a lot to be desired. The teaching was rigid and unimaginative and almost rote; the syllabus and instruction methods had not changed, I think, from the way things were done when they started the university in 1558. Each major subject was boiled down to fifteen propositions, and at the end of each course you had to defend any one of those fifteen theses that the examining professor picked at random, just as students before you had done for the past four hundred years. The approach was the same, whether you were studying logic, metaphysics, cosmology, epistemology, or anything else. And yet, as rigid and old-fashioned as the Gregorian was, it provided me with good, intellectual discipline and a wonderful grounding in classical scholastic philosophy and in theology. As a result, I've always felt intellectually and theologically secure when reading new or experimental theological treatises, as, for example, some writings of Teilhard de Chardin or Hans Küng.

Despite its slavish devotion to tradition, the Gregorian was to the Church what West Point was to the Army. The "Greg" was, and still is, I suppose, the premier school for clerics. There are more popes, cardinals, bishops, and other church leaders who came from any *one* of the Gregorian graduate schools, I believe, than from all the rest of Catholic schools combined. Within the Congregation of Holy Cross in those days, for example, those who went to the Gregorian most often ended up running things in one way or another.

But it was not until I had left the Gregorian that I came to realize just how good that university had been in comparison to Catholic universities in the rest of Europe and in the United States. Other schools were using books about the great books, they were teaching the history of theology rather than theology, they were hardly, if at all, teaching Latin. My opinions were solidified when I met a young theology student at Notre Dame who had not studied the Incarnation or the Trinity, did not know a word of Latin, and was abysmally ignorant of the books we had read at the Gregorian. Fortunately, seminary education at Notre Dame has changed a great deal and for the better since I had that exchange with the young Holy Cross theology student.

Father Sauvage made a lasting impression upon my young life.

He was a very holy man in everything he did, as close to a saint as anyone I've ever known. Beneath his brusque and no-nonsense exterior, carefully concealed, was a very warm human being. It simply took us young seminarians in his house a long time to discover that side of his personality. It hardly dawned on us at the time, for instance, that on a trip to the United States for a Holy Cross chapter meeting in 1939 he had gone out of his way to visit all our parents, who were scattered over the eastern half of the United States. When Father Sauvage returned from the United States, he bought a small table radio for the house because, as I learned much later, my father had suggested that with a war about to erupt in Europe we should be kept abreast of the news. My father offered to buy the radio, but Father Sauvage waved him off, and duly bought the radio himself in Rome. But then he forbade us to turn it on. I suppose he thought it would distract us from our studies. A few months later, however, he relented and we could hear the evening news, curiously broadcast in French by the BBC and in English by Paris Mondial.

Vaguely we realized that war in Europe was being talked about. Mussolini's residence was only a couple of blocks from the university on the Piazza Venezia, and his official quarters were right behind the Gregorian in the Quirinale. Whenever Adolf Hitler came to Rome, the university was closed down for a week because a sniper on our roof could easily hit anyone arriving at the Quirinale, as Hitler did. On one occasion, when Hitler was touring the historical sites of Rome in an open car, he passed down the Via Sistina no more than a hundred feet from the front door of our residence, Collegio di Santa Croce. Bill Shriner, a classmate, saw him from my window and called out, "Come over here and look out. Hitler is passing."

I shrugged it off indignantly as a matter of principle. "I wouldn't walk ten feet to see that bum," I replied, all my youthful idealism uppermost in my mind.

Only occasionally did we read the one copy of the newspaper *Messagero* delivered to the house. The Nazis invaded Poland on September 1, 1939, and we learned of that on the radio. The academic routine proceeded as usual, but we could feel the tension in the air. Toward the end of our third year, in May of 1940, the American consul came into our 10 A.M. class and announced that the Nazis had invaded the Low Countries. He said all Americans would have to leave Rome in exactly one week, to be evacuated on the USS *Manhattan,* which was leaving from Genoa on June 1. If we weren't on it, he warned, we might not be able to get out of Rome until the war was over, and no one could predict when that would be.

The announcement that we were going home threw us all into a frenzy. The school term would be cut short by one month and we had less than one week to prepare for our final exams, pack and get ready to leave. Fortunately, I had kept up in all my subjects and did very well in them—except for Hebrew. Because that ancient language was too difficult to retain from week to week, students traditionally crammed for that final examination during the final two weeks. Anyway, Hebrew was my last exam the day before I was to leave and I had exactly twenty-four hours to get ready for the dreaded moment.

With Europe going up in flames which would engulf the whole world, the first question was: *"Quomodo dicitur occidet hebraece?"* ("How do you say in Hebrew, 'He kills'?")

"Katal," I answered. He continued with "She kills" and "He will kill," and I was doing just fine until he got to "He was killed," and I had to say *"Nescio,"* which in Latin means "I don't know." My Hebrew teacher, a Basque Jesuit by the name of Galdos, gave me a rather disgusted look and said, *"Videamus si possis legere?"* ("Let's see if you know how to read"). He then spun a Hebrew Bible that he had in front of him so that it was facing me. Luckily it was open to the first chapter of Genesis, and he put his finger on the text of the first twenty or so lines, which I had memorized. *"Legas,"* he commanded, and I read the Hebrew text. He then asked me to translate, and I said, *"Et dixit Deus, fiat lux et facta est lux,"* which means, of course, "And God said let there be light and there was light." The little I knew of Hebrew had not fooled Galdos, but he gave me a 6, which was the lowest passing grade for the course. Still, I had passed, and that ten-minute examination fulfilled my Hebrew requirement for my doctorate years later. As

I left, Father Galdos wished me a *buen viaje* and asked me to send him a picture postcard from New York. My sister Mary, the faithful letter writer, met me at the pier in New York with a bearhug and a kiss, and together we took the train to Syracuse, where I had two weeks of homecoming celebrations with my family before resuming my studies. I had studied for three years in Rome for my doctorate, instead of eight. The next five years were slated for Washington, D.C.

By the way, I sent that picture postcard to Galdos. I owed him that much, and more.

THREE

TEACHING

I SPENT THE next formative five years of my life in our nation's capital, while we were at war in Europe and in Asia, and life was put on fast-forward so that democracy and freedom throughout the world could be saved by every man, woman, and child doing his or her bit. That was the battle cry at home in those days.

Those five years for me could be divided neatly into two periods. The first three years I studied at Holy Cross College in Washington, just behind Catholic University of America, and then returned to Notre Dame to be ordained a priest. Then I went back to Washington for another two years to study for my doctorate in sacred theology at Catholic University. Actually, it was a three-year program, but I managed to complete it in two years.

I was ordained on June 24, 1943, along with fifteen classmates in the old Sacred Heart Church in the heart of the Notre Dame campus, next to the gold-domed main building of the university. Sacred Heart, built in 1871, is one of the most beautiful Gothic churches in America. Its main altar came from Paris and its windows from Le Mans, France. It was a solemn-joyous kind of a day, one of deep, abiding feelings for me as well as for my loving parents. I gave them and my sisters and brother my first priestly blessings. Nine years before, in September 1934, I had left home with a far-off dream to become a priest at Notre Dame, and when I walked out of Notre Dame's parish church, I, Theodore Martin Hesburgh, was what I had always wanted to be: a priest. Pausing, as had so many before me, at the sculptured east side door of Sacred Heart, a memorial to the Notre Dame men who had given their lives in World War I, I read the dedication above the door: GOD, COUNTRY, NOTRE DAME. I would dedicate my life to that trinity, too.

I was a young, sheltered, but very eager priest when I returned to Washington, and truly fortunate in coming in contact at the start with so many good priests who influenced my life by their advice and example. Everyone in those days was working over and beyond his or her normal capabilities because there never seemed enough time available for all that had to be done. The older men were only too happy to avail themselves of my enthusiasm, and they really piled on the work. I was in Washington to finish my doctorate, but I soon found myself doing parish work, writing booklets for the military, serving as chaplain at a federal reform school, performing as auxiliary chaplain at Fort Myer and occasionally at Fort Belvoir, helping to run a USO club, and filling in—often on ridiculously short notice—for other priests. But, you know, there was a war on.

That first (hot) summer in Washington, I was asked on short notice to substitute for another priest in conducting a three-day retreat for high school students, which entailed three conferences a day, hearing confessions from a thousand students, and counseling the students—all by myself. I pleaded with Father Christopher O'Toole, the superior at Holy Cross College, where I was living: "Look, I've only been ordained for two months, and I have nothing with me that would be of any help at all giving this retreat." Father O'Toole was a cheerful optimist and his favorite remark, which I came to know well, was "Oh, you can do it," and he left me to my own devices. On another occasion he came to my room, where I was writing my doctoral dissertation, and asked me to fill in for someone by giving the *Tre Ore* at the local St. Martin's parish. The *Tre Ore* is a three-hour Good Friday ceremony, and starting time was a half hour away. "You mean I'm supposed to get down there in half an hour and then preach for three hours with no warning and nothing prepared?"

O'Toole just said, "Oh, you can do it," and I did.

I also wrote quite a few guidance booklets for men and women in the U.S. military. On several of them it was my pleasure to collaborate with a Holy Cross priest named Charles Sheedy, who was a few years older than I, and for whom I was to develop a lifelong fondness and respect. Charlie had graduated from Notre Dame with a major in English. He was a very savvy, worldly priest, and I learned a lot from him about the way you get things done outside the seminary. Together we cranked out a monthly news bulletin and a magazine for chaplains and a variety of publications as the need arose. On our own, Charles and I decided one day that the men in the service needed a spiritual guide, and we started looking around for one. We finally discovered a little pamphlet entitled *Pour Mieux Servir (To Serve Better)* that had been written for seminarians in the French Army. I translated it into English and showed it to Charlie, who took one look at it and said, "This is too French. I'll keep the idea, but I'm going to scratch the whole thing and start over." He sat right down and dashed off a spiritual guide that was much more attuned to our service people. We called it *For God and Country* and sent it off to the printer. The reader response was overwhelming, far beyond anything we had seen before. Three million copies of that pocket-sized booklet were eventually distributed.

While working at the Washington USO, where I met thousands of young women in the service, it occurred to me that service-women needed some sort of ethical and moral guide as much as men did. I proposed the idea to the National Council of Catholic Servicemen, a branch of the USO, and they snapped at my offer to write it. I based that little booklet on letters I wrote to my sister

Betty, who was an officer in the Waves. So, each article in the booklet began, "Dear Betty." I checked and double-checked my work with young servicewomen I knew from the USO, incorporating many of their ideas and suggestions. When the *Letters to Servicewomen* was published, copies were snapped up so fast that we were perplexed. We had printed the same number of copies as there were women in the service, something like half a million, and that was not enough. Someone finally figured out that the men were reading it, too. That was fine with us. Just a handful of us priests wrote these inspirational booklets on all manner of subjects, and overall, I would guess that between six and seven million copies of them were distributed throughout the armed forces. Judging from the incredible amount of mail they generated, I would think hundreds of thousands of lives were affected.

I became involved in the USO because Father Tom Dade, who did a radio show in Washington and was known around town as the Radio Priest, asked me to take over the operation of the Washington USO club while he went on a much-needed vacation. It was as simple as that: Someone asked you to do something and you were hooked on a new activity. I stayed with the club for the duration of the war, as a host and a friend to thousands upon thousands of servicemen and -women who looked upon USO clubs as home away from home. Our USO club was huge, located in the Knights of Columbus Hall at Tenth and K streets, which was also in Washington's red-light district. Our immediate goal was to keep the kids off the street and out of the brothels and then to give them a good time. To do that, we brought in some of the best big military bands in the country, and it was not unusual to have two or three of these top name bands playing at the same time on different floors of the club for a thousand or fifteen hundred jitterbugging men and women in the uniforms of our Army, Navy, Air Force, and Marines. It was a sight to see.

At the same time, I served as chaplain to the National Training School for Boys, which was my first experience with juvenile delinquents, and I worked with several interracial groups, mostly black, in Washington and at Howard University. I cannot measure how much or how little I helped them at the time, but for me as a young priest it was an education in itself. I added to that experience by attending seminars on racial justice held every Sunday morning at Catholic University. I had a lot to learn. Until I had gone to Rome at age twenty, I had not known a single black person.

My first parish was a two-week assignment to St. Martin's, and I considered myself lucky to have been assigned there. The worst thing that can happen to a young priest is to get put in a parish where the pastor is cynical or sour. My first pastor, whom I'll always remember as Father Bill, was a warm, cheerful, giving man of enormous energy and goodwill. Whenever he took the parish car somewhere, the backseat was filled with gifts for the needy— a layette for an unwed mother or a birthday cake for an eighty-year-old parishioner, always something for someone in need.

Father Bill, who was in his late forties at the time, told me something that has stayed with me, and I pass it on now. He never worried about being conned, he told me. If a panhandler asked for a dollar or something to eat, he always gave it to him because it was better to give the buck or the sandwich to someone who didn't need it than withhold something from someone who did. He then told me a story of a down-and-outer who approached him in downtown Washington and asked him for money to get to Virginia. The man said he'd been on the road for some thirty years, and now was terminally ill and wanted to see his mother before he died. He promised to pay Father Bill back and took his name and address. About a week later Bill got a letter from the man's mother, thanking him for his help and telling him that she and her son had had a wonderful week together before he died. Enclosed with the letter was the three dollars Bill had given.

A few weeks later, when I had been given a more permanent parish assignment at St. Patrick's Church at Tenth and G streets, my own attitude toward panhandlers was put to the test. Were they truly beggars in need or con men? I gave five dollars to a disheveled-looking derelict who had come to the door, and bore the laughter and warnings of other priests in the room who said I was naive and would never see that five dollars again. A few days later I received a five-dollar bill in the mail from him and it gave me a great deal of pleasure to wave that five-dollar bill around. Over the years some promises have been kept, some broken, but I always give, reminded of Father Bill: "Better to be conned ninety-nine times than to miss the one who really needs help." I also well remember my novice master saying, "Having taken the vow of poverty does not mean you have to be stingy."

The priests at St. Patrick's were wonderful to me, and most of them were on the fast track. One was Tom Dade, the Radio Priest, who introduced me to the USO and also signed me up for a month of his weekly radio program. Two others became chancellors. Another, Larry Sheehan, at that time a monsignor, eventually became a cardinal. The priest I replaced at St. Patrick's was George Di Prizio, the same fellow who had taught me Italian in Rome. George was keenly aware of my lack of experience, and while turning over his duties to me before leaving the parish, he gave me some advice that has served me well to this day: "Ted, don't be too professional."

At first I couldn't figure out what he meant. I'd spent my whole life becoming a professional, I told him. "That isn't what I mean," he replied. "There are a lot of priests around, probably twice as many as are really needed to do the work. But none of them is doing the work that's the toughest, the most important. When the doorbell rings, most of these fellows think that the faster they get rid of the person, the better the job they've done. That's what I mean by being too professional. A good priest will spend time with the person at the door. He won't be satisfied until he knows why that person rang the bell." *Priesthood means service, no matter who rings the bell.*

With the war on the whole time I was at Catholic University, I was really itching to get out of Washington and into the military service. Specifically, I wanted to be a chaplain in the Navy, and more specifically, I wanted to be a Navy chaplain on an aircraft carrier in the Pacific. Since boyhood my first five-minute flight in a light stunt plane, I had had a fascination with flying. But Father Tom Steiner, my provincial superior at Notre Dame, was adamant. "Get your doctorate now, or you will never get it," he told me. "Then we'll talk about your becoming a Navy chaplain."

The required work for the doctorate was supposed to take three years, but I did not want to wait that long for a Navy chaplaincy, so I decided to do it all in two years. With four years of theology behind me and my language proficiency from Rome and the Gregorian, I had a considerable advantage over my classmates. Because I had only a bachelor's degree in philosophy from the Gregorian, I had to pass comprehensive examinations which were the equivalent of a master's degree at Catholic University, but once that was accomplished, I was on my way. I read many books written in French and some in Italian and German. The most helpful texts in my chosen field of theology were written in Latin, and I reveled in reading the original versions of such classics as *De Verbo Incarnato* on the Incarnation and *De Deo Uno et Trino* on the Trinity, both by Cardinal Billot. I marveled at Billot's ability to combine his classically beautiful Latin with his French clarity of thought.

Earning a doctorate in two years loaded a lot of work into that second year. I had to take six courses, each of which required a long paper, and simultaneously write my doctoral dissertation, which would be five hundred pages, plus ninety pages of footnotes in six languages. The deadline was March 1, 1945, and the dissertation had to be perfectly typed and with five copies. If I missed the deadline, I would have to wait another six months. I worked from seven in the morning until midnight every day from October 1 to March 1 in order to finish by the due date. The only time I took off was three hours on Christmas afternoon. I could not have done it without help from some very extraordinary and kindhearted people. One of them was Jim Doll, a Holy Cross seminarian about two years behind me, who had typed most of the service booklets we had written, and banged out ninety pages of footnotes in record time and with phenomenal accuracy. All I had to do was put in the accent marks.

Jim Norris, the director of the National Council of Catholic Servicemen, which published the little booklets, was a godsend, for I was in desperate need and he came through. "Ted, you've written these booklets for the past two or three years for nothing, so here's what I'm going to do. I'm going to give you the five best typists we have until the whole thing is typed." It was heavenly music to my ears. Each day that followed, I went downtown to the office, picked up the typed pages as they rolled out of five blazing typewriters, and sat down then and there at an empty desk, proofread the pages, and put in all the accent marks.

The day the dissertation was due, the five young women were still typing and I was beginning to get apprehensive. The head of the theology department, a monsignor named Joseph Fenton, was known as a stickler on rules. A deadline was a deadline. Mine was five o'clock. No exceptions. When the women handed me the final pages of my thesis, it was ten minutes to five. No way I could make it. So I called Fenton's secretary, a wonderful woman by the name of Helen O'Connor, for whom I had done several kindnesses. I just said, "Helen, it's done."

"Thank God," she said.

I told her I was going to grab a cab and that I would be over there no later than five-fifteen. I was at the headquarters office of the U.S. Catholic Conference at 1312 Massachusetts Avenue, N.W., and there was no way I could get to the university any sooner.

"Father Ted," Helen said, "I love you dearly, but the boss told me that if any of you guys didn't get your dissertations down here by five o'clock, you weren't going to get your degree until next November." Then there was a pause, and Helen added, "But for you I'll keep the office open until you get here."

At five-twenty I rushed into her office with a heavy stack of manila envelopes more than a foot high. "Helen, here is the thesis and five copies and God bless you."

"And God bless you, too," she replied with a lovely smile.

The rest was easy. All I had to do was defend the thesis, which was on a subject that I knew more about than anyone else in the world at that time. Five examiners questioned me for an hour or so, but the defense was really a breeze. It was both the most important and the easiest examination I had ever had.

The major difficulty had come two years before when I sought approval of my topic, which was based on an avant-garde movement called Catholic Action. This was the beginning of a new lay apostolic activity in the Church. A very dear Paulist father named Gene Burke, who was my thesis adviser, counseled me against trying. "It's a great idea, but you'll never get it approved at this university, because the subject is much too practical." Up until that time, the prevalent way of thinking was that you needed a mandate from the hierarchy before you could do anything apostolic. I believed deeply that the indelible character we receive through the sacraments of baptism and confirmation—and if you are a priest, Holy Orders—is a mandate from God to build the life of Christ within yourself and also to spread the Word to others. Today this is nothing new, but it was considered fairly far-out then. I told Burke I thought I could get the topic by the committee if I dressed the subject up a little, so I thought up a long-handled title for it, and sure enough, it passed.

After defending my dissertation, I presented to Catholic University, as required, the copyright and three hundred printed copies. I copyrighted it with the glorified title and then I had a thousand more copies printed with the title *Theology of Catholic Action*. They sold out almost immediately, earning me enough money to pay for the copies that I had to give to Catholic University.

With doctorate in hand, I wrote to Father Steiner, reminding him of our talk about my becoming a Navy chaplain. Pleading my case, I wrote him that I had taken the liberty to ask my cousin, Joe Farrell, a captain in the Navy, to intercede on my behalf with a friend of his, Father Joseph Russo, who was chief of chaplains. As a result, Father Russo had promised me that with Church permission he would slip me into a chaplain class at the College of William and Mary. In thirty days I could be a chaplain on a carrier in the Pacific. It was as good as done. I anxiously anticipated Father Steiner's reply, suffering the suspense of waiting, waiting, one week, then two weeks. When his letter arrived, it was not what I had expected.

I was to go home to visit my family for a week and then report for duty at Notre Dame on July 5, my orders said. Father Steiner wrote that the Navy was sending thousands of officer candidates to Notre Dame for training, and Notre Dame was in desperate need of faculty. That sank my hopes for a carrier in the Pacific. Little did I know that a month or so later the war in the Pacific would end and I would become chaplain for all the returning veterans at Notre Dame.

It was as if the Lord were saying to me, "Your planning is terrible. Leave it up to *Me*."

Returning to Notre Dame just in time to start teaching a course on moral theology on July 5, I was expecting a syllabus or a course outline of some kind. But when I reported to the office as the new instructor, all they gave me was a textbook and six note cards with the title of the course, The Ten Commandments, mimeographed on them. With that, I was on my own. So was everyone else who was teaching the required course. In fact, as I found out later, there were as many courses in moral theology as there were teachers teaching it. In the classroom next to mine, the priest spent the whole semester on the First Commandment. Others emphasized the Sixth Commandment because they knew that any discussion of sex was guaranteed to hold the students' attention. Conversely, one priest thought it was not nice to talk about sex; when he got to the Sixth Commandment, he just said, "Purity is a wonderful virtue, and now we'll go on to the Seventh Commandment."

The text, *Moral Guidance,* written by a Jesuit, was just about the worst presentation of moral theology I had ever seen—full of casuistry and riddled with stuff like how late you could come to Mass, or how early you could leave, and still fulfill your Sunday obligation. All of this struck me as exactly the kind of thing we should not be teaching young people. They needed ideals and goals. I ignored the textbook and its minimalist moral approach as best I could, and instead stressed the Christian virtues. Teaching was brand-new to me, but fortunately Charlie Sheedy, my friend and coauthor from Washington, had already been at it for a couple of years, and he helped guide me.

The religion department at Notre Dame also offered courses in apologetics, doctrine, and the sacraments, and they were as badly taught as was The Ten Commandments. Students had a choice, a painful choice, because twelve hours of religion courses were required and one was as boring or as confusing as another. The primary reason, I thought, was that every Holy Cross priest at Notre Dame, whether he was trained in physics, economics, or whatever, was required to teach a religion course. Naturally, their hearts were in their specialties, not in the religion course. In those days the religion courses were probably the worst-taught courses at the university.

Father Roland Simonitsch, the new head of the religion department, astutely realized that the only way to shape up or at least standardize the curriculum was to design a standard syllabus for each religion course. He asked Charlie Sheedy to do the syllabus for moral theology and he had me do a syllabus for the dogma sequence. He could not very well ask us to write the textbooks, too, so very cleverly he suggested that we put down on paper some of our teaching notes to go along with each syllabus. We wrote them up and distributed them to the other priests as we went along, staying a day or two ahead of the classes. Charlie's notes became know as "Sheedy Sheets." By the end of the semester we had a whole course blocked out, which was just what Simonitsch wanted. Then, along with all our other duties, we turned those notes into books. Charlie called his *Moral Guidance.* Mine was named *God and the World of Man.* Published by Notre Dame Press, they each told over 100,000 copies, not because they were all that great, but for the lack of competition. There just were not any theology books of any consequence for college students.

When I started to teach, I was the only doctor of theology in the religion department, but I believe efforts must have been started some time before to improve the religious instruction. That was why I and others were chosen for advanced academic degrees. I was the first out of the gate. Charlie Sheedy came right after me, then Joe Cavanaugh. That was the beginning of a whole group of doctorates in the congregation. Within a few years, fifteen or twenty Holy Cross priests had their doctorates. Fittingly, I suppose, the name of the department was later changed to the Department of Theology.

But we still had a long way to go. Even after things started to turn around in the theology department, the courses were geared more to a high school level. I thought we ought to be challenging university students to learn what the Church really teaches about the great moral questions of our day and such important areas as the Incarnation and the Trinity. We should not have been ducking or oversimplifying those objects. Gradually we improved our undergraduate courses in theology, and the introduction of postgraduate courses in theology also helped raise the level of undergraduate study.

When Vatican II came along in 1962, we had to revamp everything again. Before Vatican II, the Catholic Church was mainly the work of the hierarchy in Rome. After Vatican II, we started to depart from the monarchical model and to adopt an interpretation of the Church as the People of God. I had long favored that interpretation, and I was gratified to discover that a few lines in several of the Vatican II documents were taken almost verbatim from my doctoral dissertation, especially in the document "On the Laity." It was not a coincidence, I realized, because the day after I turned in my dissertation the apostolic delegate telephoned and asked me to mail him two copies. I thought at the time I was either going to get shot or used. I was happy to be used.

After Vatican II, Father Richard McBrien, a noted theologican who later headed Notre Dame's theology department, wrote a comprehensive two-volume work called *Catholicism,* which brought the old, classical theology into modern times along the lines of Vatican II changes. Today the theology and philosophy departments are two of the largest and best departments at Notre Dame.

The first two months I taught at Notre Dame, July and August, were the last two months of the war. The Navy's V-12 program ended on campus, but the end of the war marked the beginning of the veterans era in higher education. Some came to finish degrees they had started before the war. Some were there for the first time. But they were all older men with different problems than those of the so-called traditional students. I thought these men might better adjust to campus life if they had some kind of organization they could call their own, and so I started the Notre Dame Veterans Club for the first seventy or eighty veterans on campus, and became its chaplain. We did all the usual things a vets club would do: elected officers, collected dues, and organized social events.

Our first outing was an afternoon picnic at the dunes on Lake Michigan, and it was my first experience with a beer keg party. They brought four. The first two went down just fine, but somewhere into the third, most of our young veterans became downright drunk. Feeling responsible for their welfare and fearful of what might happen, I took the fourth keg of beer and broke it open on the sand. They were too drunk to notice, I think. Anyway, I persuaded them to get back onto our flatbed truck and we drove back to campus. Worried about a truckload of inebriated students raising havoc, I ordered them to get out at Dorr Road on the western extremity of our twelve-hundred-acre campus, and then full of good cheer, I marched them up and down the roadway several times, shouting "Forward march! Hut, hut, hut. To the rear, march! Hut, hut, hut." When I judged them to be reasonably sober, I marched them briskly back to their dormitory. Years later, when I implemented my opposition to keg parties by outlawing them on campus, I could tell students that I spoke from experience. I knew that once a keg is opened, all the beer therein has to be drunk.

By the next year or so, we had so many veterans on campus that the Vets Club had a membership of something like 73 percent of the whole student body. At that point it seemed rather silly to have a club that almost everyone belonged to, so we decided to close it down. Once the Vets Club was quietly, more or less, laid to rest with a final raucous beer bust, I turned my attention to a group who became very special to me, the married veterans. I felt compassion for them. They were the first married students ever to come to Notre Dame in any substantial numbers, and there were no precedents for ministering to their needs. They also had to contend with some formidable practical problems. The worst was housing. At the time, decent housing in South Bend was so scarce that landlords could and did charge exorbitant rents for apartments that were practically uninhabitable.

I took on the vets' problems as my top priority and I learned to deal with a good many very practical matters. The first thing I did was recruit one of my students, Joe Bauer, to scour South Bend systematically by car for decent, reasonably priced apartments. For the car, I had to get him special university permission because student cars were not permitted. We were in business. In short order we had a card catalog stocked with addresses and phone numbers of acceptable landlords and apartments. Once we got our students into good apartments, we never lost control of those rooms. As graduation day drew near, we'd send a new couple over to the vet's apartment to sign a sublease. That way, good accommodations never stood empty and never were advertised in the paper.

Next, we started on housing of our own. We trucked in some surplus Army barracks and set them up along the east side of Juniper Road, which in those days ran just west of the place where the Hesburgh Library now stands. Each barrack was eighty feet long and divided very nicely into three apartments of two bedrooms, a bathroom, and a combination kitchen–living room–dining room. They weren't much, but they were on campus and rented for the unheard-of low price of twenty-eight dollars a month, compared to sixty-five dollars for a roach-infested dive in town. The vets and their wives were in heaven. Only the makeshift walls left something to be desired. They were so thin the vets used to say that you could hear the person in the next apartment changing his mind. And, of course, you could hear everything else, too. The young couples had a lot of laughs about that.

I thought the married couples also needed a social hall to ease the tension of combining schoolwork, married life, and baby care. So I got lucky. On a trip to Washington on some other business, I dropped in at a newly created federal agency called the General Services Administration. I think I was the GSA's first customer. With the war ended, the GSA was charged with getting rid of surplus government property. They were just getting off the ground when I showed up; in fact, they didn't even have the desks moved in or the phones connected. But they did have requisition forms. So I took one of the forms off the pile and applied for a recreation building. A few weeks later I learned that the GSA was sending a large surplus recreation hall to Notre Dame; all we had to do was put in some footings and hook up the plumbing and the electricity. It was as simple as that in those days.

The building was exactly what we needed. It had a couple of offices, a concrete floor, a stage, and a high ceiling. It was absolutely perfect for dances. Every Saturday night, student musicians would come over and play for practically nothing. Our admission charge was twenty-five cents, and that covered the cost of soft drinks. We always kept our costs at break-even or below, because hardly any of these young couples had any money. A married man on the GI Bill received $105 a month from the government, $125 if the couple had a child. When women's hemlines went from knee level or so to mid-calf, I had to make a rule that no young lady would be admitted to a dance in one of those longer dresses. I did that because there were only about two girls in Vetville who could afford to go out and buy a new-style dress.

One very worrisome problem among the married vets was the high incidence of miscarriages. I really had no idea what to do, but I thought I ought to do something. I dug around and found an old ritual blessing for pregnant women, and then put the word out that on the first Monday of the month any woman who was pregnant, or even thought whe was pregnant, should come to Apartment 1A at one in the afternoon to be blessed. We did this every month and, believe it or not, the miscarriages stopped just like that. We kept careful track and we had thirty-nine normal deliveries in a row without a single miscarriage.

Many of these Vetville wives were so young and inexperienced that they knew very little about their own bodies. It didn't help, of course, that their mothers were hundreds of miles away or more. Betty Lane was one example. She and Joe, who was studying law, had gotten married during the war when Joe was training on B-24s in North Carolina. When Betty first started experiencing morning sickness, she had no idea it was because she was pregnant with Kathy. A celibate priest by the name of Hesburgh had to tell her.

The more involved I got, the more I found myself functioning as a marriage counselor in Vetville, and that led me to an interest in the dynamics of marriage—the spirituality, the psychology, and the sociology involved in holy matrimony. These young couples, I decided, needed a course on marriage at the university. They knew so little. Good marriages were terribly important in the lives of these young people and the children they would produce.

I went to see the director of studies, who at the time was Doc Kenna, and told him I wanted to teach a course on marriage, but that I needed to bone up on the subject first. He advised me to go out and buy all the books I needed and when I was ready he would put the course in the bulletin and I could teach it. That's how the Marriage and the Family course got started at Notre Dame. In the meantime, of course, I was continuing to counsel couples at Vetville, so I had a nicer combination of theory and practice to undergird my classroom lectures.

Every once in a while a couple would have a big fight and would call me up, usually in the middle of the night, to come over and untangle it. This was always a delicate situation, like walking on eggs, for I had to be careful not even to appear to favor one side over the other. As chaplain, I was for the marriage, not for one participant or the other. Probably I dealt with some five hundred couples in Vetville and I'm proud to say that hardly any of them broke up during those years. Some did later on, but they were a relative few considering the national average. To this day I meet people who come up to me and say, "I'm still happily married, and thank you for straightening us out," or "Thanks for the course," or "I'm so glad for that course my husband took from you; he learned a lot." We also started marriage retreats in several residence-hall chapels on campus.

The Vetville community became a tightly knit group at Notre Dame, all of them veterans about the same age, facing pretty much the same kinds of problems. They were newly married. They had babies. They were trying to make ends meet on a tight budget. Dad was in school. Mom was at home. When tragedy struck, you could really see how deeply they cared about each other. I shall never forget the day I saw Joe and Betty Lane out wheeling their beautiful little nine-month-old Kathy in a stroller. At midnight they telephoned me from the hospital to say she had just died of spinal meningitis. They were distraught, naturally, but their friends in the Vetville community rallied behind them and helped them get through their tragedy, both emotionally and financially. Joe and Betty wanted the funeral and burial in Connecticut, where Joe was raised, but they did not have the money. I went door-to-door with a milk bottle to take up a collection. By the time I had visited all 115 apartments, the milk bottle had enough money in it to get them to Connecticut and back. A happy footnote to this story: Betty and Joe had six more children, and by the time they were on the second or third one they obviously didn't need Hesburgh to tell them anything. I still hear from them every once in a while, and occasionally we see each other. They always say that, despite the problems, their Vetville years were the best of their lives.

While chaplain of Vetville, from 1945 to 1948, I lived in Badin Hall, where I had the responsibility for the good behavior of a dormitory for unmarried veterans attending college on the GI Bill, which financed their education. They were a fine group of young men who studied hard, swapped war stories far into the night, and had an occasional need to let off steam which disrupted everyone around them. When I was named chairman of the religion department in 1948, I was required to give up my chaplaincy at Vetville and move out of Badin. I shifted into Farley Hall as rector of an explosive mixture of 330 seventeen- and eighteen-year-old freshmen, stuffed two and three to a room, away from home for the first time, innocent and ignorant of caring for themselves. "What should I do with my dirty laundry?" or "Where can I get some Epsom salts?" And so on. I was trying to write *God and the World of Man* at the time, but it was practically impossible to get anything done on it during normal hours. After dinner I had freshmen in and out of my office until lights went off at eleven. It took them another hour to settle down for the night. At midnight I would start working on the book, bang away on the typewriter until two or so, and then drop into bed and sleep until seven. Then the next day started with Mass in the hall chapel.

It never occurred to me how valuable this hands-on experience with students would be to me years later as I rose, mostly against my will, in the hierarchy of Notre Dame.

FOUR

LEADING

WITH MY teaching, writing, and chaplaincy at Vetville, I was more than content. I was as busy and happy as I had been at any time in my life. I considered myself fortunate indeed, and was perfectly happy to continue for the rest of my life doing what I was then doing—teaching, writing, and ministering. But Father John Cavanaugh, the president of the university, had other ideas for me.

One day, without any warning whatsoever, he told me he wanted me to be dean of the College of Arts and Letters. At the time I was an instructor, not even an assistant professor. To jump a mere instructor into the lofty position of a dean hardly seemed appropriate. I knew he wanted to replace that particular dean, who just was not up to the job and happened to be his brother, Frank. No matter. I felt an aversion to all the paperwork that goes with being a dean; I didn't want to be an administrator of any kind, and I told Cavanaugh that. Kindly, he did not persist, and that was the end of it, or so I thought.

But you could never tell what was going on in his mind. Father John had been a vice president of the Studebaker Corporation when he had given up a very promising career to take up a "late vocation" in the priesthood. He was marvelous at getting along with people and at the same time getting what he wanted, doing it so casually one would hardly suspect him of ulterior motives. He gave me enough time to forget about the Arts and Letters position and then he made me rector of Farley Hall. That entailed supervising 330 freshmen in the dormitory and some administrative work. But that did not bother me. Then about a week later he suggested that I give up Vetville because of my other responsibilities. I protested that I was coming along fine on the book, and that when it was finished I could handle the teaching, the chaplaincy at Vetville, and the rectoring with no trouble at all. I liked working with the married vets. Not hearing anything more about this, I thought that was that. Busy as I was, my life was pretty well organized. What I didn't realized was that Cavanaugh hadn't forgotten about me.

One day in September of 1948 I met him in front of Sacred Heart Church as we were both on our way to Corby Hall for prayers. We fell into step together and he remarked, "Ted, how would you like to go into administration?" It was a simple enough question and I thought it had just popped into his mind. Then it occurred to me that perhaps he did not fully realize how much I liked what I was doing. So I gave him a long, considered answer.

"Look, Father John, I didn't want to get a doctorate, but they said I should and I did, and now I'm glad I did. I didn't want to go into teaching because I wanted to do something more active, like being a Navy chaplain. Isn't it curious that by doing what I was told to do, rather than what I thought I wanted, I've managed to have a happy life. I'm enjoying teaching, I'm enjoying offering Mass for the students in the hall every morning, and I'm enjoying the counseling I do every evening. I like the student clubs I'm involved with. And I'm engrossed in writing this theology book, and looking forward to writing two more. I like what I'm doing. I don't want to sit behind a desk and write letters and do all those other things that administrators have to do. I'd much rather teach and stay active with the students. With all due respect, I must say, I really don't want to be an administrator."

Cavanaugh heard me out and then with a sigh just said, "Well, it isn't all that bad, Ted."

"I'll take your word for it, but it's not for me," I replied.

The next thing I knew, he made me chairman of the religion department, in charge of more than forty professors, succeeding Father Simonitsch, who had decided to finish his doctoral studies in Washington. Simonitsch may have recommended me for the job; I don't really know. But as I was now a department head, that was the end of Vetville for me. Cavanaugh would not let me continue as chaplain there.

I had been heading the religion department for only a year when I had another one of those chance meetings with Notre Dame's president. It was at the end of the school year in June of 1949. I was just coming out of the Main Building, and there he was. We were both heading for the basement chapel of Sacred Heart Church, as were all the other priests, to receive our "obedi-ences," as they were called, from Father Ted Mehling, the provin-cial. An obedience was an assignment that you received as a priest of Holy Cross for the coming school year.

When we got inside the chapel, Cavanaugh turned to me and said, "By the way, Ted, you're going to be made vice president today."

"What?" I said.

He repeated it for me: "You're going to be made vice president today."

"Oh, come on, Father John," I said, "you've stuck me with a department and a hall, but vice president? God in Heaven, I don't want to be a vice president."

Unbeknownst to me, Cavanaugh had reshuffled the whole organizational structure of the university. As Father Mehling worked his way through the obediences, I became aware, as I am sure everyone else did in the chapel, that there were several job descriptions we had never had before—vice president of academic affairs, vice president of student affairs, vice president of finance, vice president of public relations. By the time Mehling reached the fourth new vice presidency, I relaxed, convinced that Cavanaugh had been pulling my leg. There was no vice presidency left for me. There wasn't anything left to be vice president of. But obediences were handed out according to house age or when you had joined the order. He had not yet worked his way down to the youngest priest sitting in that chapel. Finally he did, announcing: "Ted Hesburgh, executive vice president." I was stunned, just as I had been twelve years earlier when Mehling had told me so matter-of-factly that I was going to Rome.

When it was over and we were standing outside, I asked Cavanaugh what an executive vice president was. He said, "Oh, that's the vice president who's in charge of the other vice presidents."

My first job was to write up an administrative procedure and a job description for each vice president's area of responsibility, including my own. The university had never had an executive vice president before. Now they had one who was thirty-two years old. Father Cavanaugh was a sophisticated and able man, severely overburdened by the postwar demands being made upon a sluggish, tradition-bound university. In his office he explained what my job would be. "Ted, I'm really going to load it on you, and you're going to hate me, but best you learn in a hurry." I assured him that I would never "hate" him. Starting right in, he asked me to forgo my summer vacation and to draw up new articles of administration for the athletics department, and then to attend every game in the fall to observe personally how well or poorly my new rules and regulations were working out.

I was not looking forward to reorganizing any of the departments, least of all the athletics department, which I'll get to later, but when I did that, Cavanaugh informed me, "Now I want you to do the same thing for the other four functional areas of our vice presidents: academics, student affairs, finance, and public relations. I want articles of administration, lines of authority, organizational charts, and areas of responsibility, the whole works."

It did not take a genius to realize that I would encounter degrees of resentment. After all, the new vice presidents were still feeling their way and, worse yet, I was younger than any of them:

Who was I to be telling them what to do? Ah, but they had taken vows of obedience, too. Father John Burke, head of the finance department, for example, was a friend and colleague and told me off in no uncertain terms: "The reason you don't know where to begin is because you're brand-new and totally green. I worked in a bank before I came to the community, and I think it's preposterous for you to come in here and try to organize my area."

"You're singing my song, John," I responded, "but all I can tell you is that this wasn't my idea. I was instructed to do this by John Cavanaugh, who happens to be the president, and if you find it bothersome, I think you ought to take it up with him." Burke must have known that I had my orders from Cavanaugh, and he cooperated with me, albeit grudgingly at first.

Organizing the major departments of the university turned out to be the beginning of an intensive three-year training program that Cavanaugh had devised for me. He also introduced me to the world of benefactor relations. During the time I was executive vice president I had to travel with the football team to all the away games. Before each game Cavanaugh would call me in and say, "Oh, I've got some people I want you to meet while you're there," and I would telephone ahead and see potential benefactors. Cavanaugh never described them or thought of them as such, only that they were friends of Notre Dame, often widows of former trustees or donors. He believed in treating all friends of the university well. The rest would follow.

The next thing Cavanaugh put me on was buildings. As with almost everything else he had me do, I knew next to nothing about getting a building built, nothing about construction or contractors, nothing about materials, nothing about finance, and nothing about architects. It probably wouldn't have been so bad if I'd had only one building to worry about, but Cavanaugh gave me five—Nieuwland, O'Shaughnessy, Fisher, the Morris Inn, and last, but certainly not least, the power plant.

My education in the complex world of architecture, design, construction, and building materials was swift and awesome. I learned because I had to. Being new at it, naturally I questioned how things had been done in the past. I found that for any new substantial building, we had used only one firm of architects in Boston and one or another local building contractor in South Bend on a cost-plus basis. The architects would draw up a beautiful Gothic exterior for the size building needed, and only later would someone try to figure out how best to make it functional. And there was no way to check on what our buildings should cost. The more I looked into the situation, the more I became an advocate of "function before form." On one of the first building projects I sat down and wrote up sixteen pages of instructions to the architect, based upon my own interviews, on the functions needed in the building.

The smartest thing I did was get help. A young engineer named Vincent Fraatz, who had just earned his master's degree in engineering from Catholic University, was on campus to advise us on building a small animal house behind the biology building, and he was so good that I hired him to help me on our multimillion-dollar building projects. Then I changed the way we did things. I opened up the bidding for the design of our four building projects and we ended up hiring three different architectural firms, based upon the best design and the lowest price. I also ended our building on a cost-plus basis and took sealed bids on all construction contracts, and that saved us heaps of money. All these were radical changes in procedures, and then, to top it all, the Korean War broke out, building materials were rationed, and I had to go to Washington and cut through a tangle of bureaucratic red tape in order to get signed government permits for such items as sixteen thousand tons of steel and thirty thousand feet of copper tubing.

During those three years, Cavanaugh assigned me to a multiplicity of overlapping projects, both large and small, more than I thought I could handle, and I sometimes wondered about his seemingly unbounded faith in me. And yet, somehow, I rose to the occasion; a job had to be done and one did it, and learned something on the way. For the better part of one summer I found myself alone in the administration and presumably in charge of the whole university. Father Cavanaugh had gone to Rome for a worldwide meeting of the Holy Cross Congregation. While he was away, he never called or checked up on me, which was his way of demonstrating his trust in me, although I did call him once about a crisis of some kind.

Then there was that cold day in January 1952 I will long remember. He called me to his office and said, "I hate to do this to you, Ted, but I'm sick, just feel terrible, and they don't know what's wrong with me, but my doctor wants me to go down to Florida and get some sun." He looked dreadful, ashen, worn out. Saying he would be gone six to eight weeks, he asked me "to take care of things." He brought me up to date on pending matters and then rose from his desk, put both hands under a huge pile of unanswered mail, and, with a big grin spreading across his Irish face, dumped the letters in my lap and said, "Well, you can get started on these." No matter how sick he was, he had not lost his sense of humor.

In late June, six months later, Cavanaugh's six-year term in office was completed. There was no search for a successor, no committee meetings, nothing of that sort. The decision was made by our religious community, headed by Father Ted Mehling, the provincial, with, I am sure, the strong advice of John Cavanaugh. At the end of our school year's annual retreat, Father Mehling once again handed out our obediences. This time, however, he had forewarned me and asked me whom I would want as my vice presidents. Nevertheless, my stomach flipped over when I heard him announce, "Ted Hesburgh, president." Perhaps no one in the room was surprised, for it was fairly obvious that I had been groomed and tested for the job over the past three years as executive vice president. But I was shaken with an attack of nerves. I had turned thirty-five just a month earlier. Fortunately, Father Mehling also appointed all the men I had requested as vice presidents.

As we walked out of the chapel, Cavanaugh reached into the pocket of his cassock and pulled out the key to his office and handed it to me. "By the way," he said, "I promised to give a talk tonight to the Christian Family Movement over at Veterans Hall. Now that you're the president, you have to do it. Good luck. I'm off to New York."

Just like that, I was president of the University of Notre Dame.

No convocation, no installation, no speeches. Just go right to work. That's the way it was done in 1952. And it was not entirely a bad idea. Thirty-five years later, when with a large coterie of academic officials I attended the installation of the new president of Yale University, Benno Schmidt, I heard a wonderful story of Benno's six-year-old daughter asking him the next morning: "All these people, all this fuss, just to put this silly medal around your neck . . ." Out of the mouth of babes . . .

I took the key, walked over to the hall, and gave a talk to a group that called itself the Christian Family Movement. It was my first official act as president of Notre Dame, and fortunately, it also turned out to be the launching of a new national movement.

During my first days in the president's office I found myself reflecting from time to time upon my predecessors. Through them I could trace back how Notre Dame had changed over the years, very much through the personalities, outlooks, and abilities of the priests who had served in this office.

When I arrived at Notre Dame in 1934 as a freshman, the president was John O'Hara. I saw him only at a distance and met him only once as a student; afterward we became very much better acquainted. What struck me about Father O'Hara was that he saw everything in black and white, never gray. He was very much an apologist for whatever came out of Rome, very fierce about anything having to do with morality, especially when it concerned sex. The tales about his going to the library as the university chaplain and pulling certain sociology books off the shelves and actually disposing of them are true.

On the other hand, he was probably the first president who realized, or at least realized more than anyone who came before him, that the president of Notre Dame had to go out and raise money if the university hoped to reach academic excellence. He also recognized the need to attract top faculty if Notre Dame were going to be known and respected beyond the Midwest. Third, Father O'Hara exemplified a tremendous religious spirit, especially by his dedication to daily Mass and Communion. His nickname with the students was the Pope. They idolized him. After serving

Notre Dame, he went on to become cardinal archbishop of Philadelphia.

O'Hara's predecessors were Father Charles O'Donnell (1928–34), a poet; Father Matthew Walsh (1922–28), a historian; and Father James Burns (1919–22), who later became provincial of the Indiana Province of the Congregation of the Holy Cross. Though he served only three years as president of the university, Father Burns, who had a doctorate in the history of education, was the first to introduce the practice of sending Holy Cross priests and seminarians on to higher education so that they could become better teachers at Notre Dame. He was directly responsible for my going to Rome to study theology, and he had a hand in sponsoring other young priests in the pursuit of higher learning. He proved, to my mind, that one person can change the whole direction of an institution, and he did it in a mere three years in office.

When I returned to teach at Notre Dame, the president of the university was Father J. Hugh O'Donnell, a good man and a good priest, but, in my opinion, a leader with very real limitations. He was a large, forceful figure of a man, with a magisterial way about him, plus a very exalted sense of what it meant to be president of Notre Dame. He wore a cape which he would flourish and fling about as he strode across campus during World War II, when a large portion of the student body were Navy officer-candidates in the V-12 program. The naval officers loved him and he kept them happy and Notre Dame alive during the war, when we trained and commissioned more than twelve thousand naval officers.

Father John Cavanaugh (1946–52) I came to know best, of course, since he was my immediate predecessor and I worked under him for those three years and with him for years afterward. He was a marvelous priest and man in every way—honest, bright, good, charming, funny. He literally earned a four-year scholarship to Notre Dame by working as personal secretary to the then president of the university for three years. And because his father had died when he was young, Cavanaugh had never completed high school. After graduating magna cum laude from Notre Dame, and also president of his class, he joined the Studebaker Corporation, then headquartered in South Bend, and rose through the ranks to become its vice president of advertising and sales in three years.

Rejecting business for the priesthood, Cavanaugh rapidly distinguished himself as a priest and an administrator at Notre Dame and became its president. Though he had a kind heart, he brooked no nonsense when it came to performance. There is a story I like about a professor who complained to Cavanaugh about a salary increase Cavanaugh had authorized for him. The professor said something like "I think this raise is disgraceful. After all, I've had twenty-one years of experience."

Cavanaugh apparently knew the professor's track record. "Professor," he said, "you've had one year of experience repeated twenty-one times. You're doing the same thing today as you did the first year you taught."

It was unusual for him to be unkind to anyone, but he wanted the best for the university. During a talk at the Carroll Society in Washington, D.C., he asked aloud, "Where are the Catholic Salks, Oppenheimers, and Einsteins?" He thought we had a long way to go at Notre Dame, and I think he regretted that he did not have the time or the health to take the university further, faster. Nevertheless, he was truly the father and pioneer of modern, professional fund-raising at Notre Dame. He propelled us into a new age. Academic excellence was his goal and he knew it would cost money.

Father Cavanaugh retired with even less ceremony than I received in succeeding him. He had not bothered even to move his things out, perhaps because he felt as if nothing in that office really belonged to him. He had cleaned off his desk, but his books were on the shelves. In fact, when I retired thirty-five years later, some of them were still there. Perhaps unconsciously, that was my way of keeping John around.

Those first six months of retirement John made himself very scarce. He took himself off to California to work with Robert Maynard Hutchins in launching the Fund for the Republic, which Hutchins, a great educator, liked to refer to as "a totally disowned subsidiary of the Ford Foundation." I think Father Cavanaugh did not want even to appear to be hovering over me. He would never have done that, but I knew that we needed him at Notre Dame. We were getting ready to plunge into our first large-scale professional fund-raising drive for the Notre Dame Foundation, a Cavanaugh idea, and we needed Father John, his personal magnetism, his business acumen, and his wide network of friends. I did not think he would turn us down, but just to make sure, I asked Father Mehling, the superior, to issue the "invitation." Cavanaugh accepted, and performed superbly, as everyone knew he would. With great prescience, he then attracted Jim Frick, a young alumnus and Navy veteran, to our fund-raising efforts, and long after John Cavanaugh was gone, Jim Frick distinguished himself as director of the Notre Dame Foundation. He became the first lay vice president at the university.

I regularly turned to Cavanaugh for advice and he shared his wisdom and counsel freely on a wide range of university matters. He knew so much more than I did. But he never offered advice unless asked. In many ways he was like a father to me.

As I settled into my new office and position, I evolved a goal for myself. What did I want to accomplish for Notre Dame? That was the question. The answer came silently as a kind of vision. I envisioned Notre Dame as a great *Catholic* university, the greatest in the world! There were many distinguished universities in our country and in Europe, but not since the Middle Ages had there been a great Catholic university. The road was wide open for Notre Dame, I told myself.

To be great, a university needs a great faculty, a great student body, and great facilities. In order to have those things, it needs a substantial endowment, which means you have to learn how to raise money—lots of it. And finally, a great university needs to be imbued with a great spirit, which is an inspirational and cohesive kind of ambience, and not be just a lot of separate parts that operate around a central heating plant. The spirit we had. The rest we didn't.

At the core of a university is its independent-minded faculty. To them, they *are* the university. They see the administration as primarily being responsible for fund-raising and support of faculty needs. The students generally hold an even fuzzier perception of what the administration does. Yet the president is subject to unremitting, conflicting pressures from these two groups, as well as from the university's trustees, alumni, donors, parents, townspeople, and others. Because of these disparate pressures, the job of running a university requires personal, hands-on management, at least until the content, focus, and style of a new administration is well in place.

The best time to make major changes in any organization is at the beginning of a new reign. That's when they are expected. That's when a new broom can sweep clean with the least amount of personal resentment. The hardest thing I had to do when I became president of Notre Dame was to shunt someone aside, or to talk someone into resigning, or, worst of all, to outright fire someone. Unfortunately, it had to be done. We had a lot of people teaching and administering colleges and departments who should not have been. They were not keeping up with the scholarship in their fields, or not working hard enough, or they were simply miscast in the first place. Worse, it always seemed that the more incompetent they were, the less they realized it. But as sympathetic to their plight as I was, I knew that if Notre Dame was ever to become the university it is today, we had to bring in new deans and start upgrading the faculty. That was my job as I saw it.

To give you an idea of what it was like around Notre Dame at this time, let me quote from something I wrote in applying for financial aid from the Ford Foundation. It is as good a summary as any:

> Our student body had doubled, our facilities were inadequate, our faculty quite ordinary for the most part, our deans and department heads complacent, our graduates loyal and true in heart but often lacking in intellectual curiosity, our academic programs largely encrusted with the accretions of decades, our graduate school an infant, our administration much in need of reorganization, our fund-raising organization non-existent, and our football team national champions.

The process of weeding out ineffective deans and department heads actually began six months before Cavanaugh retired. He wrangled the resignation of the dean of the Law School, who was an enormously attractive man and a popular teacher, and replaced him with Joseph O'Meara, an outstanding lawyer from Columbus, Ohio. O'Meara gave us fair warning of what he intended to do to upgrade the Law School, saying we would hate him when he started making changes. "The Law School you're running here now," he said, "is a night school in the daytime." Cavanaugh and I both wanted the man and we pledged him our support.

O'Meara's no-nonsense approach caused a furor. He felt that too many of the students were not serious about law and were not working hard enough. So out they went. He expelled half the students in the school, those who already had flunked one or more courses, including two sons of a Notre Dame professor and the brother of a Holy Cross priest who happened to be a very dear friend of mine. More flunked out shortly after O'Meara took over. He wasted no time in tightening up everything: entrance requirements, curriculum, exams, and new standards for faculty performance.

By the time he had finished, he had changed the place from a rather easy-going gentleman's club to a demanding, earnest school of law. And he accomplished it almost overnight. His sweeping changes upset a good many people, but I backed him and took the heat. In retrospect, perhaps the Law School became too stringent, with too many requirements and not enough flexibility. But O'Meara did accomplish his mission nobly, and his successor, William Lawless, was able to ease up a bit without sacrificing quality at the Law School.

The LOBUND (Laboratory of Bacteriology at the University of Notre Dame) project of raising germ-free animals in an antiseptic environment for scientific research was one of Notre Dame's outstanding research ventures, known throughout the scientific world, and it was my unpleasant duty to have to fire LOBUND's director. Not only was his work advancing the cause of germ-free research, it also was helping to disabuse people of the notion that a Catholic university had to be automatically against science. But there was some flimflam in the way LOBUND was financed, and I wanted that changed. Eventually we settled that point, but one of the casualties along the way was LOBUND's director. He refused to change, and he had to go. Otherwise, he was a very good director, and years later we gave him an honorary degree. He was among the first, it not the first, faculty or staff member I had to dismiss for one reason or another. And that is, without doubt, the worst part of administration: dismissing people.

Another director of a campus institute, this one in history, was a similar case. The institute was doing high-quality work, but he was running what amounted to an independent operation, even to funding and financing. There was no hint of impropriety, but the institute needed to be brought under university control and regulated the same way that all other departments were. When the director, who had been operating with virtual autonomy for years, resisted our changes, he had to go. I particularly suffered with this situation because the man I had to let go had done a great deal to promote the archives at Notre Dame. In retrospect, perhaps I could have handled this and similar situations with more finesse, but I did what needed to be done as best I could at the time.

Similarly, the Bureau of Economic Research on campus consisted of exactly one person, who had total control over funds, research, publications, and everything else. One day I told him we could not continue that way. A "bureau" was supposed to have more than one person, and the university had to have control over it. We took control and, to his credit, he never expressed any resentment at all. He was a good man in my book.

At one point in all this restructuring I learned that the dean of the College of Business Administration had gathered his faculty together the day before and declared, "Well, we've had two bad presidents in a row. We can't stand a third. But we probably won't have to worry about that, because we'll outlast Hesburgh." The next day I had him stop by my office and I asked if the report I had heard about his comments was correct. He admitted that it was.

"Then I guess you know who's finished around here," I said. That was the end of him as dean, but since he had been around so long, I offered him a position as a fund-raiser and public relations consultant for the Business College at the same pay, which he accepted.

When I became president, John Cavanaugh had advised: "The first thing you should do is replace my brother Frank." I knew he was right about his brother's performance as dean of Arts and Letters, but that didn't make it any easier to ask for his resignation. Frank was a loyal soldier, though, and we remained good friends. I replaced Frank with Charlie Sheedy, and Charlie served as an outstanding dean of Arts and Letters for the next nineteen years. Others I appointed included Phil Moore as academic vice president, Paul Beichner as dean of the Graduate School, Jim Culliton of the Harvard Business School as dean of the Business College, Mario Goglia as dean of the College of Engineering, Larry Baldinger as chairman of the Department of Pre-Med, and Bernard Waldman as dean of the College of Science. I would have appointed Doc Kenna to a key position—the Graduate School, probably—but by then he was assistant superior general of our Holy Cross order and was not available for a university job.

My new deans all had two things in common: They had high aspirations for Notre Dame and they had the ability to lead. John Cavanaugh used to say that leadership was a very simple matter. All you needed was a vision of where you wanted to go and the ability to inspire a lot of people to help you get there. When I reflect on that definition, I always think of men like Charlie Sheedy and Paul Beichner, whose high aspirations and leadership abilities never flagged over long years of service to Notre Dame.

Once the new deans were in place, we were ready to upgrade the schools and departments with new faculty, new curricula, new everything. The first grant we received for education came from the Carnegie Corporation to fund an in-house study for the College of Engineering—thirty-five thousand dollars. At about the same time, the Ford Foundation gave us twenty-five thousand dollars for improvements in the liberal arts program. We brought in Professor Jerome Kerwin, a fine Catholic scholar, from the University of Chicago to help us strengthen our social sciences. Later, in 1960, when the Ford Foundation awarded the then stupendous sum of twenty-five million dollars to advance higher education at five promising universities, Notre Dame was one of the chosen recipients. Vanderbilt, Stanford, Denver, and Johns Hopkins were the other four. We put one million dollars of that money into our social sciences and part of the rest into building our new library.

In 1956 we upgraded the College of Business Administration: The traditional business courses were made more demanding and we required 50 percent of the college's curriculum to be in the humanities and social sciences. We overhauled the biology department from an old-fashioned taxonomic operation to an experimental one with emphasis on molecular biology. Within five years we transplanted a completely new faculty there. The department kept changing with the ever-increasing advances in the biological sciences, though not, I admit, always as quickly as we might have wished.

Mathematics has always been a strong department at Notre Dame, and I think it has continually improved over the years. I don't recall any wholesale housecleaning in that department, ever. In the sciences, chemistry had been our strongest department for many, many years, going back to the time of Father Nieuwland, the inventor of synthetic rubber. It probably slipped a notch or so in the ratings as the years went by, not because it wasn't strong, but because our other science departments caught up with it and, in some cases, surpassed it.

The physics department made a big leap forward in 1955 when it acquired a new, state-of-the-art accelerator, its third, from the National Science Foundation, which thereafter continued to support the department. Later, physics got a boost in reputation when it became associated with the Argonne National Laboratory outside Chicago.

Early on, in 1953, we established our Distinguished Professors Program, designed to lure the best people in all academic fields to Notre Dame. We started from zero endowed chairs and it took a long time to raise enough money and to get the word out far and wide. We barnstormed around Europe and America, searching for the right people to come full-time or as visiting professors. It was a long process, but it is really amazing what the very best people can do for a university. They attract other outstanding professors. They attract outstanding students. And they attract more research and endowment money for more special faculty. When I retired as president, we had established more than one hundred named distinguished professorships, each one endowed for a million dollars or more.

In those early years we forged ahead on all fronts and, I think, made tremendous progress academically. Year after year we attracted better people, bigger grants, more endowed chairs, and raised our admission standards for students. We let it be known that we expected more from our deans, our faculty, and our students than ever before.

The model for much of what we were trying to do was the Ivy League, and more specifically, Princeton. Both Yale and Harvard had enormous graduate schools, which we did not, but Princeton was more our size with a superb undergraduate school and only about fifteen hundred students in graduate studies. That's about where we wanted to be, with our focus on undergraduate studies. We wanted to be a Catholic Princeton, if you will.

As time went on and the better we became, more and more students applied for admission. We always had many more applicants than we had room for, but the situation worsened considerably beginning in the seventies. Geometric progression had set in. Those postwar babies were beginning to reach college age. Every loyal alumnus had three or four sons who wanted to go to Notre Dame, qualified or not. We never solved the problem, and future administrations never will, either. The best we were able to do when I was president was to set aside 25 percent of our undergraduate capacity for the children of alumni. We are still doing that. I am equally sure our admissions office is still getting letters from people of influence who think they can get someone's son or daughter into Notre Dame. Sometimes a youngster or his parents will have several influential people write letters of recommendation. In the admissions office, this has led to the saying "The thicker the applicant, the thicker the file." Over the years our undergraduate enrollment has grown from some five thousand students to half again as many, seventy-five hundred, and our postgraduate students from fifteen hundred to twenty-five hundred, but we are holding the line there, as best we can.

At the same time that I was going full tilt on academic improvement, I was drawn into educational activities beyond Notre Dame, and one worthwhile activity led to another and to another. These projects took me away from campus a great deal, but every one of them helped me do a better job in some way at Notre Dame. The first outside organization I joined, which was only natural, was the International Federation of Catholic Universities, and I became very active in it, too, eventually becoming its president. Then I became active in the American Council on Education as a board member, and I joined the board of directors of the Association of American Colleges and later became its president. I joined a committee on Academic Improvement in the Quality of American Education, and the Ford Foundation Committee for Liberal Arts Grants, and the scholarship committees sponsored by Ford and General Motors, and the Carnegie Commission on the Future of Higher Education. Half the members of that Carnegie commission were educators, and the other half were public members. We met every month for three days over a period of six years, and during that time we produced the best and most comprehensive study of American higher education ever done— one hundred volumes' worth. On the Rockefeller Foundation, where I served for twenty-one years, there were always five or six university presidents on the board.

By the late sixties, I was personally acquainted with the president of every significant university in the country. These friendships were invaluable to me in many ways, particularly during the student revolution in the late sixties and early seventies. If you were a university president in those turbulent years, you needed all the friends you could get. Seriously, though, in serving on a broader scale to improve higher education throughout the United States (and in some instances, the world), I always felt I was not only representing Notre Dame but serving her as a citizen in the world of higher education.

How did I get all my work done? People often ask me that and

I don't know if I've ever come up with a simple answer. What they are really asking about, I think, is my administrative style. I never consciously developed an administrative style; the term did not exist when I started. But from the very beginning I realized that I could not run Notre Dame all by myself, and so I placed heavy reliance on the people around me—the vice presidents, the deans, the department chairmen, and the directors of the important nonacademic functions. I appointed the best person I could find for every position and then let him or her do the job. Once that person was in place, he or she had my trust; rarely, if ever, did I overrule a decision or insist on a change in personnel. Good people accept this kind of responsibility. They do not need me looking over their shoulder all the time. That attitude, I think, helped to enhance the extraordinary loyalty that we have always enjoyed among the deans, department heads, and officers at Notre Dame. I have made it a practice never to have two people worrying about the same thing.

How did I pick the best people, the ones I relied on so much, for those jobs? That's a good question. First, I sought intelligence. If you put someone in a position of power and that person is not intelligent, you have problems. I looked for imagination, creativity, and enthusiasm. I wanted people who had ideas about how their jobs should be done, who were not afraid to try something new, and who would throw themselves into the work body and soul. I used search committees and screening committees and that sort of thing to find those kinds of people. And I reached out and found the right man for the job simply by looking around me. Both methods worked.

I found my right-hand man in John Cavanaugh's office back in 1949, three months after I became executive vice president—a tall, smiling, ebullient priest my own age—and when I became president of the university, I appointed Ned Joyce, magna cum laude in the class of '37, as my executive vice president, the number-two man in the university. Ned, a certified public accountant, was the university's financial vice president at the time, and he was good at everything I wasn't, particularly financial matters. While I focused on academics, Ned reigned over finances, buildings and grounds, university relations, athletics, and everything else. We disagreed on matters many times, more over short-range tactics than long-range strategy, but we never fought, never had an argument. People said we complemented each other perfectly because I am, supposedly, "reasonably liberal" and he is "reasonably conservative." His restraint often saved me from making mistakes I would have regretted, and I know we worked well together because we served as president and executive vice president of Notre Dame for thirty-five years.

The other "brilliant" administrative move I made was to inherit Helen Hosinski, who was John Cavanaugh's secretary. Some say I was just plain lucky. Helen, who also backed me up for all thirty-five years in the president's office, is enormously efficient at everything she does; and as I have frequently proclaimed, Helen's memory made it unnecessary for me to have a computer in my office. She ran the office and she ran much of my life with nary a misstep or mistake, an extraordinary woman.

Thanks to people like Ned and Helen and Tim O'Meara, who became provost of the university in 1978 (giving up the chair of the math department), and all the other key people who handled their jobs so well, I was able to extend myself beyond the normal work hours in a day at Notre Dame and away. Actually, I once added up the hours and found that I was away from Notre Dame not more than one third of the time, but my activities apparently were of such high visibility that to many it seemed like more.

There was a popular, amusing gag at Notre Dame about my outside activities, which went something like this:

"What's the difference between God and Hesburgh?"

"God is everywhere; Hesburgh is everywhere, except Notre Dame."

Highly disciplined by nature and training, I could fly to New York or Washington for a day's work and return that night to Notre Dame. I always preferred the late-evening or nighttime quiet hours, say from 6 or 7 P.M. to 2 or 3 A.M., to get my real work done—to gather my thoughts, to reflect, to do my paperwork, and, not infrequently, to be available to those venturesome students who climbed the fire escape late at night and tapped on my office window for a midnight chat. I maintained an open-door (and open-window) policy, keeping myself available on a one-to-one basis for anyone—student, professor, or administrator—who wanted to see me.

In order to devote as much of my time as possible to education in general and Notre Dame in particular, I very deliberately made two important choices at the outset of my presidency. I decided not to follow in John Cavanaugh's footsteps when it came to socializing locally in South Bend. I felt I could not afford the time, and if I accepted one invitation, I would have to accept the next. So for all my years there, with very few exceptions, I did not go to parties or social events in South Bend.

The other decision, which was much more significant, was to more or less abdicate as religious superior of Notre Dame. Traditionally, the president was given the power of religious superior so that he would have, if he needed it, absolute authority over everyone in the community. Theoretically, it made sense. But I did not agree with this custom, even though I had to abide by it. I didn't think I would be able to devote all my energies effectively to the university if I had to do all the work of the superior, too. So I asked Father Richard Grim, who was a very good friend of mine, to take on the job.

During the six years that I exercised the power of the superior, I acted only when I felt strongly that we needed to make a change of some kind. For example, given the hours many of us had to keep as rectors and prefects in the dormitories, I thought it unduly burdensome for all priests to be required to attend meditation prayers every morning at five-thirty, so I changed meditation to the afternoon. I also rescheduled some of the other community events so that they were more realistic—or humane, if you will. After I ceased being superior in 1958, I asked Dick to loosen up on the purse strings a little. The vow of poverty was one thing; having to scrounge for pennies was quite another. I thought it disgraceful the way previous superiors had made our lives so unnecessarily difficult by giving us only enough money to carry out an assignment, and not a single penny more. So I changed it.

One last word on executive style—in academia, on corporate

boards, or in government, anywhere. My predecessor John Cavanaugh taught me the essence of how to make a decision. "You don't make a decision because it's going to be popular, or because it's going to be cheap or expedient. You make a decision because you think it is right."

Over the years I have learned how to handle a multiplicity of problems at the same time. You concentrate your fullest attention on one job while you are doing it, you do the best you can, and then you go on to the next one. When I have said or done something, it is over; I don't worry about it anymore. I doubt that I have spent more than half a dozen sleepless nights in my life. I put my worries aside. I say my prayers and I go to sleep.

FIVE

ON THE PLAYING
FIELD

Sᴘᴏʀᴛꜱ ᴀʀᴇ an important microcosm of life, for on the playing field all of the important values of life come into play in a tightened, heightened framework called the rules of the game. You win or lose on the playing field in front of thousands of spectators and they see, too, how you play the game. It is a fine training ground for developing character and responsibility in youngsters, which often derives from the character and integrity of the coach and the college or university behind them. One of the most important personality traits required of everyone on the playing field is courage, and that is precisely what I needed when as the newly appointed executive vice president in 1949 my first assignment was to go out there and reorganize the athletics department of Notre Dame. I dreaded the assignment. Philosophy and theology were my fields; I knew virtually nothing about the athletics department, except that the director of athletics also happened to be our head football coach. So, essentially, my job was to "reorganize" the domain of Notre Dame's football coach, who happened to be the most famous, most talented football coach in the country—the great Frank Leahy. At the time, he had three undefeated seasons, three national championship teams, and an unbeaten string of twenty-six games. He had coached Notre Dame from 1941 to 1943, gone off to war, and returned in 1946 to become the most outstanding football coach in the nation. He was a man no one, least of all a very green executive vice president, could expect to push around.

Nevertheless, Cavanaugh was displeased about various kinds of minor irregularities he had heard about in the department. He told me that the departmental statutes had not been brought up to date since 1924. The problem, as Cavanaugh explained it to me, was that while the administration theoretically controlled athletics, and had its own representative as an overseer, the reality was that Frank Leahy was doing whatever he pleased. Not that he was doing anything wrong, only that he was operating independently of the university administration. In other words, he was running what amounted to an autonomous fiefdom.

My job, Cavanaugh went on, was to install an athletics director over Leahy and have that athletics director report directly to me. Then I was to update all the statutes of the athletics department— finances, schedules, eligibility requirements, the number of players on the traveling squad, the authority of the team doctor, every-thing. I got the feeling that Cavanaugh wanted me to update the statutes not only because they were old, but also because he wanted to serve notice that the administration was reclaiming its rightful authority over the athletics department.

When Cavanaugh explained all this to me, I pointed out my dilemma. "Father John, let me bring you back to reality. Frank Leahy is one of the best-known men in the country. Around here, they think he is God. He's got enormous prestige everywhere. I find it a bit unlikely that he will take kindly to being ordered around by an unknown priest who just turned thirty-two." I went on to say that I would do it, if that's what he wanted, not that I had any choice in the matter, but that I expected Leahy to hit the ceiling and that he, Cavanaugh, was going to have to decide whether he was going to support Leahy or me. Cavanaugh said he had considered that possibility and had already concluded that in a showdown he would support me. "You might very well lose your football coach in the process," I pointed out, to which he replied, "Well, we can survive that."

I spent the greater part of that summer writing new regulations for the athletics department. By the time I was finished, I probably didn't have a friend to call my own in the department. I was prepared for that. I did not expect to be popular as I sought to find out how money was being spent. To do that, I insisted on initialing every single payment they made for anything. Once I got a fix on where the money was going, I started making some cuts. One noted area of abuse, for example, was in the handing out of too many complimentary tickets to games. Some people were getting wads of them because they were on several different lists. The mayor of South Bend, for instance, received complimentary tickets from the athletics director and from the football coach, who were one and the same person at that time, plus free tickets from the basketball coach, the business manager, and the president of the university. I whittled the distribution of complimentary tickets down to about half as many as there had been before. I wrote a plain and clear statute saying that from then on, all complimentary tickets to any official or friend of the university had to be cleared through me, and mailed with a card from the president. All future complimentary tickets would have to come from the president himself, no one else. That put an end to the patronage system that had grown up around complimentary tickets.

I asked Ed "Moose" Krause to relinquish his head coaching job in basketball to become our athletics director. A two-sport all-American as a student at Notre Dame, Moose loved being our head basketball coach, but he accepted the job I thrust upon him like the good sport he was. It was clear to me that Leahy was not going to like what I was doing. One new statute I wrote gave the team doctor absolute authority in deciding whether or not an athlete could play. If the doctor said an athlete could not play, he did not play. Period. The coach did not have anything to say about it.

The critical new statute that I knew would send the football coach up the wall was the one that stated we would abide by the Big Ten Conference rule governing the number of players on the traveling squad. The number was thirty-eight. Supposedly we were following the rule, but there was no way to know for sure. So I specified that the coach would submit to the executive vice president the names of all the players chosen to make each trip. The executive vice president would then instruct the registrar to give those players excused cuts in their classes. I did this for two reasons. I did not want our players traveling if they were in academic trouble. Secondly, I wanted to make sure that we were not exceeding the thirty-eight-player limit.

Our first away game that year was against the University of Washington in Seattle. Because it was so far from South Bend, our team was scheduled to depart Wednesday out of Chicago. I would be traveling with them to represent the university, a fairly common practice in those days. By Tuesday, when I had not yet received the list of players who were going, I telephoned Herb Jones, the business manager of the athletics department. How many players, I asked, were on the list? Forty-four. I told him forty-four players were not going to Seattle, only thirty-eight were going, and that he had better go and find Leahy, wherever he was, and tell him. Leahy was out on the practice field, he told me. That was another thing I was against, but I would handle that later. The players were going to miss a week of school as it was, and I did not think they should be out practicing when they were supposed to be in classes. But at the moment, all I wanted was the travel list from Leahy. That was crucial. Jones said he'd go find him.

"He says he's too busy to get you the list. He's getting ready for a big game," Jones reported back.

"I'll give you a shorter message for him," I shot back. "Just tell him to give me the names of the six players who are going to reduce that number to thirty-eight, because if he does take all forty-four, the six extra players are going to be out of school for good because they will have missed classes without excused cuts. I'm approving only thirty-eight for excuses."

Before I left to catch the train out of Chicago, I stopped by

Cavanaugh's office to warn of the showdown I had predicted in June. "If he takes forty-four players, you're going to have a nice choice to make," I said. "You're either going to get a new coach or a new executive vice president."

Cavanaugh grinned at me. "Oh, that's easy," he said. "We'll get a new coach."

Boarding the Chicago, Milwaukee, St. Paul & Pacific Railroad, I ran into Jones and asked him how many players were making the trip. He said "Thirty-eight, but Frank is very angry. He's ready to explode."

I did not see Leahy on the train. It could have been he was avoiding me, or simply chance. I was traveling with John Kiley, president of the railroad, in his presidential car, and when he invited me to dine on pheasant, I asked him to extend the invitation to Frank Leahy. He came, but was cold and uncommunicative, which made everybody uncomfortable, especially me.

The game itself is one I would very much like to forget. It was the only time I ever saw the officials deliberately try to do us in. The first half was especially tough. When we watched the films back at Notre Dame, it was plain to see that on practically every play where Notre Dame had the ball, one of the officials pulled his penalty flag out of his back pocket, ready to throw it before our center even snapped the ball. Every time he pulled out his flag, no matter how early, he threw it. We won the game anyway.

Frank really gave a great deal of lip to the Seattle officials that day, and they deserved it. Some of his wrath might have been due to my cutting his traveling team, but in any event, his criticism of the officiating at the game generated an adverse reaction from both the press and much of the public. I received a bushel basket full of mail on the subject, and it took us a long time to assuage feelings out West. I staunchly defended our team and Leahy, because they had been badly wronged, and that brought Frank and me closer together. We made peace with each other, and it lasted.

One bright side to that long, grueling trip to Washington was that it later helped me persuade Cavanaugh that the team ought to fly to its away games. The train ride made the players sluggish.

They exercised too little and ate too much. A big fellow like Leon Hart, who played end, would go into the dining car and order a dozen eggs, two pounds of bacon, and a quart or two of orange juice. Other players were doing the same thing. And that was just breakfast. At night they had to squeeze themselves into those cramped berths that are too small for average-sized people. So they were not getting much sleep, either. But the worst part was that they were missing too many classes. Traveling to Seattle, playing one game, and returning by train took up a whole week. Today, flying to away games, the team leaves on Friday night, plays Saturday afternoon, and is back on campus in time to do some studying and participate in the usual Saturday night festivities on campus.

Looking back on it, bringing the athletics department to heel was much like a great many other decisions that an administrator has to make. In this case Father Cavanaugh saw a department that was unregulated and he wanted it brought back under university rules. Frank resented having his authority diminished, which was very human and understandable, but he finally accepted the new way of doing things. After that we became fairly close. When he had a problem, he would often call me up and say, "Let's take a walk around the lake." I spent a good deal of time with him, not just on football trips, but on other occasions, too. Frank was a very intense man, a classic type-A personality, and I often found myself in the role of friend and confidant. Above all, Frank was a winner and he had the record to prove it. He was one of the most successful football coaches of all time, and I think his intensity had a lot to do with it.

It was during Leahy's time, or just afterward, that there were some stories going around that I was de-emphasizing football at Notre Dame. Not true. I never deliberately did anything to cut back on football. My belief is, and always has been, that the university ought to do everything—academics, athletics, you name it—in a first-rate manner. That means doing everything not only well, but honestly, too.

I did have another run-in with Frank, which became fairly well known and might have caused some people to question my allegiance to Notre Dame football. When I took over the supervision of the athletics department as executive vice president, I reviewed all the files and found a letter from Leahy saying that he had an extraordinary group of candidates that year and would like to accept forty-one players instead of the usual thirty. (There were no NCAA regulations at that time.) The next year he would take only nineteen players, which would average out to thirty per year for the two years. His request was approved. When I arrived the next year, Frank came in with the usual thirty candidates, not the nineteen he had promised. I did not blame him for trying, but I could not allow it. I sent him a copy of his letter and told him I expected him to hold to the agreement. My restricting him to nineteen players became fairly well known on campus, but very few seemed aware that we had taken forty-one players the year before. That is probably why I was accused by some people of trying to de-emphasize football at Notre Dame. But in my book, when you run an honest athletics operation, you are emphasizing athletics, not de-emphasizing them.

With our checks and balances, we set up an honest system in our athletics a long time ago and we have kept it that way. We expect no less from our coaches. In my day, before officially signing on a football or basketball coach, I would sit down with him privately and ask if he had read our rules and was prepared to keep to them carefully. The response almost always was that our system for integrity was what attracted him to Notre Dame in the first place. Then I would insist that we wanted only *student-athletes*. We expected all the players to be students, and we expected all of them to graduate—not 50 percent of them, not 30 percent of them. All of them. I would tell him that if he followed the rules and made sure his players graduated, he would not have to worry about alumni pressure. If he lost some games, or even had a losing season occasionally, I would take the heat, not he. If hired, he would be assured of a five-year contract. With the same assurance I also warned each coach that if he cheated, he would be gone before midnight of the day I caught him at it. That Notre Dame precept in hiring coaches has not gone out of style, nor, I trust, will it ever.

The young Hesburgh and two of his sisters, Betty and Mary, pose for a childhood photograph at their home in Syracuse. (Hesburgh family photograph)

A Hesburgh family photograph taken at Selkirk Shores, Lake Ontario, following Father Hesburgh's ordination in 1943. Front row: Betty, Mary, Theodore B. Hesburgh, and Jimmy. Back row: Anne Marie, Mrs. Hesburgh, and the author. (Hesburgh family photograph)

Theodore M. Hesburgh and fellow seminarian Thomas McDonagh of East Chicago pose just before sailing for Europe in September 1937 on the SS *Champlain* to begin studies in Rome. (Hesburgh family photograph)

Theodore M. Hesburgh (second row, center) and fellow seminarian residents of Collegio di Santa Croce in Rome, photographed with their superior, Father Georges Sauvage (second row, right). (Hesburgh family photograph)

Father Hesburgh (third from left, back row) and other members of his ordination group being ordained at a Mass in Sacred Heart Church in 1943. (Courtesy of Notre Dame Archives)

Frank Folsom and Father Hesburgh at a meeting of the International Atomic Energy Agency (IAEA) in Vienna in the 1970s. They were delegates to the IAEA from the Holy See.

Four-year-old Socheat Long of Cambodia is blessed by Father Hesburgh at the 1982 Jefferson Memorial ceremonies, at which he was given the Jefferson Medal for service to education. In 1979–80, Father Hesburgh chaired a group that raised money to stave off mass starvation in Cambodia. (Associated Press)

Father Hesburgh celebrating Mass at the baroque altar in the Lady Chapel of Sacred Heart Church on the Notre Dame campus. (Bruce Harlan)

Father Hesburgh as principal celebrant at an outdoor Mass for students in the Main Quadrangle of the Notre Dame campus. (Bruce Harlan)

At a 1980s commencement in the Athletic and Convocation Center, Father Hesburgh blesses the graduates. Near the end of each graduation exercise, he would invite parents to join him in blessing their children, a poignant moment that brought tears to many. (Bruce Harlan)

Father Hesburgh and Father Edmund P. Joyce, C.S.C., executive vice president, plan physical expansion of the 1,250-acre Notre Dame campus in the late 1950s. New construction averaged $10 million a year in the Hesburgh era. (Bruce Harlan)

Notre Dame athletics officials and Fathers Hesburgh and Joyce break ground for the Athletic and Convocation Center, an $8.7-million sports building completed in 1968. (Bruce Harlan)

Notre Dame's vice president for business affairs, Holy Cross Father Jerome Wilson (right), and Father Hesburgh surveying the campus from the newly constructed fourteen-story library, circa 1964. (Bruce Harlan)

In 1972, Father Hesburgh called a Washington, D.C., news conference to complain about the lack of White House progress on civil rights. A few months later, he was removed as chairman of the U.S. Commission on Civil Rights by President Richard M. Nixon. (Courtesy of U.S. Commission on Civil Rights)

That's our philosophy and it has worked well. We have run an honest program and have managed to turn out winning teams with athletes who graduate. Our coaches have appreciated the integrity involved. They know we will not wink at a rule violation. When Ara Parseghian resigned as football coach, he made it a point to let me know that there had never been anything under the table while he was coach and that whoever came in after him would find an absolutely clean operation. I received the same assurance from Dan Devine and Gerry Faust when they left, and I have no doubt that Lou Holtz will be able to say the same thing some day.

The coaches we hire know that Notre Dame does not put winning above honesty, or the health of a player—or their own health. Both Ara Parseghian and Frank Leahy won a lot of games for Notre Dame, and both of them could undoubtedly have won a lot more. That would have been nice for us, but bad for them. The pressures of coaching a high-profile, winning team like Notre Dame, plus their own fierce personal desire to excel, eventually took their toll on the health of both these men. When that happened, I encouraged each of them to quit. Ara told me about his health problems; Frank did not. When Ara told me in 1974 that his coaching was adversely affecting his health and he thought he ought to quit, I agreed with him. His health was more important than winning football games for Notre Dame. He had given Notre Dame ten of the best years of his life. He thanked me and said he appreciated my support.

Frank Leahy, on the other hand, did not say a word to me about his health problems. He didn't have to. During a home game against Georgia Tech in 1953, he collapsed in the locker room during halftime and had to be taken to a hospital. When they got him there, he had practically no pulse. On another occasion, in Baltimore playing Navy, he again collapsed in the locker room. They had to give him an injection to bring him around. Frank often worked himself into a frenzy of worry and concern over an upcoming game, even when Notre Dame was heavily favored to win. I saw that one night when we were down in Bloomington, getting ready to play a so-so Indiana University team. I ran into

Frank pacing the hotel corridors around midnight. There was absolutely no reason for him to be up at that hour worrying about that game, but that's the way he was.

Because of these incidents, I resolved to do something to keep Frank from killing himself. He had eight young children under college age. Knowing I could not persuade Frank myself, I enlisted the help of Arch Ward, the prominent Chicago sportswriter, and Art Haley, our long-time director of public relations, both great friends and admirers of Frank. They took him and his wife, Floss, to dinner and, in essence, confronted him with the stupidity of risking his life to continue coaching football when he could retire, regain his health, and live happily ever after. To their surprise, Frank agreed with them. He had no money worries at all and there was no reason he could not continue to earn a good deal on the lecture circuit.

After conferring with Ned Joyce, I offered the job to Terry Brennan, our freshman football coach, with a major proviso. I told him we all knew him well and liked him. As a matter of fact, I had had Terry in one of my religion classes and knew his wife from when she was a student at Saint Mary's, across the lake from Notre Dame. Terry had had a successful career on our football team, and his famous runback of the opening kickoff for a touchdown against Army in 1947 was well remembered. It was a very popular victory at Notre Dame. Terry had gone into high school coaching, where he led Mt. Carmel High School in Chicago to three straight city championships in the highly competitive Catholic League. Then he came back to Notre Dame as our freshman coach. He was good, very good. The one reservation we had about Terry, however, was his age. He was only twenty-five.

I told him I would understand if he decided to take a pass while he got a little more experience, and that if he did, we would consider him to be the prime candidate the next time the top job came up. But Terry did not want to wait. He said he could do it, and that if Father Joyce and I offered him the spot, he'd accept it. We made him the offer—and Notre Dame had the youngest head coach in its history.

I gave Terry only one piece of advice. I suggested that he surround himself with the best people available and not be concerned if they were older and more experienced than he; that's what I had done when I became president of Notre Dame at thirty-five. But Terry hired a group of new assistants, some of whom were even younger than he was. He did very well his first two seasons, but the third year the team won two games and lost eight. We stayed with him two more so-so years and then, with little hope of turning things around, we had to let him go.

I came off like Scrooge when the announcement of the end of Terry's Notre Dame coaching career came just before Christmas in 1959. The timing was actually at his request. I wanted to announce it early in December, but Terry told me his wife had already planned a Christmas party on something like the sixteenth or seventeenth of the month. She did not want the party to be ruined by the news, so I gave in on the date. I should have known better. It was a slow news day, and the media played the story big. I got bushels of mail accusing me of pushing the Brennan family out into the snow. Many years later we met as friends.

After three disappointing seasons with a young, inexperienced coach and staff, we swung completely around and hired a veteran from the pro ranks, Joe Kuharich, coach of the Washington Redskins. Joe was known for emphasizing the fundamentals, something we were told our teams had lacked under Terry Brennan. If we were to continue losing, at least it would not be because our players didn't know how to block and tackle. Joe brought a lot of experience to the job, but somehow he lacked the fire or the spark or whatever it is that a college coach needs in order to create a winning team. After a few years it was clear both to him and to us that he was not the right man for the job, and he resigned. Joe came through it with his reputation intact and subsequently landed an attractive ten-year contract with the Philadelphia Eagles.

Ara Parseghian was a popular and winning coach at Northwestern University when we eyed him for the job. He had defeated Notre Dame four years in succession. After the 1963 football season, Ara called Father Joyce, whom he knew well, and inquired if Notre Dame would be interested in hiring a nonalumnus as its head football coach. He told Father Joyce, who was overseeing our football activities as executive vice president and chairman of the faculty board in control of athletics, that he had decided to leave Northwestern and was considering several offers. Would Notre Dame be interested in him? Would we!

Father Joyce arranged for Ara to meet with him and me privately to discuss the matter further. I had always made it my business to participate in the hiring of head coaches, even though the primary responsibility for athletics was Ned's. I also believed that when you want to talk seriously to somebody else's coach, you should let that somebody know about it. I called Roscoe Miller, president of Northwestern at that time and a friend of mine. Miller said Ara was a fine, wonderful guy, and that he could stay there forever, but he knew Ara wanted to move on. Then he thanked me for calling. "Father Ted, you're the only guy I know who doesn't go hunting without a license. The rest of them talk to Ara all the time, but never inform or ask me."

Parseghian had agreed to meet us on neutral ground, which turned out to be in a Chicago motel at nine-thirty at night. I won't soon forget that night. Ned and I drove some eighty miles in a blinding snowstorm to keep that appointment. And it was worth it, if only to hear Ara's reason for wanting to leave Northwestern for Notre Dame. This is Ara's story:

Northwestern had beaten a tough Ohio State team in an important game, and Ara was feeling very good about it on the plane heading back home when a sportswriter bet him a steak dinner that no celebration would welcome them back at Northwestern. Ara took the bet, confident. Then he got word on the plane that bleacher seats and a PA system had been erected outside Dyche Stadium in preparation for the team's arrival. Ara gave the sportswriter a chance to withdraw the bet. But the sportswriter said it made no difference. He still did not think the Northwestern fans would be there and the bet was still on. When they arrived at the stadium, not a single person had showed up to congratulate the team for its victory over Ohio State.

When he finished relating this anecdote, Ara said to us, "I've gone as far as I can without school spirit. I'm a believer in emotionalism in athletics, and I know they have it at Notre Dame, and I know I can do better there." Ara was right, of couse, and he proved it many, many times.

Dan Devine also had a very good record as a coach. As I recall, he was on Ned's list when we were looking for a replacement for Joe Kuharich. Then, because Ara coached for eleven years at Notre Dame, we more or less forgot about Dan. When Ara retired, Dan's name came up again. He was the only coach we interviewed. Like the others, Dan brought in good student-athletes and never put us in an embarrassing situation with regard to the rules. But a campaign to discredit him began almost immediately after he arrived. We were getting calls from Green Bay, Wisconsin, about rumored irregularities. Ned and I checked out all of them and, of course, they were simply not true. Dan just was never accepted at Notre Dame. I don't think it was his fault. It was just something to do with the chemistry, or lack of it, between him and the fans. Nor do I know what you can ever do about that. In six seasons with us, from 1975 through 1980, Dan won three bowl games and a national championship. His overall record of fifty-three wins and sixteen losses is not great by Notre Dame standards, but it's not all that bad, either.

Gerry Faust was another coach I thoroughly admired, even though his record after five seasons was just over .500. He was totally dedicated to Notre Dame, almost with a passion, and he was terribly enthusiastic, totally optimistic. He was the high school football coach with the best record in the country, and Ned and I thought it was worth taking a chance on him. It did not work out, and after two or three years we were under a lot of pressure to drop him. In the fourth year he came to me and said, "Padre, I'd love another season. I think this year's going to be great. All my friends say I ought to have another year."

I assured him that he did not have to ask for a fifth year. "We told you when we hired you that we'd give you five years, as long as you kept the program honest, and you've certainly done that."

"That's true," he said, "but at any other school in the country, they'd buy me off."

"I know, Gerry, but we aren't any other school. We said five years. Five years it is."

We took a lot of heat for not buying him out after four years, but in the long run I don't think it hurt us. It showed people that when we made a contract, we stood behind it, and that while winning was important to us, it was not the only thing we cared about.

When Gerry Faust did resign at the end of the fifth year, he told me he was very concerned that he would not be able to afford to send his son, a high school senior, to Notre Dame, where the boy yearned to go. I knew he would find another coaching job without difficulty, but he was such a good human being that I blurted out, "Gerry, don't worry about it. Your son just got a four-year scholarship."

Lou Holtz is another marvelous gentleman. Judging from his spectacular performance so far, he looks like he's going to be another Ara Parseghian. He is a great teacher and motivator, and he loves his players like a father. He has that intense desire to win, like every great coach, but not at any cost. I have no doubt that he meant exactly what he said after the USC game in 1989 when he told his players that he would resign if there were any more pushing and shoving with another team in the tunnel beneath the stadium. I am equally sure that there won't be any more incidents like that, because the players have so much respect for Lou. He is not only a superb coach but also a man of great dignity and integrity. How many Division I college football coaches do you know who would tell two starters to skip the Orange Bowl if the practices were getting in the way of their studies? Lou did exactly that as Notre Dame was preparing for the 1990 Orange Bowl.

One of the peculiar myths about Notre Dame athletics I would like to lay to rest is that when we have a bad season, contributions from alumni decrease. That may or may not be true at some other schools. I don't know. It is not true at Notre Dame. In all the years that I was president, we raised more money during the bad seasons than we raised during the national championship seasons. I'm not saying that people consciously give more money when we're having a bad season. Our benefactors do not, to my knowledge, count wins and losses when they decide when and how much they're going to give. Notre Dame is an academic institution, and it will continue to grow and prosper as long as it continues to do an outstanding job academically.

It goes without saying that the standards we established for our football team apply with equal force to all sports at Notre Dame. In the nineteen years that Digger Phelps has been coaching basketball, for example, all athletes who finished their collegiate playing careers at Notre Dame have graduated. When I say "all," I mean 100 percent. I don't know of another coach in the country who can make that claim. A few of Digger's players left early, but they all eventually graduated. I remember Adrian Dantley for one. After his final season he still needed about six hours to graduate. I ran into him on the campus and told him if he didn't get those six hours I would boot him around the block. "Yeah, you on one side and my mom on the other," he replied. He was well aware of what was expected of him, and he came back and finished his degree.

Our attitude toward the relative importance of academics and athletics is borne out, too, by the way we have handled our physical facilities. Ned Joyce had long believed that for a school of our athletic prominence, we deserved and needed better athletic facilities, and he was right. The Old Field House was a disgrace and the Rockne Memorial was much too small. Beyond that, after Notre Dame went coeducational, we needed an athletic facility that would accommodate the needs of women.

For years, Ned kept talking about it and I kept saying that we needed a new library more than we needed a new athletic facility. When we were in the planning stages for a new library, in 1960, I told Ned he could start doing something about an athletic facility. But I set two conditions: One, I personally would not raise a nickel for it; I had too many other things to do. Two, the facility had to cost considerably less than the library. This second condition was a little unfair, I admit, because building costs were rising by some 10 percent per year at that time, and I should have taken that into consideration. But I was concerned that outsiders might be led to believe that Notre Dame favored an athletic facility over a library.

Ned went ahead with the Athletic and Convocation Center. He

and Moose Krause, our athletics director, raised the $9.5 million it took to build it. They brought it in well below the $12.5 million that the library cost, as promised, and we had an excellent facility at a bargain price. We made only one major mistake with that building, and it was my fault. At the last minute I insisted that they eliminate the planned swimming pool. That saved $500,000, but I regretted it later. Swimming is an important winter sport, and the pool we built twenty years later, donated by the Rolf brothers, both Notre Dame alumni, cost ten times as much, although it was considerably bigger than the pool I had vetoed.

Blame the football stadium on me, too! There's no question that it is small and outdated, especially when you compare it to the stadiums of the teams we play. I understood that a bigger, more modern football stadium would more than pay for itself and was justified financially. But at a crucial time in our academic resurgence, when we were working very hard to improve our curriculum and faculty salaries, I was concerned that a new or bigger stadium would send out the wrong message. I feared it would reinforce the widely held misconception that Notre Dame was emphasizing athletics at the expense of academics. I was not about to do anything that would send this message. The time will probably come when we will enlarge the stadium, but I never could face that decision.

Do we take athletes who don't meet our normal admission requirements? Yes, but not very many. Every year we accept a small number of students who excel at something—music, art, whatever—but who do not meet our normal academic require-ments. We once, for example, admitted the best high school tenor in the country. He did not have the grades or the test scores that we normally require, but we felt he deserved to come to Notre Dame because he had a tremendous talent. Yes, we do make exceptions to our admissions policy, but we are always forthright with those students. We tell them they have no guarantee that we will keep them; if they don't make passing grades, they will flunk out. And we accept no one who obviously has no chance to succeed. The ones for whom we make exceptions, including the athletes, are deemed intelligent enough to graduate, if they study hard enough. Often their low grades or test scores in high school were due to poor motivation or substandard school systems. All those we accepted did earn their degrees, almost always in four years. Since 1965, 99 percent of our scholarship football student-athletes were graduated. Our graduation rate for *all* recruited student-athletes in 1987–88 was 91.57 percent, and that was a better record than the 90.94 percent graduation rate for the entire student body.

The whole question of recruiting and supporting athletes who do not qualify for college, including charges of chicanery, fraud, payoffs, special privileges, and the like, rose once again from the swamp of dishonesty in the late 1980s. It cast a dark shadow across many, if not all, of our college athletic fields. To find the answers, in 1989 the Knight Foundation, an offshoot of the Knight-Ridder news organization, established a twenty-two-member Commission on Intercollegiate Athletics, comprised largely of university presidents from the conferences and independents, where the problems chiefly exist. I am cochairing the commission with William Friday, president of the University of North Carolina at Chapel Hill. Between us we have sixty-five years' experience presiding over clean athletics programs, he in a public institution and I in a private one.

We have high hopes of eliminating once and for all the various kinds of duplicity and fraud that seem to pervade collegiate sports from time to time, if our fellow university presidents across the country will commit their institutions to three basic and binding regulations:

1. Academic Integrity: The college must graduate at least the same percentage of student-athletes as it does students who are nonathletes.

2. Fiscal Integrity: All funds derived from athletics (tickets, television, contributions of boosters) must go directly to the university and be dispensed only by the university.

3. Continuous Auditing: Just as academic programs are checked and accredited, just as university financial accounts are audited regularly, there shall be a continuous, ongoing audit by an outside agent, under the NCAA, with an annual report on the state of

athletics from an academic, financial, and moral point of view. Thus can the public have confidence that colleges are doing what they say they are doing.

Undoubtedly there are subsidiary problems, but these three commitments could eliminate all the current scandals that are destroying the integrity of so many of our universities.

Only the university president, with the complete backing of the trustees, faculty, students, and alumni, can insist on these principles. That is why we call our reform program 1 + 3.

SERVING OTHERS

EVERYBODY KNOWS about the Peace Corps, but relatively few people know that Notre Dame played a pivotal role in the earliest beginnings of the program. President Kennedy provided the initial inspiration for the corps in a campaign speech at the University of Michigan. The idea was simple, bold, and inspiring: The U.S. government should set up a "Peace Corps," calling upon young Americans to enlist for two years of service abroad in the underdeveloped countries of the world. They would wage peace instead of war. Taking their own native American intelligence, education, skills, imagination, and goodwill, plus a few months of training provided by the U.S. government, young American men and women would move into poor villages and rural areas and try with their American ingenuity to improve the lives of the people living there.

It was a brilliant idea, just the kind of thing this country needed. It was a period when America's reputation as leader of the free world was declining and many of our own young people needed a constructive outlet—for their own pent-up idealism. Also, there was a clear need for this kind of personal help and American know-how in the developing nations. The Peace Corps idea was a campaign promise of high visibility, and when John F. Kennedy was elected, it became one of the top-priority items on his agenda. He asked Sargent Shriver and Harris Wofford to draft an executive order, after which it would need congressional approval.

I had introduced Wofford to Shriver, who was JFK's brother-in-law, and then "lent" him to JFK for his campaign. And, I must say, he was never "returned." Actually, Harris Wofford was a brilliant, idealistic lawyer out of Yale who was my legal assistant on the Civil Rights Commission when I asked him to give a speech for me. Sargent Shriver had invited me to speak on civil rights for the Catholic Interracial Council of Chicago (of which Shriver was president), and when I could not make that date, I sent Wofford in my place. Wofford apparently impressed Shriver to such an extent that when Kennedy was running in the Wisconsin primary early in 1960, Shriver asked Jack's father, Joe Kennedy, to ask John Cavanaugh, a friend of the Kennedy family, to persuade me to persuade Wofford to join Kennedy's campaign as an adviser on civil rights. That's the way things are done in politics. I demurred. I explained to Cavanaugh that I had already asked Wofford to do too many things for me, and suggested that either Mr. Kennedy, Sr., or Shriver call and ask Wofford directly. Shriver did, and Harris Wofford joined the Kennedy campaign. As it turned out, I learned, it was Wofford who suggested that Jack Kennedy telephone Martin Luther King, Sr., and offer his help when Martin Luther King, Jr., was put in jail for leading a sit-in demonstration in Atlanta. That phone call is generally credited with winning Kennedy hundreds of thousands of black votes and giving him the margin he needed to win the presidency over Richard Nixon, who did not make a similar phone call.

One day not long after Kennedy was inaugurated, I was in Washington on some Civil Rights Commission business, and I caught sight of Shriver and Wofford as I walked through Lafayette Park, across from the White House, on my way to the airport. They were waving a piece of paper at me, looking very excited as they tried to attract my attention. When I went over, they showed me their draft of Kennedy's executive order for the Peace Corps, and said it would not be long before it would be signed and under way. Later that same day—actually, it was late that night—they phoned me at Notre Dame to ask if I could provide them with a pilot project with which to begin the work of the Peace Corps. "I certainly can," I told them, feeling my own enthusiasm rise. "You can have your pick: Bangladesh, Uganda, or Chile. Which do you like?"

They chose Chile, and the next day I set up a luncheon meeting of Notre Dame's Latin American group, a collection of people, mostly academics, who were knowledgeable about Latin American affairs. We settled on the idea of using radio to teach reading and writing to the rural people in the central valley of Chile. Most of them had little or no education, and had fallen under the spell of the local communists. The project was my idea, borrowed from a similar venture I had seen work in Colombia. Later on, possibly, we could move into television. We called it Education of Rural People through Radio. Then we rushed it off to Shriver as a model program for the budding Peace Corps.

Five or six weeks went by and we heard nothing. Then one day when I was in Washington, meeting with the National Science Board, I received a call from Shriver asking me to come over to the Peace Corps office right away. I told him we were discussing a ten-million-dollar project and that when that work was finished, I would come directly to his office. When I arrived there, Shriver was very excited. "We have to get moving right away," he said. "We like your project and we'd like you to go down there and get the Chilean government to approve it; everything we do has to be at the invitation of the government."

At least one of the others, Bill Josephson, legal counsel of the Peace Corps, was not excited at all. He seemed to have the idea that this was our pet project and that the Peace Corps would be involved only to foot the bill. He complained about some kind of "vicious circle" whereby Notre Dame would send its own projects over and the Peace Corps would pay for them. It did not take long for my dander to start rising. I had heard all I wanted of that kind of talk. We had responded to Shriver's request; we had devised a pilot project, put it in writing, and rushed it off. They had sat on it for five or six weeks. And now Notre Dame was being accused of trying to use the Peace Corps to its own advantage. I told Josephson that he need not worry any longer, because I was going to break the "vicious circle" by going back to Notre Dame. With that I got up and left.

As I walked down the hallway toward the elevator, passing Shriver's office, he came charging out. Apparently he'd been tipped off that I was leaving. He grabbed my arm and asked me where I was going. I told him what had happened, but he persuaded me to come back to his office. I was still pretty hot, but I said I'd give him five minutes. When he had shut his office door, he admitted that his people were gun-shy about the "Catholic factor." He was Catholic, I was Catholic, the President was Catholic, and the project had been put together by a group of Catholics at a Catholic university. Was there any way, he asked, that we could bring in another school besides Notre Dame so the project would not be exclusively Catholic?

I told him I was pretty sure I could get the Indiana Conference of Higher Education, which was made up of all the universities and colleges in Indiana. That would provide Anglicans, Lutherans, Baptists, Presbyterians, Mennonites, and Fundamentalists of all kinds—all backing a nonsectarian Peace Corps. Would that satisfy his colleagues? I asked. Shriver liked that idea and asked me if it would be a problem for me to handle the situation that way. No problem at all, I said. Using his phone then and there, I called the secretary of the conference at Indiana University, explained the problem, and asked him to call around to see who was interested. He promised to have everyone lined up by the next morning. I hung up and told Shriver it was all set. The project would be sponsored by the Indiana Conference of Higher Education, but it would be headquartered at Notre Dame.

The next thing Shriver wanted was someone other than Uncle Sam to pay for my trip to Chile. After all, this was not official business until Chile "asked" for Peace Corps help, and Chile could not "ask" until I got down there to tell someone. Anyway, I think

Shriver got Henry Crown of Chicago to put up five thousand dollars for traveling expenses. Then Shriver suggested that I get someone to go with me—a non-Catholic. So I invited Herman Wells, president of Indiana University. Herman had to go to a meeting in New York, but offered me someone even better, Peter Frankel, his assistant, who spoke Spanish. Shriver said he also wanted to send someone else down on government money "to keep an eye on us," whatever that meant. For that he picked the dean of the Yale Law School, where Shriver himself had earned his law degree.

In Chile we soon discovered that none of the universities wanted anything to do with our program, nor did any of the radio stations. But there was something already in existence called the Institute for Rural Education that intrigued us. It consisted of special schools that a private organization managed specifically for the underprivileged, undereducated rural youngsters so they could learn about things like crop rotation, animal husbandry, hygiene, and nutrition. Given the indifference of the radio stations and the universities, we felt the best way to help the rural people of Chile would be to plug into the Institute for Rural Education. To do that, we needed the cooperation of the Minister of Education, the Minister of Agriculture, and the assistant to the President, Julio Philippe, who, we were told, was the most powerful man in the country after the President.

We called the American Embassy for help, but the only appointment set up for us was with the Minister of Education, and somehow that was botched. Perturbed, I telephoned Mark Mc-Grath, a Holy Cross priest who had grown up in Panama, spent virtually all of his priesthood in Latin America, and now was dean of theology at Catholic University in Santiago. Mark was a friend of both the officials who, the American Embassy said, could not or would not see us. Mark asked when we wanted to see them. I said tomorrow, because we had to fly back the following day. A ten-minute appointment was arranged with Julio Philippe. We then discovered that Philippe, not the President, actually ran the government. Philippe thought our program was the best thing he had ever heard of, and our ten-minute appointment stretched into an hour and a half as he pressed us for details. As we left, he urged us to send the program down right away and he would have the President approve it. The Minister of Agriculture was equally enthusiastic and we spent an hour with him.

When we returned to Indiana, we wrote up the project. Peter Frankel translated it into Spanish and sent it down to Julio Philippe. He cabled us back almost immediately: "Send your volunteers down whenever you are ready." At our own end we still needed the approval of the State Department. That meant somewhere in the neighborhood of thirteen people had to put their signatures to the agreement. Harris Wofford walked that agreement through the State Department, desk by desk, garnering signatures, and got us State Department approval in forty-eight hours, which might have been a record. Several staff people at the State Department scoffed at our rush. It would take months, if we were lucky, they said, to hear anything back from Latin America. But they did not know of our prior discussions with Philippe and the government minister. We cabled the project down there at 1 P.M. on a Thursday afternoon, just before a long weekend was to start. We had an affirmative reply at 3 P.M. the same day—two-hour service. So much for stereotypes of Latin American inefficiency.

The day the project was approved here and in Chile, I picked up the phone and called the man I wanted to lead and direct this all-important first overseas venture of the Peace Corps. Walter Langford was the chairman of our Department of Modern Languages and a professor of Spanish and Portuguese. He heard me out as I explained my deep interest in the success of the Peace Corps and why I thought he was the man to lead it. I asked him if he, his wife "Dit," and their teenage daughter Liz would be willing to move to Chile temporarily. I wanted Walter to organize and direct our volunteer training program, then to take the first Peace Corps group to Chile and supervise them for two years. Walter, bless him, asked me to hold the line. And I held on while he talked to his wife and daughter. Generously, they all said yes. And that, to my mind, guaranteed the success of the project.

Walter and Dit worked together as a team and did a terrific job. The volunteers loved them. They still do.

All forty-five volunteers for the project were selected and approved by the Indiana Conference of Higher Education. We trained them at Notre Dame. Each year we would pick a new group of students from all over the nation and repeat the process. I made it a practice to welcome the new volunteers when they arrived at Notre Dame. I also attended some of their training classes and picnics. I wanted to see what they were like, but I also wanted to learn what I could for my own benefit. We soon discovered that there was a great need for an education program in the cities as well as the rural areas of underdeveloped nations, especially in the slum sections, and we started up and staffed a second program that was designed to educate people who lived in urban slums.

It seemed to me that our young volunteers deserved more than just a pat on the back for their selflessness, and so just before Peter Frankel and I left for an official visit to Chile, I called up Sargent Shriver, the head of the Peace Corps, and asked him if the President would be good enough to write a letter of thanks and appreciation to the volunteers that I could take down to Chile with me. I wanted them to have visible proof that they were appreciated, not only by us but by the President himself. I planned to have the letter photocopied so each of them could have one. On my way to Chile, I stopped in Washington to pick up Peter Frankel and the letter. Then we boarded our flight for Chile and opened this big packet that Peter had brought from Shriver's office.

Inside, instead of photocopies, was a personal letter on White House stationery to each of the forty-five volunteers, and each was signed by Jack Kennedy. Peter and I traveled more than a thousand miles in the interior of Chile, visiting the various duty stations, spread from one end of the central valley to the other. As soon as we arrived at each school, I would hand the volunteers their letters from home and say, "I have a letter for you, and it's from the boss." They were thrilled, of course, and many years afterward when I visited some of them in their homes, they had Kennedy's letter framed and hanging on the wall.

Those original forty-five volunteers were some of the greatest youngsters I have ever known. One I'll never forget was Tom Scanlon. He graduated magna cum laude from Notre Dame and, as I remember, earned an M.A. from the University of Toronto. He had planned to enroll at the London School of Economics, but changed his mind. Instead of more schooling, he decided to get out in the world and do something for his fellow human beings. He asked me if I had any ideas. I suggested the Peace Corps. If he showed up at Notre Dame that weekend, he could begin training, I told him, and he did show up and join that first group. At that time he did not know a word of Spanish. But he mastered the language quickly, and in a required language proficiency test he took at the end of his service, he scored the highest grade possible.

Tom's job was to set up agricultural cooperatives. He hardly knew a horse from a cow, but he organized farm cooperatives that are still in existence today. He did all kinds of other things, too. One of his best-remembered exploits involved helping some poor people who lived in three remote villages at the top of a mountain. When Tom heard they were up there, he climbed the mountain and approached the Communist leader of the villages, saying, "I'm Tom Scanlon with the Peace Corps. I'd like to bring one of our nurses up to your villages to treat the sick people."

The Communist fellow, who probably had never seen an American in his life, scoffed at Tom, complaining that he was like all the other Americans—all talk and no action. "If you want to visit my villages," he said, "come in July." That is the middle of winter in Chile, when the mountain snow is several feet deep. Tom said he'd be there.

When July rolled around, Tom and a nurse rode up the side of the mountain until the horses were up to their bellies in snow. When the horses could not go any farther, the two of them dismounted and pulled the animals the rest of the way up. When they reached the villages, the Communist expressed his astonishment. He allowed Tom and his nurse to treat the children of the village, almost all of whom were afflicted with yaws, a tropical infection that eats into the skin and bone. The nurse, fortunately, had come well supplied with penicillin, and in forty-eight or so hours all the children had clear skin. This was too much for the Communist. "I may be a Communist," he exclaimed, "but if you two are any example of what Americans are like, I'm all for America."

When I think of Americans abroad, I always like to think of Tom Scanlon as a true representative of what is best about our country. And he was not different from so many of the other idealistic young men and women I knew in the Peace Corps.

A group of young women worked some similar magic at schools of the Institute for Rural Education. They discovered that half the kids were missing classes because they were bedridden with diarrhea. They knew exactly what to do about it. They cleaned up the school kitchens, got rid of the flies, and made sure the dishes were washed in hot water. They put an end to the schools' practice of having fresh produce delivered; what the schools were getting were the vegetables left over at the end of the day. Instead, the young women drove to the market in their Jeep at 6 A.M. and picked out the produce themselves. They took over the cooking, and did that better, too. Then they taught the local women at these schools basic sanitation. And it was done in a spirit of one-on-one friendship, and accepted as such.

I told Tom's story, among others, to Shriver, who related it to Kennedy. The President later used it in a widely quoted speech he gave on the Peace Corps. That made Tom Scanlon famous for a while. Among his fellow volunteers in Chile, though, he was best known for his humorous imitations of me. He really had me down pat. I did not mind a bit, because someone once told me that imitation is the sincerest form of flattery.

We were involved with the Peace Corps for five years, but each year the bureaucracy in Washington chipped away bit by bit at our role. First they wanted to pick the Peace Corp volunteers. Then they wanted to train them their way, not ours. Then they wanted to supervise the projects in the field, and eventually they were haggling over minor items in the field budget. After five years of this, we decided to back off and let them run the program. We had made our contribution.

Typical of interference from Washington was a call I received one afternoon from Frank Mankiewicz, a well-known writer handling public relations for the Peace Corps. He informed me that the Peace Corps was getting static from Congress and he wanted our corps volunteers taught the Latin American history course by anyone other than Professor Samuel Shapiro, whom we had hired. The objection to Professor Shapiro was that he had been dismissed from Oakland University in Michigan because of his views on Communist Cuba. Professor Shapiro had a fine educational background, including a Ph.D. in diplomatic history from Columbia University, and we were well aware that he had been blackballed by universities in the Midwest when we hired him. Apparently his enemies in Michigan were still pursuing him. But I was not about to give in to that kind of pressure.

In no uncertain terms, I informed Mankiewicz that the Peace Corps had a contract with Notre Dame and that we would decide who would teach what. If Washington had any difficulty with that, they could take their contract and give it to someone else. Then I hung up.

I should mention that Frank is one of my good liberal friends. To his credit, he called me back the next day to apologize. "We were out of line," he said. "Please just forget it." I tried to forget it, but in writing this thirty years later, it all came vividly back to me. The incident raised the ever-recurring issue of academic freedom, about which I have always had strong feelings.

The Notre Dame project volunteers did a great job in Chile during those first five years, and afterward, too. Some of the agricultural cooperatives they founded are still operating. Most of the volunteers are still using their Spanish in one way or another. About a third of them came back and went to graduate school. About a third are working on projects today that are connected with Latin America. Two or three married Chileans and some still live there. In 1981 we celebrated a twenty-year reunion at Notre Dame. About fifty of them came back for it, and swapped stories about what their Peace Corps experiences had done for *them.* I hear from many of them at Christmas, too, and Walter still writes them round-robin letters.

Over and beyond the immediate good it did in far-off places of the world, the Peace Corps has continued to influence the global and environmental awareness and attitudes of many Americans to this day. To my mind, the Peace Corps is one of the most significant legacies of the Kennedy administration. John F. Kennedy brought the glow of youthful enthusiasm to the country, and the thousands of volunteers in the Peace Corps came away with the experience and knowledge that young people, all people, can do good for others less fortunate, and in so doing reap the personal gratification and satisfaction of knowing they have helped their fellow men.

The Peace Corps was such a good idea that it served as a paradigm for other programs. Notre Dame's Council for the International Lay Apostolate (CILA) took the Peace Corps as a model and sponsored many students on volunteer projects throughout Central and South America. Holy Cross Associates does the same thing in Asia, Africa, and Latin America. Also, I take pride in the fact that Notre Dame has sent more volunteers to the Peace Corps than any other Catholic university. All these programs are continuing today at Notre Dame and on campuses of other universities. About one quarter of our students venture out in South Bend each year helping the sick, the aged, wayward youth, and local students who need tutoring. It is still an integral part of their extracurricular education at Notre Dame, and when I hear the stories these youngsters bring back from their volunteer work with the needy in our own community, I think back fondly to that group of eager youngsters who comprised that very first contingent of Peace Corps volunteers a generation ago.

It was, and still is, a beautiful concept, a fitting legacy: Wage peace, not war.

I knew Jack Kennedy fairly well because of the closeness of John Cavanaugh to the Kennedy family and through my dealings with the President relating to the work I did for the government. Aside from the Peace Corps, I was serving on the Civil Rights Commission, the National Science Board, and the State Department's Commission on International Educational and Cultural Affairs. From time to time I would see Kennedy in the Oval Office on business, but more often we would greet each other at social functions. Though we were friendly, I wouldn't say we ever became close friends.

On occasion I took him to task for what I considered at the time his reluctance to commit the federal government to an all-out fight against racial discrimination, particularly in the Deep South. I thought he was too cautious in leading the country on civil rights because of the perceived political liabilities inherent in such a battle. On the other hand, I was frequently surprised by the depth of his knowledge on the subject. At one meeting, relying on information from a commission researcher, I protested vigorously to Kennedy that there was not a single integrated school in all of the South. He shot back at me: "Yes, there is one; you're wrong!" We checked it out and he was right.

Actually, I knew Dwight D. Eisenhower better than I did Jack Kennedy, and I always felt that Ike was one of the most underestimated presidents in modern times. He got things done, and he did not shout about it from the rooftops; and knowing that he was smarter than most people thought him was enough to satisfy his own ego. That, too, helped him get things done. I would not say Ike was a great champion of civil rights, per se, but he possessed a very strong sense of fairness and justice, which he applied to all people regardless of race, origin, or color of skin. He was not a small or mean man.

It was Eisenhower who in 1954 appointed me to the National Science Board, comprised of twenty-four of this nation's leading scientists and me. When I protested that I knew nothing about science, word came back from Ike that he thought the scientists, formulating a national policy on scientific research, needed a man like me versed in the humanities. I served on the National Science Board for twelve years, garnering a vast education in the sciences, and as the years went by I realized more and more the wisdom of Eisenhower. Every science policy-making body should have a humanities person there, if only for help in guidance.

Three years later, in 1957, when civil rights, segregation, and racial discrimination became visible, volatile issues, with filibusters in the United States Senate and the country being split politically between North and South, Congress created the U.S. Civil Rights

Commission to study the subject, report back, and make recommendations. Eisenhower offered me a spot on that six-man commission, neatly split between Northerners and Southerners, Democrats and Republicans, and I served there long and hard for the next fifteen years.

Eisenhower was the butt of many jokes because of the way he would torture the English language on occasion. Few people ever knew that early in his career Ike wrote speeches for his superior officer, General Douglas MacArthur, one of the great orators of our time. Actually, Ike himself was a speaker well above average. When he gave a bad speech, it was usually because he had a prepared text that was of little interest to him or was just the product of an uninspired speechwriter. But I heard Eisenhower speak from the heart on civil rights on more than one occasion, and those talks were superb. His speech at the Republican National Convention in 1960, when he was leaving office, caused a national sensation because it was so unexpected. With his experience as the Supreme Allied Commander in World War II and a two-term President, Eisenhower left office warning the American people of the dangers inherent in the buildup of what he called the military-industrial complex in this country. It was a magnificent speech because Ike knew the subject well and was deeply concerned about it. On another occasion, I heard him say, "Every dollar spent for armaments comes out of the hide of some hungry child or some underdeveloped nation." I used to quote that line in my own speeches and most people thought that statement came from a pope or a peace activist, but I had it straight from Dwight D. Eisenhower.

SEVEN

STUDENT REVOLUTION

THE HIGH idealism, vigor, and youthful hopes that marked the inauguration of John F. Kennedy in 1961 ended in disillusion, anger, and finally violence when the 1960s came to an end. College students, our traditional hope for the future, questioned the established values upon which they were raised, and then at least some of them revolted against everything that represented adult authority. Proclaiming their distrust of everyone over thirty, they fled parental authority, wore ragged clothing, used foul language, turned to mind-altering drugs, disdained the work ethic, family and marriage, and more—all to find a new meaning and a new way to live their lives. These were, for the most part, the children of affluent and well-educated parents. When they wanted to voice their protests, they struck out, of course, at what was nearest to them: the colleges and universities from Berkeley in San Francisco to Columbia in New York City. Why did it happen?

There is, of course, no simple answer. But in the 1960s John F. Kennedy, his brother Robert, and Martin Luther King, Jr., the nonviolent, charismatic leader of the blacks, were assassinated. Senseless murders. It shook to the core all thinking, feeling people, especially impressionable young people on our college campuses who had time to read, to think, to discuss, to question, and to criticize. These were young men and women who grew up believing in the American dream, reciting daily: "one nation, under God, indivisible, with liberty and justice for all." And then they grew up and suddenly came upon the realization that this nation was not one and indivisible. It was clearly divided between the whites and the blacks, the affluent and the poor, the hopeful and the hopeless. They saw inequalities all around them which contradicted what the "older generation" was telling them in and out of our universities. All this was exacerbated by the escalating war in Vietnam. In their view, America became the big, bad bully trying to impose its will upon a primitive, rural country called Vietnam. (Ironically, our government was drafting blacks, Hispanics, poor whites to fight in a far-off war while affluent college students were exempted from military service.)

Through it all, I never thought the student revolution was all that bad. And I said so on many occasions. These young people were demonstrating their enormous energy, commitment, and dedication to ideals with which few of us could argue. Oh, I did not approve of their methods and excesses. But that was really nothing new. If only our historians had helped us put the cataclysmic upheavals of our youth into historical perspective!

Ancient Greece, the first democratic society, also had trouble with its youth. Plato complained in his day: "What is happening to our young people? They disrespect their elders, they disobey their parents. They ignore the laws. They riot in the streets inflamed with wild notions. Their morals are decaying. What is to become of them?" He spoke for us today and that was twenty-four hundred years ago.

A generation later Plato's disciple, a philosopher named Aristotle, tried to explain youthful excesses this way: "Young people have exalted notions, because they have not yet been humbled by life or learned its necessary limitations; moreover, their hopeful disposition makes them think themselves equal to great things.

They would always rather do noble deeds than useful ones; their lives are regulated more by moral feelings than by reasoning—all their mistakes are in the direction of doing things excessively and vehemently. They overdo everything—they love too much; hate too much; and the same with everything else."

How apt and right they were, old Plato and Aristotle! Nevertheless, even historical perspective would not have eased the distress and anguish of going through our own student revolution. It was a very painful, troubling time to be associated with a college or university. And the higher you were in the administration, the more you felt the pressure and suffered the pain. At Columbia, students took over the office of the university's ill-fated president, Grayson Kirk. After they barricaded themselves inside, they proceeded to ransack his files, drink his sherry, smoke his cigars, and defecate on his rug. Similar outrages were carried out against several others among my colleagues of that time, including Clark Kerr, president of the University of California, and Edward Levi, president of the University of Chicago.

The day after the students left Levi's office, I called him up. "You're back in your office, I assume," I said.

"No, I'm not," he said. "I'm in a temporary command post while they're cleaning it up." Ed had a great sense of humor and he was also a very wise, patient man. I asked him how he had handled himself during the two weeks that the uprising was at its height and when the students had taken over his office. "Well, Ted, I'll tell you how," he said. "I got up every morning and I asked myself what's the worst thing I can do today. I figured out what it was—say, calling the police—and I didn't do it."

My office was never attacked or taken over, but we did confront a very real threat from some students who planned to burn down our ROTC building. The threat came to my attention late one Sunday night after some really draining confrontations during the day. I should have been back in my little room in Corby Hall sleeping, but instead I was in my office working. I often worked late those days. Shortly after midnight I heard a knock on my door. When I opened it, a student was standing there. "You know," he said, "tomorrow they're probably going to burn down the ROTC building." I asked him if he was in favor of that. "Hell, no," he blurted out, "I'm student commander of the Army ROTC. I just came over because I thought you ought to know." After he left, another student came to the door at about 2 A.M. He told me that one of the more radical groups on campus was planning a big rally on the mall early in the afternoon. They were going to ask me to speak, but their real purpose was to set me up for some kind of embarrassment or humiliation, he said, perhaps by shouting me down or bombarding me with overripe tomatoes.

Sure enough, about 2:30 or 3:00 A.M., I got a call from the head of the student government, who, I later found out, was a closet revolutionary. Very matter-of-factly, almost innocently, he said, "Oh, Father, we're going to have a big rally out on the main mall at one or two tomorrow afternoon and we thought maybe you'd like to speak."

I said, "Of course I'd like to speak; thank you."

I often spoke to groups of students on one subject or another and frequently gave little homilies with my celebration of the Mass at one dormitory or another. Almost always I talked off the cuff, but this was one time I sensed that I had better prepare carefully what I wanted to say. I wrote out the whole talk, including a list of recommendations that I thought would help defuse the situation. As I began to write, my thoughts expanded to the whole dilemma facing all universities and colleges: Where do students' rights begin and where do they end? What role, if any, should the government play? I finished about four-thirty, left it for my secretary, Helen Hosinski, to type, and went to bed.

The next day when I got to the main mall on campus, a large throng of about two thousand students had already gathered. The first part of my talk was conciliatory; the second part was a set of practical steps that I thought the government should take to address the students' grievances. I also said I would present them to President Nixon if they wanted me to. Basically, I told the students that like them I was against the war in Vietnam, but unlike them I was in favor of the ROTC on college campuses. Why? Because as long as nations needed armies, I believed the United States should have the best Army possible, run by the best people possible, and that meant the Army having people who had studied philosophy, theology, and the other humanities in our colleges and universities. Ideally, all military officers would possess this kind of education. In the best of all possible worlds, of course, there would be no wars, no need for a military, but we had not yet reached that point.

When I finished speaking, I went to the campus barbershop to get a haircut, then walked back to my office. When I arrived, a large group of students had gathered outside the door, waiting for a copy of my speech. Helen had sent it downstairs to be mimeographed. The students told me they thought my speech made sense to them and that they had decided to take a copy of it to every house in South Bend, ask the people to sign it, and then have me send the signed copies to President Nixon.

Later that week a huge contingent of Notre Dame students organized what they promised would be an orderly and nonviolent march through South Bend. I asked them to route the start of the march so it would pass in front of the Main Building. It took them more than an hour to file by, but I stood there on the front steps, smiling, waving, and wishing them well. They were exercising their right of free speech. And they made a very favorable impression on the residents of South Bend, I was told. By the end of the week they had gathered more than twenty-three thousand signed copies of my speech, and I did mail them off to the White House.

The next item on the students' agenda was a scheduled all-night meeting to decide whether or not to burn down the ROTC building. The various factions on campus agreed to decide the question democratically: Majority would rule. Anyone at the meeting could talk and the others would have to listen, and at the end they would vote and the vote would be binding. The hard-core revolutionaries argued for torching the ROTC building. Most of the students said no, and voted that way, and that was that. It seemed that the predominant sentiment on campus switched over from violence to nonviolence in that one single week.

That was not the end of student dissension on campus. There was no shortage of ugly incidents, mostly in the form of boorishness and incivility. One night in my office, while engrossed with someone on the phone, I was startled to look up and find a student standing in front of my desk, taking a swig out of a can of beer. "I want to talk to you," he demanded.

I put my hand over the receiver and told him I had exactly four points I wanted to make to him very bluntly. It went something like this: "One, you are never to walk into my office again, or anyone else's, without first knocking. Two, it is not polite to listen in on another person's conversation, ever. Three, it is bad form and bad manners to come in here with a beer in hand, besides which it is against the rules to drink beer on campus, and for that you could be suspended. Four, I want you right now to get back out in the hall until I am finished with my call. After that, if I'm cooled off sufficiently, I may come out and talk to you."

Without a word, he turned around and walked out. When I went out to see him, he said he wanted his paper back, which referred to some five hundred copies of an obscene sheet that he had written and distributed around campus. What he had written was really disgusting; every other word started with f. Apparently, the campus security people had picked them up wherever they found them and thrown them in the trash bins. I told him we were not about to provide the facilities for him to distribute that screed, and that if he didn't like it he could go to court. With that, he mumbled a few obscene words and left.

Once a meeting of our board of trustees was disrupted by a student mob banging on the door, demanding to voice their grievances to a trustee. One of our trustees at that time was Bayard Rustin, the long-time black civil rights activist. "Well, if they want to talk to a trustee, I'll go out and talk to them." Another trustee, Tom Carney, went with him. They walked with the group down toward the cemetery, then came back to the auditorium in the Center for Continuing Education, where the radicals had gathered. There Rustin found himself in a kind of two-man debate with one of the radicals, while students in their bare feet and shirts open to their navels interrupted with questions and jeers. At one point the youngster said to him, "We're talking strike here, but that's something you wouldn't know anything about." Obviously he had no idea who Bayard Rustin was.

Bayard, who had been a labor leader before the student was born, said, "Sonny, I've got more scars on my head from being in strikes than you've ever had thoughts in that head of yours about strikes."

Things got worse, not better, as students nationwide became more objectionable and more violent in their challenges to authority. Notre Dame seemed to be consumed in controversy. Here and everywhere the students were trying to take over. And the toll was heavy. It seemed to me that the time had come to draw the line. It was time to spell out very clearly the conditions governing protests. It was time to say to students: This is it; you can go this far, and no farther. I was in favor of the right to protest, but not when the protest interfered with the right of students being able to attend their classes or administrators being unable to get into their offices.

Up until then, no college president had really taken a firm stand. Some, I think, feared that they could not enforce any edict they put out; some doubted the degree of support they would get from faculty, students, and alumni. Many were simply indecisive, and that, too, played into the hands of the student rebels. The total university community was shaky and uncertain. I feared that if I did not do something, my administration would eventually find itself in deep trouble with an irate public, with the National Guard, with the local police, and with the majority of students, who really wanted to resume their normal classwork.

The fundamental question was where to draw the line. How did I intend to enforce it? How could I make it clear that students had a right to protest, but not to impose their will upon others? How could I stop their sit-ins and lie-ins and rowdy behavior, which prevented others from attending classes, and still not abrogate their rights? And, even more fundamental was the question of who governed the university, who had the final say over university affairs—the administration or the students?

I decided I would take neither a hawkish nor a dovish approach; I would try to appeal to the best in both camps. In order to enforce where the line was drawn, I decided to canvass the entire university community to make sure I had a broad base of support. I would ask each constituent body—faculty, students, and alumni—to declare its support openly and for publication.

I talked to all of them, explaining my stand and the need to take action, and it took some arm-twisting, but finally all of them—with one exception—said they would back my stand, each with its own misgivings. Of the five constituent colleges in the university, only Arts and Letters (we have a distinct College of Science) voted not to openly support my proposals. But I did have the backing of the Academic Council (our highest academic body) and the Faculty Senate. We were between meetings of trustees, but I knew they would favor my position, too. With that support behind me, I sat down and carefully composed a letter to be sent to every student and faculty member, every administrator and trustee.

Somehow that letter touched a live nerve. It was the first of its kind from a university president, the first firm drawing of the line on student protests, and it was widely taken as a blueprint of sorts for other colleges and universities. Perhaps it was merely the right tone of letter at the right time. Whatever, within two days of being sent to the students, the letter was reported in every newspaper in the country. The *New York Times* carried the full text. Unfortunately, as so often happens, most of the press overemphasized the tough part of the letter and hardly mentioned the portions which spoke of the legitimacy of protest. I came off sounding like a superhawk, which I was not. Judge for yourself from these highlights of that noted letter, addressed "Dear Notre Dame Faculty and Students," and dated February 17, 1969.

. . . My hope is that these ideas will have deep personal resonances in our community, although the central problem they address exists everywhere in the university world today and, by instant communication, feeds upon itself. It is not enough to label it the alienation of youth from our society. God knows there is enough and more than enough in our often nonglorious civilization to be alienated from, be you young, middle-aged, or old.

The central problem to me is what we do about it and in what manner, if we are interested in healing rather than destroying the world. Youth especially has much to offer—idealism, generosity, dedication, and service. The last thing a shaken society needs is more shaking. The last thing a noisy, turbulent, and disintegrating community needs is more noise, turbulence, and disintegration. Understanding and analysis of social ills cannot be conducted in a boiler factory. Compassion has a quiet way of service. Complicated social mechanisms, out-of-joint, are not adjusted with sledgehammers.

The university cannot cure all our ills today, but it can make a valiant beginning by bringing all its intellectual and moral powers to bear upon them: all the idealism and generosity of its own people, all the wisdom and intelligence of its oldsters, all the expertise and competence of those who are in their middle years. But it must do all this as a university does, within its proper style and capability, no longer an ivory tower, but not the Red Cross, either.

Now to the heart of my message . . . I now have statements from the Academic Council, the Faculty Senate, the Student Life Council, some college councils, the Alumni Board, and a whole spate of letters from individual faculty members and a few students. Some of these are enclosed in this letter. In general, the reaction was practically unanimous that this community recognizes the validity of protest in our day—sometimes even the necessity—regarding the current burning issues of our society: war and peace, especially Vietnam; civil rights, especially of minority groups; the stance of the university vis-à-vis moral issues of great public concern; the operation of the university as university. There was also practical unanimity that the university could not continue to exist as an open society dedicated to the discussion of all issues of importance if protests were of such a nature that the normal operations of the university were in any way impeded, or if the rights of any member of this community were abrogated, peacefully or nonpeacefully.

I believe that I now have a clear mandate from this university community to see that: (1) our lines of communication between all segments of the community are kept as open as possible, with all legitimate means of communicating dissent assured, expanded, and protected; (2) civility and rationality are maintained as the most reasonable means of dissent within the academic community; and (3) violation of others' rights and obstruction of the life of the university are outlawed as illegitimate means of dissent in this kind of open society. Violence is especially deplored as a violation of everything that the university community stands for.

Now comes my duty of stating, clearly and unequivocally, what happens if. I'll try to make it as simple as possible to avoid misunderstanding by anyone. May I begin by saying that all of this is hypothetical and I personally hope it never happens here at Notre Dame. But, if it does, anyone or any group that substitutes force for rational persuasion, be it violent or nonviolent, will be given fifteen minutes of meditation to cease and desist.

They will be told that they are, by their actions, going counter to the overwhelming conviction of this community as to what is proper here. If they do not within that time period cease and desist, they will be asked for their identity cards. Those who produce these will be suspended from this community as not understanding what this community is. Those who do not have or will not produce identity cards will be assumed not to be members of the community and will be charged with trespassing and disturbing the peace on private property and treated accordingly by the law.

The judgment regarding the impeding of normal university operations or the violation of the rights of other members of the community will be made by the Dean of Students. Recourse for certification of this fact for students so accused is to the tripartite Disciplinary Board established by the Student Life Council. Faculty members have recourse to the procedures outlined in the Faculty Manual. Judgment of the matter will be delivered within five days following the facts, for justice deferred is justice denied to all concerned.

After notification of suspension, or trespass in the case of noncommunity members, if there is not then within five minutes a movement to cease and desist, students will be notified of expulsion from this community and the law will deal with them as nonstudents.

Lest there be any possible misunderstanding, it should be noted that law enforcement in this procedure is not directed at students. They receive academic sanction in the second instance of recalcitrance, and only after three clear opportunities to remain in student status, if they still insist on resisting the will of the community, are they then expelled and become nonstudents to be treated as other nonstudents, or outsiders.

There seems to be a current myth that university members are not responsible to the law, and that somehow the law is the enemy, particularly those whom society has constituted to uphold and enforce the law. I would like to insist here that all of us are responsible to the duly constituted laws of the university community and to all of the laws of the land. There is no other guarantee of civilization versus the jungle or mob rule, here or elsewhere.

If someone invades your home, do you dialogue with him or call the law? Without the law, the university is a sitting duck for any small group from outside or inside that wishes to destroy it, to incapacitate it, to terrorize it at whim. The argument goes—or has gone—invoke the law and you lose the university community. My only response is that without the law you may well lose the university—and beyond that—the larger society that supports it and that is most deeply wounded when law is no longer respected, bringing an end to everyone's most cherished rights.

I have studied at some length the new politics of confrontation. The rhythm is simple: (1) find a cause, any cause, silly or not; (2) in the name of the cause, get a few determined people to abuse the rights and privileges of the community so as to force a confrontation at any cost of boorishness or incivility; (3) once this has occurred, justified or not, orderly or not, yell police brutality— if it does not happen, provoke it by foul language, physical abuse, whatever, and then count on a larger measure of sympathy from the up-to-now apathetic or passive members of the community. Then call for amnesty, the head of the president on a platter, the complete submission to any and all demands. One beleaguered president has said that these people want to be martyrs thrown to toothless lions. He added, "Who wants to dialogue when they are going for the jugular vein?"

STUDENT REVOLUTION

So it has gone, and it is generally well orchestrated. Again, my only question: Must it be so? Must universities be subjected, willy-nilly, to such intimidation and victimization whatever their good will in the matter? Somewhere a stand must be made.

I only ask that when the stand is made necessary by those who would destroy the community and all its basic yearning for great and calm education opportunity, let them carry the blame and the penalty. No one wants the forces of law on this or any other campus, but if some necessitate it, as a last and dismal alternative to anarchy and mob tyranny, let them shoulder the blame instead of receiving the sympathy of a community they would hold at bay. The only alternative I can imagine is turning the majority of the community loose on them, and then you have two mobs. I know of no one who would opt for this alternative . . .

May I now say in all sincerity that I never want to see any student expelled from this community because in many ways, this is always an educative failure. Even so, I must likewise be committed to the survival of the university community as one of man's best hopes in these troubled times. I know of no other way of insuring both ends than to say to every member of this community, faculty and students, that we are all ready and prepared and anxious to respond to every intellectual and moral concern in the world today, in every way proper to the university . . . We only insist on the rights of all, minority and majority, the climate of civility and rationality, and a preponderant moral abhorrence of violence or inhuman forms of persuasion that violate our style of life and the nature of the university . . .

May I now confess that since last November I have been bombarded mightily by the hawks and the doves—almost equally. I have resisted both and continue to recognize the right to protest—through every legitimate channel—and to resist as well those who would unthinkingly trifle with the survival of the university as one of the few open societies left to mankind today. There is no divine assurance that the university will survive as we have known and cherished it—but we do commit ourselves to make the effort and count on this community, in this place, to uphold the efforts that you have inspired by your clear expression of community concern. Thanks to all who have declared themselves, even to those who have slightly disagreed, but are substantially concerned as well . . .

I truly believe that we are about to witness a revulsion on the part of legislatures, state and national, benefactors, parents, alumni, and the general public for much that is happening in higher education today. If I read the signs of the times correctly, this may well lead to a suppression of the liberty and autonomy that are the lifeblood of a university community. It may well lead to a rebirth of fascism, unless we ourselves are ready to take a stand for what is right for us. History is not consoling in this regard. We rule ourselves or others rule us, in a way that destroys the university as we have known and loved it.

> Devotedly yours in Notre Dame,
> (Rev.) Theodore Hesburgh, C.S.C.
> President

After the letter was distributed, the crisis on campus quieted down, at least temporarily. Resistance to violence, incivility, and boorishness began to stiffen. The letter was at least partially responsible for that. But it had another effect that I never anticipated. It made me a kind of folk hero among the hawks, who saw the solution to the student revolution in terms of truncheons and police action. Maybe that explains why I spent so much time after 1969 trying to get people to understand why the students were legitimately upset and what was good about their concerns. A hawk I was not.

The worst part of it all, however, was that the Nixon administration started thinking about federal legislation as a means of clamping down on the campuses and some people there wanted me to lead the charge. It was just one week after I sent that letter to the students that I heard from President Nixon. It was somewhat embarrassing because as it happened I was spending that afternoon at a racetrack—my first visit, I hasten to add. On my way to an annual meeting of the Conference on Higher Education in the American Republics, held that year in Bogotá, Colombia, I stopped off in Miami to spend a day with one of our trustees. He had a horse running at Hialeah that day and asked me to accompany him to the track. By the time we reached our seats, I must have run into at least five delighted alumni, who couldn't resist the greeting: "Hi, Father, putting a few bucks on the ponies today?"

When we returned to the hotel, the staff people at the front desk all said at once, "The President has been calling you all day and we've just been telling him you're out at the track." I thought to myself, If my life history is written, it will probably say I was at the track when I should have been tending to a crisis at my school. A four-page telegram then arrived from President Nixon congratulating me on my stand on student violence. He added that he was leaving for Europe, but that in a few days Vice President Agnew would be heading a meeting in the White House with all state governors on what to do about student violence on campuses across the nation. Would I please advise the Vice President regarding federal legislation to regulate turmoil on the campuses.

My heart sank. Repressive legislation was the last thing colleges wanted or needed. I certainly wanted no part of it. But I had to leave for Bogotá in a few hours while Agnew was getting ready to sell the idea to the governors of the fifty states. When I arrived in Bogotá, the first thing I did was to prepare a cable opposing any and all kinds of federal action on the campuses. My position was that the universities and colleges should handle their own problems, make their own decisions, without the intervention of the federal government except upon invitation. My objective was to persuade the governors not to go along with any restrictive legislation on this sensitive issue.

Fortunately, two old and very capable friends at the Bogotá conference agreed to read and edit my initial draft: Sol Linowitz, then the American ambassador to the Organization of American States, and Alex Heard, chancellor of Vanderbilt University. They were both very helpful. Once the final draft was ready, I asked the American ambassador to Colombia to send it. He said he was having trouble with communications, but would try. (It never arrived.) I became very concerned that my views would never

reach the governors conference in time. I tried a different route.
That didn't work, either, although I did not know it at the time.
But my instincts were working overtime. The morning of the
governors conference in Washington, I met Sol Linowitz and his
wife, Toni, checking out in the lobby of the hotel in Bogotá. Sol
assuaged my worries. He promised to hand-deliver my cable to Pat
Moynihan, then President Nixon's chief adviser on domestic policy, who, Sol was certain, would convey my message to the
conference. Moynihan did just that. Sensing the importance of my
cable, he had fifty copies made immediately and took them to the
governors meeting at the White House.

Once again, begging your indulgence, here are the highlights of
the cable:

Bogotá, Colombia
February 27, 1969

Dear Mr. Vice-President:

President Nixon has asked me to give you my views regarding
campus unrest and possible action on the occasion of your meeting
this week with the governors of the fifty states . . .

Writing from such a distance and in the midst of a busy
conference, I shall make my comments as brief as possible.

1. The best salvation for the university in the face of any crisis
is for the university community to save itself by declaring its own
ground rules and basic values and then enforcing them with the
widest and deepest form of moral persuasion for the good life of
the university, and consequent moral condemnation with academic
sanctions for any movement against university life and values—
especially violence, vandalism, and mob action, which are the
antitheses of reason, civility, and the open society which respects
the rights of each and all.

2. When moral persuasion and academic sanctions fail to deter
those who show open contempt for the life-style and self-declared
values of the university community, there should be no hesitation
to invoke whatever outside assistance is necessary to preserve the
university and its values. However, it is the university that best

judges its need for outside assistance and invokes this assistance, much as it would call for help in a three-alarm campus fire. Here the concern is survival against forces bent on destruction.

3. It is important to see and judge universities today as they really are, not as they appear to be. The bizarre and widely publicized antics of relatively few students and relatively even fewer faculty are accepted as the stereotypes of all students and all faculty, much to the disgust of this widely maligned majority of faculty and students. The vast majority of university and college students today are a very promising and highly attractive group of persons: They are more informed, more widely read, better educated, more idealistic, and more deeply sensitive to crucial moral issues in our times, more likely to dedicate themselves to good rather than selfish goals than any past generation of students I have known.

Many of them are bothered by some aspects of American and world society and current values or the lack of them—with good reason in most cases. They would work very hard, I believe, if given a real opportunity to participate in changing this world for the better. They would also find out how hard it is to do and would quickly discard some of their more naive present solutions to our problems. Even those most far-out students are trying to tell society something that may also be worth searching for today if they would only lower the volume so we could hear the message.

Anyway, the great majority of our students need better leadership than we or the faculty have been giving them. In a fast-changing society the real crisis is not one of authority but a crisis of vision that alone can inspire great leadership and create great morale in any society. A rebirth of great academic, civic, and political leadership, a sharing of some of those youthful ideals and dreams (impossible or not) would be good for our universities and good for America, too. It might also help us all remove some of the key problems that underlie most of the unrest. The campus is really reflecting America and the world in hi-fi sound and living color.

4. Part of the vision I have been speaking of must certainly include law and order. But curiously enough, one cannot really

have law and order without another part of the vision: greater achievement of justice in our times, more compassion for all, real love between generations. All elements of the vision are interdependent. Moreover, the vision must be whole and real for everyone. Lastly, a measure of humor would help from time to time to break the deathly seriousness of the present scene.

5. As to the present action: I would make the following two suggestions:

A. Assume for a few months that the university community—faculty, students, administration, and trustees—is capable, in most cases, of laying down its own guidelines and effectively maintaining them in its usual free and independent university style. Things will be messy from time to time, but we will make it as universities if we determine strongly to maintain our freedoms and our values. That determination is growing on every campus, every day now. Give it elbow room in which to grow and operate in its own good way.

B. Where special help is needed, let all assume it will be asked for and given quickly, effectively, and as humanely as possible, given the provocations that surround the need for such outside help, as a last alternative to internal self-correction. But let it be understood that the university, and only the university, public or private, makes this determination.

If my two assumptions are correct, the crisis will pass without the further requirement of actions other than those contained in my assumptions, especially not repressive legislation, or overreaction in its many forms . . .

My best personal regards, and prayers, too, for you, Mr. Vice-President, and all the governors.

Devotedly yours,

New York's Governor Nelson Rockefeller later told me what had happened at the governors meeting. At first the discussion had centered on the need for federal legislation. More than forty governors were ready to vote for sending in the National Guard to quell outbreaks of violence and for other repressive legislation against the universities. Then Pat Moynihan arrived with the cable. The governors took time to read it, and the sentiment in the room seemed to do an about-face. When it came time to vote, more than forty of the fifty governors voted against asking for federal legislation to deal with student dissidents. Moral of the story: Follow your instincts and thank God if you have friends like Sol Linowitz and Pat Moynihan.

At Notre Dame a month passed and no one challenged our resolve to do what I said we would do in my letter to the students. Oh, there was plenty of vocal sounding off by the militant minority—really a small group—but no violence, no blocking classrooms or offices. Students were still concerned about their right of free speech, especially their right to criticize the Vietnam War, and there was a great deal of debate on whether the right of violence was guaranteed by the First Amendment as a form of free speech.

Late in March of 1969, about a month after my letter was circulated, some students called and said they had something important that they wanted to discuss with me in the Student Center. I got many calls of this kind, usually from students who wanted to vent their rage about something or to make some unreasonable demand. I always attended to these calls, when I could, because I was determined to keep an open mind to deal with this crisis. When I entered the Student Center, I was somewhat surprised to come upon forty or fifty student activists there, including leaders from the more radical groups such as the SDS and the YAF.

"We've been having a meeting about Vietnam and we've discovered that there's one thing we can all agree on," one of them said. "We think that as part of our educational experience here, we should have a course offered on nonviolence, plus programs on nonviolence and maybe a new library collection of materials that relate to nonviolence. We asked you over here to see what you think about it."

I immediately responded that I thought it was a great idea. I was all for nonviolence.

"Will you do it?" they asked.

"Sure, I agree with your idea," I said, "but the world is full of great ideas and you can't get them all done before midnight." I tried to acquaint them with the logistics involved in getting new courses into the curriculum. First, I said, we needed to bring in several people who could put together some intellectually satisfying courses on the subject. I even suggested the names of three teachers who I thought would be very good. I explained that it was not enough just to announce the courses. We would need the faculty behind us. Then the courses had to be approved, the library started, the money found. It was already the middle of the semester, so minicourses would have to do for the near term. The budgets were already set, so there was no loose money lying around.

"Well, then, the ball's in your court," they said.

"No, the ball's in both our courts," I countered. "You start working on the faculty. I'll take care of the money." They gave me their position paper with all their signatures and affiliations on it, and that was the end of the meeting.

The very next morning, purely by happenstance, or perhaps as a gift from God, I received a call from Alex Lewis, the vice president at Gulf Oil who was in charge of their charitable foundation. He wanted to see me, and soon. Fine, I said, as soon as you want. He said he'd get a company plane, fly in from Pittsburgh with some other vice presidents, and meet me for lunch. We had lunch at the Morris Inn on campus and conversed about our student situation. When it was over, he asked for a quiet place to talk. I booked a quiet corner room at the inn and we all went up. I still didn't know what he had in mind.

As soon as we sat down, Alex said, "We had a board of directors meeting yesterday and it was unanimously decided to give you and President Hayakawa [of San Francisco State University] a hundred thousand dollars each to do with as you please."

I did not agree at all with Hayakawa's hard-line approach at San Francisco State, but the gifts were separate and this one certainly was timely. "Alex," I said, "I can use that money and, as a matter of fact, I have a specific purpose in mind right now. But you gentlemen may not feel comfortable with it, so I'd like to tell you about what it is and get your approval beforehand, so you're not embarrassed later when it comes out."

I handed him the paper containing a summary of the program on nonviolence studies, with the students' signatures and affiliations affixed to it. I had brought it along—just in case. He read through it, commenting with great familiarity where each of the student organizations fit into the political spectrum, and then said, "You know it's extraordinarily positive that they want to get together on doing something about nonviolence. It's hard for me to speak for my colleagues, but it seems to me that you're making a move that Gulf Oil would be proud to be a part of."

To top off my day, the telephone rang when I stepped into my office, and I had on the line a reporter for the *Observer,* the Notre Dame student newspaper, who wanted to check out a story he was writing about my meeting yesterday with students about nonviolence studies. He went over the salient points and then got to the crucial question: "And you said you'd take care of the money, right?" That was correct, I told him. "What I need to know, then," he said, "because my editors are sure to ask me, is how long it's going to take you to get it—six days, six weeks, or six months after we're dead?"

Obviously he thought I had given the students the usual line about being on the side of the angels, but being conveniently unable to follow through because there wasn't enough money. "What would you say," I asked him, "if I were to tell you that I already have the money?" He said he'd be very surprised and wanted to know if I had the amount I had told the students it would take to get the program going. "I have in my hands right now a check for a hundred thousand dollars," I said.

"My God!" he exclaimed, and hung up.

I love that story because it's such a great example of the way the providence of God works. There's a famous line that I like to quote when I try to persuade cynics to have faith in the future: "The one thing we really know about tomorrow is that the providence of God will be up before dawn." The studies in nonviolence, with new books and new faculty, were started and then expanded each semester, and thousands of Notre Dame students signed up for one or more of those elective courses. They accomplished, too, what we all wanted: a sane and nonviolent learning experience which, I am sure, deepened the intrinsic personal values we were trying to instill in our students at Notre Dame.

It was fully nine months after my letter went out and into the beginning of a new school year, in November of 1969, that a group of students chose to test and challenge the university on my policy governing student violence. During those nine months there were many protest meetings, peace rallies, incidents of picketing, and students who made a nuisance of themselves walking up and down the hallways wearing placards in one kind of protest or another. All that was permitted, if not encouraged. Over the months I had had many talks with the dissidents and they knew where I stood. Time and time again I would tell them, "You can protest, but you have no right to burn down the ROTC building: You don't own it." They could speak out on any subject, but they had no right to try to stop the ROTC or the CIA or Dow Chemical or any other organization from also speaking out and trying to recruit students on campus. There were, believe it or not, students who wanted to work for the CIA and Dow Chemical after graduation. I also made it abundantly clear they had no right to prevent other students from attending classes or to stop faculty and staff from doing their jobs.

What happened was that an unthinking clerk had arranged for the CIA and Dow Chemical to conduct job interviews at the same time for three days on campus. We had a special placement office for graduating students' job interviews, and for the first two days student protesters had carried signs and marched in front of the door to that office. But that did not stop some other students from seeking job interviews there.

Tim, the leader of the protesters, came to see me in my office late that second night and outlined his plans for a lie-in to block entry to the office starting at eight o'clock the following morning. Actually, he wanted my permission. Surely I could not object, he argued, because lying down in front of the door was a nonviolent protest.

"Tim, there are two kinds of violence: physical and spiritual," I told him. "Physical violence is easier to deal with. Spiritual violence is more difficult." Why? Because I would not walk on the bodies in front of that office under any circumstances, and I doubted if any students would either. Therefore, he and his friends were depriving me and those students of our rights, and I, as president, had to uphold everyone's rights.

Sure enough, the next morning it was reported to me that twelve students were stretched out in front of the door to the placement interview office, challenging anyone wishing to enter to walk on their bodies. There was no other way to get into that office.

So, the issue was clear. The students lying in front of that office, blocking anyone from entering, were in clear violation of university regulations. Certainly I did not want anyone stepping on them or over them to enter. I instructed the dean of students, Jim Riehle, to put the widest and most lenient interpretation on everything, to give the protesters the benefit of every conceivable doubt. I told him I did not care if fifteen minutes became twenty or if five minutes became ten. I wanted them away from the door, but I was not really concerned about strict enforcement of the time limits. I also told him to be sure to reiterate to them the terms of the letter so there would be no suspensions or expulsions because someone had not fully understood the terms.

Riehle went back to the scene of the lie-in, read them the rules of university policy. He asked them to meditate and think over what they were doing, and said he would be back in fifteen minutes. When he returned twenty minutes later, they were still there, stretched out on the floor, blocking the office. He picked up their ID cards and said they were suspended for the rest of the semester. Then he said he was going to leave again for five minutes and anyone who was still there when he came back would be expelled permanently.

When he came back this time, all of them were gone. He then sent them notification of their suspensions. They demanded and received a hearing, but the rules were clear and they were out. All of those suspended returned the next semester and went on to graduation. And that was the end of the challenge to the university's right and ability to govern its students.

It is most difficult, if not near impossible, to summarize or generalize what happened during those three or four years of student rebellion on our college campuses. There were some outright political radicals dedicated to Marxism or Communism and they perhaps had ulterior political motives, but by and large most of the protesting students at Notre Dame and across the country were really good, dedicated youngsters who had high, very high, ideals, and very little practical sense as to the ways of the world. Some of them met tragic ends—victims, in a way, of their own dedication.

I think of two young men in particular. One was my friend Tim. He was always on the front lines of the protesters, but somehow he had never gone to jail, and I think that disappointed him. Finally, on graduation day, he got his wish. He and some other students showed up at commencement carrying a coffin, and were promptly arrested by our campus security force. The first thing they did after their release, however, was to stop by for their diplomas.

Tim was in and out of my office many times while he was at Notre Dame, but we never had harsh words. He was always there out of concern, not because he wanted to show off or make a scene. I admired him because he practiced what he preached. He had the courage of his convictions. On one occasion he and five other students and a professor from the sociology department went down to a poverty-stricken town in Texas on a summer research project. The students each received a living allowance of twenty dollars a day plus the price of a motel room. Tim did not think it was right to live better than the poor people they were trying to help, and so he bought a few cans of beans for himself and slept outside. The money left over from his food and lodging allowance he gave to the poor people. He was a great young man, and on top of that, very bright. Despite his suspension for one semester, he graduated magna cum laude.

After Tim left Notre Dame, he went to one of the California universities to work on a master's degree. He had been there only a couple of months when he was found dead. We were told that he had committed suicide, though I found that hard to believe. In fact, I don't believe it still.

Another young man of that era who really lived the Gospel was Tom. He also came up to my office frequently, greatly concerned about the people starving in Biafra and later in Bangladesh. As a sophomore he was involved in all the world hunger activities on campus, so much so that he stopped going to class. Late one night in my office, I asked him when he'd last been to class. About six weeks ago, he said. I told him that was not fair to his parents or to himself. They were spending good money for an education that he was not receiving. And that was doubly unfortunate because by going to class and graduating, he could be learning things that would help him do something about the hunger problem that was haunting him.

I suggested to Tom that he drop out before he flunked out, that he go to Biafra and spend six months getting some field experience, distributing food to the starving. I even arranged for him to work with a relief group for one school semester. Six or eight months after his return, a tidal wave inundated Bangladesh and once again there was a terrible hunger crisis in that poverty-stricken country. Tom came up to my office right after it happened, and I greeted him with "Well, I guess we're going to have to do another leave of absence, aren't we?" He said yes. So, once again, I set it up, but this time I told him that when he came back I wanted him to stay and finish his degree so he would have the kind of preparation he needed to have some lasting impact on the problem of world hunger. But he did not come back to Notre Dame. He went back to California, fell in love for the first time, and was jilted. That, added to all the anguish he was feeling about hunger, was too much for him. He sat down one day, wrote a ten-page letter to his parents, then went out to the garage, closed the door, and started his truck. He breathed the carbon monoxide fumes until he was dead.

I don't think those young men would have died the way they did if they had been at Notre Dame. There would have been many people they could have talked to here, people who felt the same way they did, or understood their youthful enthusiasm. Out in the secular world one does not often find that many caring people, certainly not all in one place as you do here.

People have asked me how I survived the student revolution when it ended the careers of so many other college presidents—almost all of them. There are several answers to that question, all of them true to one extent or another. During those years it was a very lonely job for each and every college president. You sensed that many people were for you, but there were no great rallies of support. Very few spoke out publicly in your behalf. Even so, there were quite a few like Tom Stritch, for example, head of the American studies department, who wrote very welcome and encouraging notes of support. Or I could walk across the hall to Ned Joyce's office and he would give me words of consolation or encouragement. I always believed that most of the students knew I agreed with them on many issues and that I had a great deal of sympathy for them. I am not sure how well I communicated that, but it was there. I was always available to talk to anyone who wanted to talk, and at any time of day or night. I did participate in some fairly visible events, like the campus Peace Mass, and I spoke out in favor of granting the vote to eighteen-year-olds, for civil rights, for an end to the military draft, for nonviolent protest, and for other things I have already mentioned.

But I feel that I owed my survival as president of the university to great good luck, the grace of God, and the very special love, respect, and caring that our people have always had for one another at this very special place called Notre Dame.

I harbor no rancor about those years, nor do I harbor resentment toward those who made my life so difficult. Actually, I am rather friendly with many of them. One was a student named Robert Sam Anson, the editor of the student newspaper, the *Observer*. He used to attack me in every issue. When I wrote that letter to the students and faculty, I got this telegram from Anson:

Statement on student protesters betrays utter disregard for due process. Will succeed only in provoking further disruption. For good of all, sadly but strongly suggest your immediate resignation.

In August of 1970, Anson was captured by the Khmer Rouge in Cambodia while covering the Vietnam War for *Time* magazine. His editor cabled me, asking me to do what I could to get Anson released. Uncertain as to what, if anything, I could do, I sent a fairly lengthy telegram to Pope Paul VI about Anson. He put the Vatican diplomatic corps on it. They contacted Prince Sihanouk's exiled government in Peking and Hanoi. Three weeks later Anson was released. He showed up late one night at Notre Dame and thanked me. In a signed article that he wrote about the experience, he mentioned our late-night conversations and voiced his amazement at how much I had changed in the last few years. It made me think of something very similar that Mark Twain had once said about his father: "When I was a boy of fourteen my father was so ignorant I could hardly stand to have the old man around. But when I got to be twenty-one, I was astonished at how much he had learned in seven years."

EIGHT

FLYING HIGH

W H A T D O I do for fun? What do I enjoy doing most, outside of work? Flying! No, I am not a licensed pilot, although I have been at the controls of some very sophisticated aircraft. I have probably logged three million miles in airplanes, most of them on routine commercial flights, and for my money all commercial flights should be smooth, routine, and on time. I get writing and paperwork done when I am flying somewhere, and I have no need or desire for any excitement.

But commercial flight has nothing whatever to do with the kind of flying that excites me most. I always jump at the chance of flying fast in military planes—bombers, jet fighters—and in highly sophisticated surveillance aircraft. The thrill, excitement, and catharsis of high-speed flight is like nothing else; it is a world unto itself. To give you an idea, I've flown in a Navy torpedo bomber from the flight deck of a carrier, in a Navy weather plane (PB4Y-2) through the crater of a volcano, and in the backseat of an Air Force SR-71 at supersonic speed. I am also quite fond of biplanes and stunt planes.

My love of flying probably began when I was a boy building model airplanes, eager for a taste of the real thing. I was about ten years old when I took my first ride in a plane. I went up with my friend Eddie Naughton, who shared my love of airplanes and lived just down the street. One day we talked our dads into taking us to the Perth Amboy airport near Syracuse, where a well-known barnstormer was appearing. He was one of those daredevil pilots who went from airport to airport performing stunts and giving rides. The star attraction that day was a flier named Tex Perrin, and he was decked out like no one we had ever seen before: tight-fitting helmet, goggles, leather jacket, white scarf, flared cavalry pants, and high, laced boots. He was Lafayette Escadrille all the way. And we were impressed.

The plane was a creaky biplane with a wooden propeller, probably with one of those old de Havilland Liberty engines left over from World War I. Anyway, Eddie and I talked our dads into letting us take a ride. It cost five dollars for each of us, which was quite a bit of money in those days. But they could see how eager we were, and did not have the heart to say no. The pilot said we were small enough to take the ride together. He strapped us into the front seat—riders always sat in the front, the pilot in back—and we roared off down the runway and lifted into the air. Eddie had one side of the open cockpit to himself and I had the other; we both had window seats—without the windows. The view was stunning—farms, woods, cars, people, downtown Syracuse, the neighborhoods, and, of course, Lake Onondaga, which is right next to the city. The ride could not have lasted more than fifteen or twenty minutes, but I was hooked for life.

Not until the mid-forties, some twenty years later, when I was teaching at Notre Dame, did I go up in an airplane again. It was a typical commercial flight for those days, but quite different from what we know today. To get from South Bend to a National Catholic Students convention in Boston, I took a United DC-3 from South Bend to New York. It was what they called in those days a milk run. We stopped at Toledo, Cleveland, Buffalo, Rochester, Syracuse, and Albany before landing in New York. In New York I changed planes for the last leg to Boston, and we made two more stops in Providence and Hartford. I had left South Bend at nine that morning and landed in Boston at eight-thirty at night. Today you could fly from New York to Tokyo in the same amount of time, or in half the time if you were to take the Concorde.

My first jet ride was in a T-33 trainer from Bryan Air Force Base in Texas to Notre Dame in 1953. When we came in to land in South Bend, there was water on the runway. The pilot set the plane down perfectly, but when he hit the water he lost control. We kept sliding and fishtailing down the runway, which was only five thousand feet long. When we passed the 2,500-foot mark, we were still out of control and going at a hundred knots. We were still going pretty fast when we ran out of runway and plowed into mud and weeds. Fortunately, neither of us was hurt.

A few years ago I took a ride in a supersonic F-14 Tomcat, the same type of advanced fighter they used in the filming of *Top Gun*. The plane was at the South Bend airport in connection with an air show, and our Navy ROTC captain had arranged a ride for me. The pilots were not allowed to break the sound barrier, because the sonic boom would have caused damage on the ground at low altitude. But it was a lot of fun anyway, because we did some aerobatics. We looped right over Notre Dame, coming in at four thousand feet and over the top at nine thousand and then right down and through again. The G meter read 4.5 Gs, which meant that my normal weight of 185 was equivalent to almost a thousand pounds. My head was so heavy I could not hold it up. But it was a great ride.

The biggest thrill I ever had in my early days of flying was off the deck of an aircraft carrier not long after World War II ended. I had long been fascinated by aircraft carriers, and just a year earlier had narrowly missed getting myself assigned to one as a chaplain. Remember, my greatest desire during the war was to be a chaplain on an aircraft carrier. And, as I said before, God provides in mysterious ways.

I had been at Notre Dame for a year or so, and my dream of duty aboard an aircraft carrier had faded completely when Father

Cavanaugh, the president of the university, called me, right out of the blue, and said, "Ted, the Secretary of the Navy has asked me to join an ROTC cruise. It'll be out in the Pacific for six weeks on the carrier *Princeton,* and I just don't have the time for it. Would you mind doing it for me?"

There must have been a long pause on the line as thoughts raced through my mind. It was an opportunity I had long cherished, but I was the youngest member of the order and I did not think it fair to someone perhaps more deserving. "Father John, that's like offering a steak to a hungry dog. But I'm sure some of the older fellows would feel terrible if you didn't offer it to them first."

Three days later Father Cavanaugh called me back and said, "I offered the thing to about five others and none of them was interested. So how about it?" So off I went by train to San Francisco, or rather to Alameda, and a few days later I was aboard the USS *Princeton,* headed for Hawaii, where most of the naval exercises were to take place. I could hardly wait for the opportunity to see what it was like to take off and land on a carrier.

On the way over, though, I somehow managed to get on the wrong side of the air officer, by the name of Rooney. Despite his Irish ancestry, he did not take kindly to priests on naval vessels, or at least to this one, and I did not endear myself to him in our after-dinner game of chance, called Pogey Bait. All it amounted to, really, was shaking the dice to see who would pick up the tab for the cigarettes and candy that were passed around after the meal. Everything was very cheap aboard ship. A carton of cigarettes cost a dollar; candy and gum were mere pennies. So if you lost at a table of six, your tab would rarely amount to more than a dollar or two. But Rooney wanted more than anything, it seemed, to stick me, and after dinner each night he would challenge me. "Let's put these two tables together and just shake once, and the loser pays for both tables." Almost invariably I'd win, and he'd lose.

He did not take his losses very gracefully, and this worried me a little. I knew I would need his permission before I could climb into an airplane. He made me squirm a little first, but I kept prodding him. Finally he said, "Well, damn, I'll let you fly, but

I'm going to give you the worst pilot in the fleet." The guy he gave me was a Polish kid from Chicago named Kujac. I had no way of knowing if indeed he was the worst pilot aboard the carrier, but he sure must have been the youngest. I felt a little sorry for him; he had to know that Rooney did not think he was much of a pilot.

Despite Rooney's animosity, I finally found myself exactly where I wanted to be—strapped into the backseat of a torpedo bomber, roaring down the deck of the carrier. The plane dipped a little, as if hitting an air pocket, when we sped past the deck, but we had plenty of airspeed and we soon turned and climbed to our assigned altitude. At last I was airborne in a TBM off a carrier, realizing the dream of a lifetime.

But Rooney was not through with me yet. As we came in to land, there was Rooney on the deck, waving us off. It looked to me as if Kujac had the plane lined up perfectly, and he probably did. The seas were calm, the wind was negligible, and Kujac obviously knew his stuff, despite his age. But Rooney waved us off. So we climbed back up and came around again. Same thing. As we neared the deck almost ready to touch down, Rooney waved us off. Up we went to make another approach, and once again he waved us off. Finally after four go-arounds, Rooney let us land. He had put us through some tense moments, which was exactly what he had wanted to do, but come to think of it, it was wonderful practice for the young pilot.

The highlight of the maneuvers was a mock attack by the Navy's carrier planes on Pearl Harbor, which was designed to duplicate the sneak attack by the Japanese in 1941. And I wanted to get in on it. The plan was to attack from the northwest, just as the Japanese had done, and to use every plane on the carrier—the fighter planes, the torpedo bombers, the dive-bombers. I finagled to get myself assigned to one of the planes as a radio operator. What I overlooked was that the names of everybody participating in the mock attack would be published in a list Rooney would see.

He really hit the ceiling. "What's going on here? Who's this radio operator, Hesburgh?"

"Well, you know," I said, "I'm out here by order of the Secretary of the Navy to study naval aviation and training, and I can't do that if I don't do a little flying." That didn't help at all. If anything, it probably made Rooney madder.

"By golly, you are really something," he said. "The Army is going to send planes up to intercept ours, and they are going to be chasing us all over the sky. What do you think will happen if a couple of them collide and you're killed?"

"If I'm killed I won't worry about it."

"*You* won't worry about it," he screamed, "but *I'll* worry about it. The Navy would raise holy hell with me. Forget it. You're scratched." He drew a line through my name and that was it. The warplanes of the *Princeton* launched their mock attack against Pearl Harbor, but Hesburgh stayed aboard ship.

When the maneuvers were over we docked in Hawaii, and I said Mass at Hickam Air Force Base. I finished about noon, then walked over to lunch. The Navy had scheduled a cocktail reception before the lunch and there were numerous high-ranking officers and several educators in attendance. Because of a mutual aversion to martinis, I hit it off with an admiral named John McCrea, who was deputy commander-in-chief of the Pacific Fleet. Just before lunch he asked me if I would say grace, specifically a short one.

"Why not one of your Navy chaplains here?" I asked.

"I have no stomach for that; they all get up and feel obliged to tell the all-knowing God everything that is going on."

I obliged the admiral with the standard Catholic grace before meals: "Bless us, O Lord, and these, thy gifts, which we are about to receive from thy bounty, through Christ, Our Lord, Amen."

Apparently, he appreciated the brevity. After lunch he asked if there was anything special he could do for me there. I told him that I'd like to go fishing and, if possible, to see the Big Island, Hawaii. He promised to take care of it and suggested that I bring some friends along. I rounded up several junior fliers who had befriended me on the carrier, and the next day we found ourselves boarding the admiral's barge, which is a very classy boat that takes admirals and other high-ranking officers to shore and back. The boat was fully stocked with food, beer, and fishing gear, plus a crew. And, of course, it was flying the admiral's four-star flag, plus several others, and that got us more attention than we wanted. As we went by Navy ship after Navy ship in the harbor, everyone on deck had to snap to attention and salute those sailing under the admiral's flag. This amused the junior officers enormously, and they returned those snapped salutes with all the laid-back, casual manner they could summon, considering our lack of rank. We did not catch any fish, but we consumed an awful amount of food and beer, which added up to a great day on the ocean, not to mention a good laugh on the Navy braid.

The next day the admiral arranged a flight for my friends and me to the Big Island. For this outing, I invited seven of my fellow academics, and, as before, everything was laid out for us first-class. At precisely the appointed time, we were picked up and driven to Hickam, where the planes were waiting. They were four PB4Y-2s, the Navy version of the B-24, used as weather planes. The squadron was known as the Tearjerker squadron because they got wet so often, flying through storms and hurricanes to collect weather information. As the nominal guest of honor, I suppose, I was assigned to the lead plane, along with George Weller, a foreign correspondent for the *Chicago Daily News*. Before we took off Commander Davis, the pilot, asked me what I'd like to do. I mentioned seeing some of the other islands between Oahu and the Big Island, including Molokai, and Haleakala, the volcano on Maui. Davis said, "Great, we'll see them all." And with that we took off, the three other bombers right behind us. I have no idea what instructions, if any, Admiral McCrae gave the pilot for this junket; perhaps Commander Davis simply had a wild imagination of his own.

Once we were airborne, Davis asked me if I'd ever flown. I said no, but that I'd love to know how. He turned abruptly to the copilot and said, "Give him your seat." He then proceeded to teach me the instruments, what they do, and how to test and double-check them. When we reached Molokai, Davis swooped down and buzzed the leper colony there. That must have frightened the lepers half to death. I was relieved when we climbed back up and joined the rest of the planes in the squadron.

As we approached the great volcano of Haleakala on Maui,

Weller, the foreign correspondent, said he would like to get some pictures of the volcanic crater because he had a special high-power camera with him that he had borrowed from the Navy. Weller went down into the Plexiglas bombardier station in the nose of the ship, and the next thing I knew Davis put this big, four-engine bomber into a dive as if it were a fighter plane. We headed right into the hole of the crater. Soon we were not only in it, but only about twenty-five feet off its bottom. This was hair-raising enough, but there were also these big cones, six hundred to seven hundred feet high, sticking up all around us. Davis saw them, too, of course, but I wasn't taking any chances. I pointed each one out as it came into view, and Davis was flying along at 150 miles an hour, dodging these cones as if they were no more significant than clouds. Some of them were just off the wing tip. "God in Heaven, what have we gotten ourselves into here," I thought. Meanwhile, George was down in the belly of the plane, taking pictures. He had to be scared witless. But he wasn't saying a thing. It occurred to me that maybe he had passed out, but I was afraid to go down there because I wanted to make sure that Davis saw all the cones.

Eventually we negotiated our way to the other side of the crater, but now we had a new problem. A thousand-foot-high wall loomed in front of us; there was no way we could climb fast enough to get over it. But Davis just calmly put the plane into a tight turn—I have no idea how he did that with that big plane— and started flying back the way we had come. I could not believe it.

"Good Lord, we're going to spend the rest of our life in this crater," I said aloud. I figured Davis would try to get us out of the crater by gradually corkscrewing up until he was above the rim. He did not do that. Instead, he flew straight toward a big V at the other end, where the lava had flowed out during the last eruption. We would never make it through, not with our wingspan. Even I could see that.

"This is it, the end," I murmured to myself. I did not even have time to pray. But at the last moment he stood the plane on its wing, so that we were flying with the wings perpendicular to the ground. He flew right through the V as if it were the most routine thing in the world.

"Whew," I sighed.

"Did you get some good pictures, George?" Davis nonchalantly asked.

"I not only got some good pictures," came Weller's reply, "I reached out and picked up a handful of lava."

With that, Davis turned to me and asked me if I'd like to go into the crater again. "No, sir!" I replied without a doubt.

Then he quipped, "Well, I was just trying to make a Christian out of you."

Davis must have thought I needed some additional faith. Flying over the ocean, he set the plane on automatic pilot, heading for Mauna Loa, the 16,860-foot volcano on the Big Island. With the chart in front of me, I could see that we were only fifteen hundred feet above sea level, and we had to climb some fifteen thousand feet more to clear the peak of Mauna Loa. Our big, heavy, lumbering bomber on automatic pilot was not climbing very fast. When we reached the coastline, we still had four or five thousand more feet to climb and I was getting worried again. Half a mile away from the peak, we were still at least three hundred feet too low, closing fast, and still on automatic pilot. Davis was not touching the controls. He just sat there saying, "C'mon, baby, climb! C'mon, baby, climb!" Naturally, I thought he should do something, that we were tempting fate once too often, but it was not my place to tell this pilot how to fly his plane. Miraculously we cleared the peak, I swear, by not much more than ten feet.

We landed at Hilo for a sight-seeing tour of volcanic tunnels, a fern forest, and an Australian rest house at the top of the volcano of Kilauea. Then we headed back home to Hickam, and I relaxed. Ah, but I had once again underestimated Navy Commander Davis. When he leveled out at fifteen hundred feet, he put the plane on autopilot and turned to me and said, "Padre, you've had a flying lesson. Now, by golly, you're gonna fly!"

He radioed the other three planes of the squadron that they were on their own and that he would see them back at Hickam. They broke formation and disappeared. I had a hunch he did not want them to see what was going to happen next. What happened next was that Davis got up out of the pilot's seat and said, "Sit down, Padre, you're it." So I took his place in the captain's seat, and Davis said, "You take us back to Hickam. I'm going to get some sleep." His nonchalance should not have surprised me after our thrill ride through one volcano and over another one. The copilot, an ensign younger than Kujac, was sitting next to me in the right-hand seat. If an emergency arose, I wondered, could we get Davis back in time? Before he left the cockpit, he cut off the automatic pilot switch and glanced at me. "You're at least going to give me a heading, aren't you?" I asked.

And he said, "Yeah, it's the one we're on right now. That'll get us to Hickam. But we're starting to sway, so you'd better get it under control." And with that he left.

Well, the first thing you learn when you're flying a plane is that you have to worry about more than one dimension. A plane not only sways to the right and to the left, it also bobs up and down. As soon as a wing drops down, you are off course. So you straighten the wings parallel to the horizon in front of you, and then you discover that you may be diving, or climbing. You have to correct that. There's a little picture of an airplane on one of the instruments that shows you what attitude the plane is in, and a wheel that helps keep you in level flight. But flying a bomber takes concentration and there is a lot to do at the same time. It is like driving a big, stubborn, ungainly truck on a narrow, winding road, only more difficult.

Eventually I got the plane under control and we were level and on course to Hickam. I was feeling pretty good, maybe even a little proud of myself. So I lit up a cigarette. (Yes, I smoked cigarettes in those days.) The cigarette was a little reward for doing so well. I was starting to relax a bit when someone handed me a mug of coffee. I did not look up from my instruments to see if it was the copilot or George Weller. At any rate, things were beginning to get complicated again. I had an airplane to fly, plus a cigarette to smoke and a mug of coffee to drink. The big bomber began to wander, and so I put the coffee mug on the seat and gripped it between my legs. This freed up one hand for flying the plane—up, down and right, left—while I sipped, smoked, sipped, smoked, using the other hand. The plane settled down once more, but I still felt like the fellow in the circus who spins saucers and juggles at the same time. Meanwhile, George was somewhere in the belly of the plane, probably afraid to come up and see what was happening; Davis was sacked out; and the young copilot was undoubtedly too scared to say anything.

But I had my flying, smoking, coffee-drinking routine down pretty well by now, and once more I was starting to relax. I probably should have known better, because at that point someone came up and handed me a ham sandwich. I was hungry, so I started eating. Now I was smoking a cigarette, drinking a cup of coffee, eating a ham sandwich, and flying an unfamiliar four-engine bomber. Something had to go; so I snubbed out the cigarette. That helped. Now I just had the coffee and the sandwich to think about while flying the plane. Then the copilot up and left. I was alone in the roaring cockpit. I gulped down the remains of the coffee and ham sandwich, and I wisely resisted the temptation to light another cigarette. It was very lonely flying alone over an empty stretch of the Pacific Ocean in a bomber I knew next to nothing about. Believe me, the tension built. I screamed to no one in particular, "Get that so-and-so of an ensign up here!" Silence. "At least you guys ought to have some regard for your own lives," I yelled. Still no reaction. Finally I bellowed, "If I make a mistake, we're all in the ocean!" That had no effect either.

Twenty minutes later, the ensign ambled into the cockpit and said, "What's the big deal?" By then we were approaching Hickam field and the ensign went back and woke up Davis, who came up and took over.

That was my introduction to serious flying. I have had only one experience that can compare. That was a ride I took in an SR-71.

The SR-71 is the Blackbird. It is painted all black, and the paint is composed of microscopic metal balls that absorb radar, which makes it undetectable. It is a supersonic reconnaissance plane that gathers military intelligence from altitudes of eighty thousand feet and higher. This bird measures 107 feet 5 inches front to back, 55 feet 7 inches from wing tip to wing tip, and 18 feet 6 inches from top to bottom. It has no weapons, not even a single machine gun. But it does carry some of the most sophisticated photographic and electronic gear ever developed.

What intrigued me about this plane was its speed. When I first heard about it in 1976, the SR-71 had just set a world speed record of 2,193 miles per hour, which translates to Mach 3.35, or 3.35 times the speed of sound. I thought how much I would like to fly in the SR-71 someday, and, even more, try to break its speed record. About three years later, on February 28, 1979, courtesy of President Jimmy Carter, I got my chance.

As had happened with my bomber tour of the Hawaiian Islands more than thirty years earlier, my flight in the SR-71 came about because of a casual remark, not a carefully thought-out plan. I had just finished several special projects for President Carter, and we were talking by ourselves in the Oval Office when the President remarked, "Is there anything I can do for you?" That is the kind of question anyone would like to hear, but it's especially welcome when it comes from the President of the United States.

The response popped right into my mind. "Yes, Mr. President, there is. You're a former submariner, and yesterday I noticed that you were indulging a fantasy of yours. You were out on a nuclear submarine with Admiral Rickover [the father of our nuclear Navy] and you went down to six hundred feet and took control of the sub yourself. I happen to be an aviation nut, and my fantasy is someday to ride the shuttle and say Mass in space. That probably won't happen very soon, so in the meantime I'll settle for a more attainable fantasy. I'd like to ride in the world's fastest airplane."

President Carter smiled with understanding. "You mean the SR-71. Well, they don't let civilians even see that airplane, much less ride in it," he said. "It's a very special airplane, and there are only about twenty of them in existence."

"I know," I said, "but you're the Commander-in-Chief, and you can order it if you want to. All I want to do is go faster than the fastest recorded time in the Guinness Book of World Records."

Two days later the chief of staff of the Air Force called me. "The boss says you want to fly in the SR-71."

"Yes, sir!"

"Well, there are some conditions. First, you've got to pass the astronaut physical and psychological tests." I agreed to that. "Secondly, you've got to know how to eject from an altitude of over eighty thousand feet." I don't remember exactly what I said, but he went on. "And thirdly, you've got to know how to operate everything in the backseat, on command from the guy in the front seat. He's busy flying the airplane, so you have to know how to do the other stuff. For openers, you've got seven radios and a transponder, plus navigational equipment, and several other things. Can you do that?"

I was not to be put off. I informed the chief of staff that I was more than willing to learn whatever I needed to know in order to make the flight. "All I ask is a chance to learn the backseat," I told him. I understood that I had to do the job of the systems officer, the other half of a crew of two, and if I failed, I'd be putting the pilot's life in danger.

"We'll set up a time for you to spend several days at Beale Air Force Base in Sacramento," he agreed. "If you pass the exam, you fly. If you don't, you don't."

"Fair enough," said I.

They wasted no time. A few days later an Air Force major who flew backseat in the record-setting flight of the SR-71 met me in Chicago. We flew commercial together to Sacramento and to the Beale base outside of the city, and all the way worked on the confidential Air Force SR-71 manuals. At Beale they put me through a vigorous and complete physical and psychological examination. At sixty-two years of age, I passed it with no difficulty. Over the next three days I was put through an intensive course of instruction. It covered everything I needed to know about the plane and about myself physically to fly as the second man in the SR-71.

This Lockheed "Recon Bird" is a long, needle-nosed aircraft in which both crewmen sit up in the point of the needle, one behind the other, with the rear seat somewhat elevated so the second man (me) can see over the top of the pilot. Two Pratt & Whitney J-58 jet engines supply the awesome power required to reach and surpass Mach 3. At that speed the SR-71 is close to the edge of just about everything. It could burn up, go out of control, or fall apart. Even in the rarified air above eighty thousand feet there is a

tremendous amount of friction. At Mach 3-plus the skin of the
plane heats up to 950 degrees. This is more than enough to burn
up most planes, but the skin of this bird is made from a heat-
resistant alloy composed of titanium and tungsten. Even so, the
heat and the supersonic speed exact a toll on every flight. The Air
Force spends an unbelievable amount of time maintaining the SR-
71. For every hour of flight time, the plane undergoes 450 hours of
maintenance. Every 200 hours the plane is taken completely apart
and put back together again.

Before long, I was under the impression that the Air Force does
the same kind of maintenance on its flight personnel. In one test,
my instructors put me into a big pressurized tank, bolted me to
an SR-71 backseat, and left. I sat there wearing a space suit and
an oxygen mask. A doctor outside, on the other side of the
window, stared in at me. They reduced the pressure in the tank
until it was equivalent to what you would experience at eighty-five
thousand feet. Suddenly a light started flashing, which meant that
either they were simulating an emergency for me or we actually
were having one. I was supposed to react the way I'd been trained.
So, I ejected. If I had actually been in the Recon Bird, I would
have been shot out faster than a rifle bullet, more than three
thousand feet per second. Then another emergency light began
flashing, telling me that the automatic ejection system was not
functioning. That meant I had to go to the back-up, manual
system: Uncap something over here; pull a lever over there; when
the hood blew off, pull another handle that in a real situation
would have blown me right out of the airplane. I did everything
correctly, and we went on.

They asked me to push my helmet visor up off my face to the
top of my helmet. That shut off the oxygen supply. Of course, I
couldn't breathe. That was exactly the point of this test: to find
out how I would react and function without oxygen. I was
supposed to go without oxygen or air for a minute, and naturally
I was apprehensive, wondering if I could do what I'd been trained
to do. I resisted the acute temptation to breathe fast, because it
wouldn't do me any good: I'd hyperventilate and fail the test. So
my task was to stay calm and breathe slowly. For three hours

before the test I had breathed in pure oxygen, and I knew my oxygen-rich blood should easily sustain me for a minute or so without breathing. But the natural inclination is to breathe; no one can deliberately stop breathing. I just took very slow, shallow breaths and kept my cool.

Next, the doctor outside the window asked me if my fingers and toes were starting to tingle. I said no, not particularly. "OK, go another minute," he told me. That extra minute really dragged. It was like trying to hold your breath under water. I was trying to almost not breathe, but it was very difficult to overcome the natural impulse. I breathed as slowly as I could. The doctor asked me again if my fingers and toes were tingling, if I was getting a little fuzzy? Again I said, "Not particularly."

Apparently, he did not like this answer. "OK, smartass," he said, "go another minute."

I focused on the third minute exactly as I had the first two, reassuring myself that I had oxygen stored in my blood, that I must keep calm, and take slow, shallow breaths. The third minute ended and I was still feeling pretty good. The doctor said, "*Now* do you have the symptoms?"

Again I said, "Not particularly." I could see his face through the window, and I sensed that my nonchalant answers were making a personal contest out of this. He instructed me to count to ten, and back again. I counted perfunctorily, but as fast as I could, because I didn't know how much longer I would be able to continue. At this point I had gone three minutes without oxygen, and I was now counting back from ten.

Finally, the doctor said, "Pull your visor down." Fresh air. Once again I was breathing oxygen. I could feel it rushing through my bloodstream, revivifying my body.

I had now passed the physical, plus two psychological tests. I reacted well under stress. If I'd panicked during the ejection exercise or the oxygen deprivation test, they would have told me ever so politely: "Well, Padre, nice try. But if you'd panicked like that at eighty thousand feet, you'd have died. Sorry, we can't let you make the flight." The dreaded words were not spoken. So far, so good. Instrumentation, navigation, and the use of emergency equipment came next.

Ejecting in the event of an emergency is one of the most crucial elements in high-risk, experimental flights. After all, your own life depends on it. With the primary system you just blow yourself out. You pull on this big ring and you're gone. If that does not work, however, you have to blow the hatch, then blast yourself out while you are still strapped in your seat. A .45-millimeter shell shoots you about 450 feet into the air, well clear of the plane. It is the same system used now by the crew on the space shuttle, if an emergency arises before they get up too high.

There is a great deal to know and remember about the fail-safe ejection system. The training teaches you to imagine yourself at eighty thousand feet, strapped every way from Sunday into your chair and traveling faster than a bullet out of rifle. A chute opens to slow your descent, and also to keep you from going too much farther horizontally, which could complicate rescue efforts, especially if you were headed toward water. If you are westbound over Rochester, for example, and you eject at that speed without a drogue, you can easily find yourself in Lake Erie by the time you land.

Your parachute pack has a radio in it that starts squawking "Mayday, Mayday." That alerts rescuers to the trouble you're in, and gives them something to beam in on while trying to find you. After you eject, there is nothing much to do, personally. You sit there and watch the clouds go by as you plummet toward earth. At fifteen thousand feet, a device that senses barometric pressure is supposed to explode another shell, which activates something called the guillotine. The guillotine is so named because it cuts all these cables that are holding you to the seat. If that fails, there is a lever beneath the chair you can pull to separate yourself from the seat. But that is trickier. There is still one more back-up system to help you, called the kick-ass. Like the others, it is an explosive shell designed to separate you from your seat with a bang. No doubt the name of the thing is akin to the feeling you get when it is deployed.

At fifteen thousand feet and clear of your seat, your parachute should open automatically. If it doesn't, you have to pull a rip cord. One way or another, when your thirty-eight-foot parachute opens, a rubber boat comes out on one side of you and automatically inflates, and on the other side of you a large survival kit pops out. You hope you will not need either of them, but they are attached to you with forty-foot lanyards if you do. When you land, you get out of your parachute immediately, turn off the radio that has been broadcasting the Mayday message, and turn on a more powerful radio in your survival package. If you land in the water, however, things become more complicated. With the lanyard you can easily pull the boat over to you. The trick is getting into it. Remember, you are wearing a bulky space suit, which is difficult enough to get in and out of on dry land. I hoped I would not have to eject, at least not over water. Ejecting over land, I have to confess, intrigued me a little. What a trip down that would be!

When I finished being checked out on the emergency equipment, one trainer paid me the compliment "You're really a quick study."

"Look, when your life depends on knowing these things, you naturally pay very close attention," I said to him. I still had to check out on all the instruments. The most difficult part of this was performing the operations wearing that bulky space suit. Every part of your body is completely covered. The helmet screws onto a metal ring on the top of the suit. Your hands are encased in thick gloves and cumbersome boots cover your feet. All of this makes movement of any kind very difficult. The gloves significantly reduce your dexterity, and this can be dangerous. You are sitting on nine different explosive charges, and you can ill afford to hit the wrong button or pull the wrong lever. Fortunately, I can read the gauges without my glasses, so I did not have to worry about them falling off or steaming up inside my helmet.

Every day at Beale I did a vigorous set of boring calisthenics, of which I am not at all fond: running in place the equivalent of a half mile or so, a hundred pushups from the knees, sit-ups, and what not. But I did them faithfully to get myself in the best possible physical shape. On my last day of training, the pilot who was going to take me up told me the good news: "Okay, we're going to fly tomorrow." He was Major Tom Allison, and he invited me to his home for dinner that night with his wife and two children. We enjoyed a wonderful time, getting better acquainted before our record-attempting flight.

The next morning was the beginning of a perfect day. No clouds and no wind. It was also Ash Wednesday, the first day of Lent. I had been up since four-thirty to give myself plenty of time to say Mass and perform the tedious exercises one more time. A final physical exam was scheduled before the flight. We were supposed to have the standard preflight astronaut breakfast of steak and eggs. The nature of my work that morning, I know, permitted me to eat a needed, substantial breakfast, even though it was a fast day. But I decided I should not, and I explained to Tom, "I'm going to be a little bit ornery this morning. There are only four fast days left in the Church, and today is one of them. I know I'm allowed a big breakfast with steak and all before the flight, but I think I ought to do what the rest of the Catholics are doing this morning, and just have a piece of toast and a cup of black coffee."

I had no idea whether Tom was Catholic or not, but he just nodded and said, "I'll do it with you."

Next we struggled into our space suits, and I do mean struggle. They are airtight, and you squeeze into them through one small opening at the back. Then you pop your head through the metal ring at the top where the helmet screws on. Somebody fastens it on for you, then zips you up in back, and you are in there to stay. A portable air conditioner is hooked into the suit to keep you cool. You talk to the outside world through a radio in your helmet. Suited up, air-conditioned, ensconced on a La-Z-Boy recliner, and breathing pure oxygen, you just lie there for a couple of hours while your blood absorbs the maximum amount of oxygen possible. At the same time, your blood is being purged of nitrogen. The idea is that with so much oxygen and so little nitrogen in your blood, you will not get the bends if the oxygen system on the plane fails, or you have to bail out.

After about two hours on the oxygen, when we were almost done with it, a young corporal walked in and plugged into Tom's helmet and started talking. Tom nodded and seemed to doze off on his couch. A few minutes later the corporal returned and gave me the message. "I apologize, sir, I was telling the major that a few minutes ago while I was pulling the pins on your parachute pack, one of the pins slipped through my fingers and fell down below the seat to the bottom of the plane. You cannot take off with that thing rattling around; it could interfere with some very sensitive electronic equipment down there. We are going to have to take off the hatch, remove the seat and all the explosive charges, and get down there and get it out." He was not about to take any chances.

"It's going to take us about three hours," he added. I winced. Two hours sucking oxygen and now another three hours of simply waiting did not endear that corporal to me, but, then again, I did not want him to feel any worse than he already did.

"Don't worry about it; it could happen to anyone," I told him, adding, "But would you give me that pin when you find it, as a souvenir?" He did, and I still have it.

While waiting, Tom and I had to unplug the oxygen and get out of our gear. Laboriously, off came the gloves, the boots, the helmets, and the suits themselves. During the wait we got so hungry, we indulged in another cup of coffee and shared a grilled cheese sandwich for lunch, still observing Ash Wednesday. Finally, when the seat and all the charges had almost been replaced, we suited up again and went back on pure oxygen. It did not take long this time for our oxygen level to reach its peak, at which point we disconnected from the oxygen tanks and carried our portable air conditioners for the walk to a van. The van was equipped with another pair of La-Z-Boys, and we made the trip to the hangar lying down.

Now you don't just turn the ignition key to start the engines of an SR-71. It takes the combined power of two Packard engines to do it, and even then you still are not ready to take off. Several automobiles have to cruise the ten thousand-foot runway to look for dead birds and beer cans, and anything else that can cause trouble after you get moving down the runway. A final check of all the instruments and systems takes another half an hour. Then a whole bunch of technicians swarm all over you, making sure that you are strapped in tight and that your feet are secure in the stirrups. To eject successfully you must be almost one with your seat; if you have a leg sticking out, you either break that leg or lose it entirely.

When we were almost ready to roll, I switched on my intercom radio and reminded my pilot, "Tom, we've got to break the world speed record today. You know that, don't you?"

"You've told me that ten times already," he said, "and I've heard you every time."

He reminded me to watch for two signals he would give me in the event we had to bail out. The amber light meant, "Caution, get ready to eject." If the red light went on, we would eject. He demonstrated first the amber light, then the red one. "You don't want me to eject here and now, do you?" I asked. "No," he said, "but if you see that red light go on, get out. I'll stay put until you're gone."

Well, I couldn't have that, especially after meeting his family. "Like heck, you will," I said. "You've got a wife and two kids, and I don't. You give me the few seconds I'm entitled to, no more, and if I'm not out, you go anyway." All during the training I never really believed I would have to eject. But the glow of the light as Tom tested it, and the tone of his voice as he talked, made me realize that it was not as distant a possibility as I had thought. As I was contemplating all this, Tom's voice suddenly came over my radio again. "OK, we're ready to roll."

And did we ever roll. Tom turned on the afterburners and I felt like someone had just kicked me in the rear. Flames shot out five or ten feet behind each one of those big J-58 engines. About halfway down the ten thousand-foot runway, maybe not even that far, we took off like a rocket. It seemed like we were going almost straight up. We got to thirty thousand feet in what seemed like only seconds. It was the closest thing to being shot out of a cannon.

At thirty thousand feet, Tom leveled off and checked in with ground control. The flight controller already knew we were at thirty thousand feet, cruising at a leisurely Mach .9. He instructed us to maintain that altitude and speed until further notice. I felt a little impatient at this because Mach .9 was a long way from Mach

3-plus, and I was anxious to break a speed record, not just go sky riding. I asked Tom what the speed limit was all about. He told me we had to take it easy until we passed over a ski area below us, or our sonic boom could precipitate an avalanche.

After five minutes or so, the flight controller radioed permission to climb to sixty thousand feet, beyond which we were on our own. There was no air traffic up there where we were going. I knew we would be climbing to eighty thousand feet, maybe even higher. Tom assured me that we were going up higher, but in a slightly roundabout way. "Padre," he said, "first I'm going to dive to twenty-five thousand and go through Mach 1. Then we're going straight up."

That was a roller-coaster ride I will never forget. I watched the Machmeter as we went through Mach 1. Then Tom pulled the stick back and, just as he said, we started climbing straight up, faster and faster. The rate-of-climb indicator on my instrument panel turned to a blur. We blasted through Mach 2, then Mach 3. I could feel the flesh on my face pulling against my cheekbones and trying to move around to the back of my head. I could hardly believe the instrument panel. As we roared through seventy-six thousand feet we were climbing at the rate of four thousand feet a minute. Tom had the plane into a climbing turn as we passed through eighty thousand feet. We were still climbing. The Mach-meter was registering 3.35. My eyes were glued to the needle, watching for the instant that it passed that mark. At last it did, and I was exultant. Major Tom Allison and Father Theodore Hesburgh had just set a new world speed record! At that speed, we could have flown from Sacramento to Notre Dame in forty-five minutes.

For security reasons I cannot reveal the actual reading on the Machmeter, except to say that it was over Mach 3.35, or much more than 2,193 miles per hour. Because we did not exceed this speed in exactly the prescribed manner—so many miles in each direction—it does not stand as an official record. But we had the satisfaction of knowing that we did it.

When we were over Seattle, I actually did something useful aboard the SR-71. The ground asked Tom what the setting was on our transponder. Tom got on our private bandwave and said, "That's your department, Padre." I looked at the transponder and told him it was set at 6644. Tom relayed this, and the controller on the ground asked us to set it at 6424. Tom came back on and said, "Can you hack it, Padre?"

I said "No sweat," and groped my way because the transponder was way back from where I was sitting and I had to do it by feel. When I had reset the thing, the flight controller radioed an OK, and Tom gave me a "Good work, Padre."

At that point the fellow on the ground exclaimed, "You got a priest up there!" It was more of an exclamation than a question.

Feeling pretty good at that point, I answered him myself. "And God bless you, too." Then we passed out of his radio range, into the wild blue yonder.

Back on the ground at Beale, I asked Tom if he had pushed the plane as fast as it would go. "My God, Padre," he said, "I went within five degrees of burning us up. What more do you want?" When we got inside, they gave me a little medal, and I had my picture taken with the wing commander pinning it on.

A few years later I managed to get myself on the list of civilians volunteering to go up in the space shuttle. Since I had already passed the astronaut physical and had flown in the SR-71, I thought I had a pretty good chance to go into space. There were only two civilians ahead of me who seemed to be my main competition—Walter Cronkite and James Michener, and I am younger than either of them. I figured my chances were pretty good. But the Challenger disaster put an end to civilian space travel, and so I probably will have to be satisfied with my unofficial speed record in the SR-71. It looks like I won't be offering Mass in space.

THE MASS

THE MASS in the Roman Catholic Church is a recapitulation of the Last Supper and Christ's sacrifice on the cross, redeeming the sins of all those who believe in Him. It is the central part of salvation, and of all the services performed by a priest, to my mind there is nothing more important than offering Mass. That was why when I was ordained in 1943 I made a personal pledge, to myself more than anyone else, that I would celebrate a Mass every day of my life, although the church did not require that of me or of any other priest. I thought it would serve as a daily act of gratitude for my being accepted as a priest, and also that it would bring me closer each day to the Holy Spirit.

I pray every day to the Holy Spirit, as my friend, to give me the light and the strength to do the right thing. And the Holy Spirit has never failed to show me the way, and to give me the strength of purpose to struggle on in the face of all kinds of adversity.

As the years went on, I discovered that when you make up your mind to do something every day, come hell or high water, your life takes on a new, purposeful fascination: You have this obligation to perform, a personal obligation you must not fail. Since being ordained a priest, I have not failed it, with the exception of one night when I was helping to keep a vigil over a premature baby. I have said Mass with atheistic Russian Communists standing around the altar; with readers such as Rosalynn Carter and Robert McNamara; in an Anglican church that had not seen a Catholic Mass since the middle of the sixteenth century; in a dining car aboard a lurching railroad train; on all kinds of ships; in the middle of an African jungle; in thousands of hotel rooms in more than a hundred countries; and in all five languages that I speak. I even figured out a way to lay out a portable altar and say Mass in space, if and when I am ever chosen to ride the space shuttle.

Saying Mass every day was not a problem when you were at home, but when traveling it could get quite complicated, especially before Vatican II eased many of the traditional rules on the service. There used to be five sets of colored vestments you had to carry for different feast days and liturgical seasons. You had to fast from midnight on and say Mass—in a church—before noon, which made things doubly difficult if you were on a plane or out in the middle of nowhere.

Because my work took me all over the globe, these rules and regulations could have posed a formidable obstacle to my saying Mass every day. Fortunately, I was not bound by them because I was ordained during the war and was able to get myself named an auxiliary chaplain, and because of military exigencies chaplains were the only priests who could offer Mass anywhere and at any time. For that I had Bishop John O'Hara to thank. Bishop O'Hara had been the president of Notre Dame when I was a student there and later became the military ordinary, which meant he was in charge of all the military chaplains in the armed forces. I got to know him well when consulting with him on the religious pamphlets I was writing for our armed forces people, and later when I was a newly ordained priest ministering to service personnel passing through Washington.

It was during this period when I was working closely with the armed services that O'Hara made me an auxiliary chaplain. This freed me from the usual rules and regulations covering the saying of Mass. I could offer Mass several times a day if necessary, even on Holy Thursday, when Mass was then (incomprehensibly) forbidden. I could drink liquids in between Masses, set up portable altars in appropriate places if I had to, and say Mass in hotel rooms, on trains, and in other unconventional places. None of this is unusual today, but back then it was. Of course, Good Friday is still the one day when no priest is allowed to say Mass, since the event that the Mass reenacts stands for itself on this day.

Years later, when I was teaching at Notre Dame and no longer an auxiliary chaplain, I found that I missed the flexibility I used to have, especially as my traveling for the university increased. Luckily I had the good fortune to run into O'Hara when he was visiting Notre Dame after the war had ended. He had become an archbishop and a cardinal, and I had recently been made executive vice president of the university. We shared a taxicab on the way to the South Bend airport, and as we sat there together I wondered if I had enough nerve to ask him a favor.

O'Hara was a commanding figure, but he never had much time for the symbols of rank. Except for a rather old-fashioned vest with a Roman collar, he was dressed exactly the same way I was, in a basic-black priest's suit. When he settled down in the cab, he took off his ring and the large cross he wore across his chest and put them in his pocket. We chatted about the steps we were taking to improve the academic quality of the university, and I felt a bit uneasy because the truth was that in improving the academic quality of the university I had been instrumental in firing almost every one of the deans and old-time faculty whom O'Hara had hired in his days as president. He could have interpreted these moves as being deliberately designed to get rid of his favorite people. I was fairly certain, too, that those affected must have told O'Hara what I was doing, but I never heard a word from him while it was going on, or afterward. He knew but he did not interfere.

I thought of these things as we rode together to the airport, and I must say I agonized a little over the prospect of asking him to grant me the faculties I needed to continue saying Mass every day.

But I finally turned to him and popped the question. I said something like "I think you'll understand when I tell you that I offer Mass every day, but because of the kind of life I lead it becomes very difficult under the normal rules, and I was wondering if there is some way you can still help me the way you did during the war when you gave me those military faculties."

What I actually said may have been even longer and more awkward than that. But if O'Hara bore me a grudge, you would never have known it. He just said, "Well, it's no big thing. When they made me military ordinary they gave me power to give these faculties, and when they made me bishop of Buffalo and Philadelphia they never took them away. So I assume I can still give them. Whenever you need faculties, just give me a call."

Over the ensuing years when I had to go to South America or somewhere like that, I would phone O'Hara and ask for faculties, promising I would take care of any American military along the way. On every trip overseas I had no trouble at all finding American sailors or soldiers who invited me to say Mass. But when O'Hara died in 1960, I was right back where I started. However, it was not long before I began doing some work for Cardinal Spellman of New York in connection with the International Atomic Energy Agency. Since Cardinal Spellman actually was the military ordinary and O'Hara had been his surrogate, I explained my situation to Cardinal Spellman and he immediately agreed to confer upon me the faculties of an auxiliary military chaplain whenever I needed them.

On one occasion, on an overnight trip aboard the Southern Pacific Railroad, I offered Mass at 5 A.M. in the train's empty bar car, attended only by a Catholic conductor. Another time, caught between planes in Dallas, Texas, I was allowed to use an empty American Airlines office to say Mass at 4:30 A.M. Just as I finished the ceremony, still dressed in my white robe, with my altar candles flickering in the dark, I was startled to see a bewildered baggage handler staring at me from the other side of the huge picture window. "What are you doing there?" he called out.

"I'm offering Mass."

"Who for?"

"For the whole world."

That seemed to satisfy him, and he got back on his baggage tractor and left.

The record for the most Masses said in the shortest period of time, and under the most trying circumstances, could very well be those I said on my first trip to Antarctica in 1963, as a member of the National Science Board. There were about thirty of us on the trip, mostly scientists and explorers, and the morning after we arrived I was scheduled to say Mass aboard an icebreaker that was sixty miles out to sea. I got up about seven, put on the usual layers of warm clothes, grabbed my Mass kit, and ran down to the helipad. I boarded a chopper for the flight to the icebreaker, which was clearing a path through 16-foot-thick ice for two loaded oil tankers en route to McMurdo Sound Station. On the way, we passed over Ross Island, Mount Erebus, and Cape Crozier, where all the penguins live. We also flew over the hut that the polar explorer Scott lived in back in 1910.

The captain of the icebreaker, I soon learned, was out of sorts about my coming to say Mass. He considered it a willful and unnecessary interruption of his mission. He would not slow down his craft, and so we had to make a delicate landing on a fast-moving ship between its ramming into an enormous ice field. The icebreaker would crash into the ice field, break off a chunk or two, then back up a thousand feet or so and charge full speed into the ice field again. The younger officer who met me said they had not had a priest aboard since the ship had left Quonset Point, Rhode Island, six weeks before, and so I decided to give them the full treatment. I heard confessions in a cabin for an hour or so, then said Mass, complete with sermonette, and handed out rosaries and some Notre Dame medals. After that, we all had breakfast together, and I got back in the chopper for our return trip to McMurdo Sound. Apparently, my visit to the ship had done nothing to soften the attitude of the captain. Even as we prepared to take off, the ship continued attacking the ice, full speed ahead.

From McMurdo I flew to the South Pole with Larry Gould, who had been Admiral Byrd's executive officer at Little America in the late 1920s. Larry was in understandably high spirits because although he had been to Antarctica four times, he had never gone to the pole. The ten thousand-foot runway at the pole is lined with oil drums every hundred yards or so, on both sides, and we were lined up perfectly between them when all of a sudden we hit something very hard. The impact threw us back up in the air and sent the plane veering sharply to the left. I was sure we were going to crash, but fortunately our pilot cut the power on the two engines on the right side and simultaneously poured it on from the left. The plane stabilized and dropped in for a perfect landing. It was one of the most beautiful pieces of airmanship I had ever seen. If we had winged over and crashed, we would have been goners: The plane was carrying fifteen hundred pounds of TNT for seismic shots. We found out later that we had hit something called a *sastrugi,* which is a Russian word for the icy spikes formed by the wind along flat areas. They use a bulldozer to clear them off the runways, but somebody must have missed this one.

Everybody was at work when we arrived and not available for my scheduled Mass, so Larry and I decided to walk to the pole, which was only about a mile away. I would say Mass later. As we trudged off into the whiteness, Larry mentioned that he felt as if he were on a religious pilgrimage. I felt a bit that way myself, and we walked mostly in silence. When we arrived at the pole, we found a flagpole supported by guy wires, and it seemed strange that this most unique place on earth would be marked so simply. Still, we went ahead and observed the customary ritual. We walked a complete circle around all the guy wires. In so doing, we had walked through all 360 degrees of the earth's longitude and had traveled literally around the world in a matter of sixty seconds. It was a silly thing, of course, but I don't see how anyone could have resisted doing it. I took the occasion, too, to say a little prayer.

When we got back to the station, I discovered that finding a suitable place to say Mass was more difficult than walking to and from the South Pole. Practically every facility was in constant use. People ate at all hours of the day, so the dining room was out. There were not enough beds for everyone, so the men slept in four-hour shifts around the clock in the sleeping quarters. Finally, I found a room, where the doctor performed surgery, which was not being used. It was a bit small for my taste, but the operating table made a perfect altar.

Before Mass I heard confessions in a small storeroom. The first scientist who came in must have been used to yelling above the howl of the Antarctic wind, because you could hear him all over the place. Not only that, but there was only a flimsy cardboard partition between us and the radio room. "Look, son," I said, "you'd better tone it down a little or you're going to be broadcasting your sins to the whole world." When confessions were over, I said Mass and delivered a sermon. We had a drink with the admiral and caught four hours of sleep.

Then back to the South Pole again, where I was to bless the ceremony marking the change of command at the station from Admiral Tyree to Admiral Reedy. It was thirty-four degrees below zero with a strong wind. I pushed back the hood of my parka and said what must have been the shortest prayer on record. Most of the others present wisely left their hoods on. We then marched back to the station and climbed into a plane for the flight to Byrd Station, eight hundred miles away. I said my third Mass of the day there. Afterward, we celebrated the birth of a baby who had been born back in the States to the wife of one of the crew.

In twenty-four hours, with only four hours' sleep, I had said a Mass in three different locations in Antarctica: at sea on a pitching icebreaker, within a mile of the South Pole, and half a continent away at an even more remote place, Byrd Station. Larry Gould missed only the first one, on the ice breaker, and when we finished the third one he said to me, "Father Ted, I think I'm doing pretty well, don't you? Here I am a Lutheran and I've been to Mass twice this Sunday."

The Antarctic was not the only place where I had to contend with snow and cold in order to say Mass. Baltimore one winter felt almost as inclement. I had delivered two lectures at Johns Hopkins University, and Milton Eisenhower, the president, had invited me to have an early dinner with him before I flew back to South Bend. I planned to leave at eight-thirty, but it started snowing heavily and within an hour traffic was at a standstill and all flights were canceled. I had no choice but to spend the night. I had given up cigarettes for Lent, but Milton gave me one of his pipes and some tobacco and we stayed up late, puffing away on our pipes and solving world problems. The next morning I was caught without my Mass kit and it appeared from the snow outside that I would be spending the day there and could not say Mass. Milton gave me directions to a chapel at Loyola College of Baltimore, which was down one hill, up another, and through the woods.

Dressed in Milton Eisenhower's trout-fishing hip boots and his football stadium coat, I struck out through the snow. I got to the chapel at 7 A.M., took off the hip boots and the stadium coat, and offered Mass. Then I put everything back on and walked back to Milton's.

Of the many hotels in which I have said Mass, there was this rather undistinguished little place in the Rome airport. I was making a half-hour stopover between planes on my way to Jerusalem and when it occurred to me that I would not reach Jerusalem until after midnight, I hurried to this small hotel and, puffing hard, spoke to the desk clerk, a woman. "I'd like to have a room for half an hour," I said, "and it's not what you think it's for."

She laughed and said, "Well then, why do you want it?"

I told her I wanted to offer Mass and invited her to come up and take part if she did not believe me. She said she believed me, and handed me the key. I said Mass, came back down to the desk, and asked her how much I owed. "Nothing," she said. "You have sanctified my hotel." I told her that I hoped one Mass would do it, thanked her, and hurried off to catch my plane.

I believe very deeply in ecumenism, in Christian unity, and I have been very fortunate to have had numerous opportunities to involve people of many faiths in the Masses I have offered. Of all places, Moscow was the scene of two particularly memorable Masses with a strong ecumenical flavor. I was never quite sure if religious services were forbidden or merely frowned upon in the Soviet Union, but while there on conferences I always held Masses in my hotel room and I almost always invited people to attend them. On one such occasion, Rosalynn Carter, our former First

Lady, turned up, among others, and she obliged me by reading the Gospel at the service.

At another conference on human rights, this one in the chancery of the Russian Orthodox archbishop of Moscow, the archbishop invited me to say Sunday Mass in his chapel the next day. Our meetings lasted all day and as we closed I announced a general invitation to all present to attend, if they wished, my saying of the Mass in the chapel of the archbishop. At eight o'clock the next morning, the first guest to appear was Robert McNamara, former Secretary of Defense and at the time chairman of the World Bank. I asked him if he would do the first reading. "I'm not even a Catholic," he protested.

"I didn't ask you if you were a Catholic," I said, adding, "I asked if you would do the first reading." He agreed.

Susan Eisenhower, the former President's granddaughter and a staunch advocate in the cause of international human rights, was the next to enter and she agreed to do the second reading. Others arriving included Yevgeny Velikhov, the vice president of the U.S.S.R. Academy of Sciences; Raoul Sagdeev, the head of the Russian space research program; Andrei Sakharov, the well-known Russian human rights activist; and a couple of American Episcopalians, William G. Miller, president of the American Committee on U.S./Soviet Relations, and Ned Hodgson, our American representative in Moscow. Ned asked me if it would be proper if they, as Episcopalians, received Communion. He had not received Communion since he had come to the Soviet Union six months before. I said, "Sure, just tell God you're sorry for all your sins." By the time I started the Mass, the chapel was full. Everyone who had been at the meetings the day before was there, even the Russian translators.

In my homily, I could not help mentioning that all of us were in a place of prayer, even though not every one of us was praying, and that we were all in Moscow for the same reason: to work for peace and against nuclear arms, poverty, and pollution. I made the point that after seventy years of trying to stamp out religion, the Russians were celebrating, or at least marking, a thousand years of Christianity. I said I thought it was remarkable that despite the active opposition of the government, Christianity had not only been preserved there but might well fuel a rebirth of the faith in Europe, a continent where churches, for the most part, were either standing empty or used as museums. I urged all present to keep Bob McNamara's wife in our prayers, because she had died recently. Bob was very moved by that. After I gave the final blessing, he came up and told me that the Mass was the highlight of the meetings for him.

Offering a Roman Catholic Mass in an Anglican church was one of the highlights of my travels in 1989, after I had retired as president of Notre Dame. I was attending a meeting of the Notre Dame Ecumenical Council in Wells, England, along with several of us from the university, including the president, Father Ed "Monk" Malloy, plus two Anglican bishops and Anglican laypeople. The Anglicans were part of Notre Dame's Institute for Ecumenical Studies through their support of something called the British Trust, which financed Anglican students during their year of study at the institute in Jerusalem. We were all staying at the Bishop's Palace, which was resplendent enough in itself, but it also had a beautiful Gothic chapel attached to it. Our host, George Carey, the bishop of Wells, graciously invited me to say Mass in the chapel for the whole group, offering me his vestments, chalices, and liturgical books.

Although I already had everything I needed, I used some of the prayers and readings that were in the bishop's books and did the Catholic ones from memory when it was time for the Offertory and the Consecration. Many of the prayers of the Catholic and Anglican rites are almost identical, so I made the Mass a blend of both traditions, which was in keeping with the ecumenism we were there for. Everyone seemed to appreciate that, and the bishop came over to me when I had finished. "You made history this morning," he said. "This was originally a Catholic monastery, but today was the first time in 450 years that anyone has said a Catholic Mass in this chapel." Well, you can never be too ecumenical, I thought. Since we were staying over, I did it again the next morning. Recently, our host, Bishop George Carey, was named Archbishop of Canterbury, leader of the Church of England.

One of the most memorable Masses in my life was one I did not even offer myself. It was during the height of the Cold War in

1957 when I was representing the Vatican at the International
Atomic Energy Agency in Vienna. The other Vatican delegate—
actually he was the delegate and I was the alternate—was Frank
Folsom, who had recently retired as president of RCA. Frank and
I had felt for some time that we ought to do something of a
religious nature at these annual meetings of the agency. For one
thing, we thought it might help reduce the acrimonious atmosphere that almost always developed. Typically, the delegates
would start out with high expectations. Then the wrangling and
the accusations would take over. By the time the first week ended,
the opposing factions—primarily the U.S. and the U.S.S.R.—were
ready to shoot each other and go home.

To help ease tensions we decided to invite all delegates to a
Mass, followed by a very nice brunch. This was in line with the
practice of each delegation holding social affairs, usually cocktail
parties, for the other delegates. For the Mass we picked Karlskirche, or Church of St. Charles, a small but very beautiful church
right in the middle of Vienna. There were larger churches, of
course, but we had no idea how many people would accept.
Among the delegates probably every religion in the world was
represented. There were Moslems, Hindus, Buddhists, Christians,
and a hefty proportion of nonbelievers. We figured that if the
response to our invitation was not good, it would be better to have
a half-empty small church than a very empty large church.

Karlskirche, when we went to look it over, was very beautiful,
as we had been told, and very dirty. We talked to the pastor about
having it cleaned up for the important diplomats we had invited.
He was unmoved. So we rounded up the maids at the agency and
had them clean the church from top to bottom. When they had
finished, I think it looked better than it had since the day Napoleon
was married there.

Then we paid visits to the nuncio and to the archbishop of
Vienna to see if one of them would volunteer to say the Mass. The
nuncio wanted no part of it, and he immediately left town.
Archbishop Franz Koenig of Vienna (who later became a cardinal)
reluctantly agreed to say Mass for the international set of delegates,
and I even persuaded him to read the Gospel in the languages of

the conference—French, English, Spanish, Russian—and in German because we were, after all, in Vienna. He balked at reading the Gospel in Russian.

"Why bother with that?" he asked. "The Russians won't even be there."

I told him I thought they would be.

"They never come to church," he said, "and don't you try to instruct me on this because I've been living here with them for ten years during the partition of Vienna and they've never been inside the church, except maybe to look around. They're atheists. Don't you know that?"

I said, yes, I knew they were atheists, but I still thought they would come to this Mass.

"And I know they won't," Koenig insisted.

We were at an impasse, but I thought I would have one more go at it. "I'll make a deal with you," I said. "If the Russians come to church, will you read the Gospel in Russian?" What could he say? He agreed, and we were all set—almost. The next problem was finding a Russian Bible. Koenig didn't have one, so I said I would provide a Russian translator who had just come over from the UN. The next problem was the Gospel itself. I told Koenig we would like it to be the Gospel of Christ the King.

He balked at that. "It's not the feast of Christ the King," he insisted.

"Come on," I said, "you're an archbishop. You can read any Gospel you want." Finally, we got to the sermon. I advised him to give a very short sermon in English, about three minutes, tops. "In fact," I said, "I've already written it out for you." I put the sermon I had written in front of him. He reached out and without even looking at it, turned it upside down on the table. By then I realized that for a young American priest I probably seemed just a tad pushy to this crusty Austrian archbishop. So I backed off, saying, "Well, anyway, you're going to be there at eleven o'clock, right?"

"I'll be there at eleven o'clock," he replied tartly. And that was all he said.

The Saturday night before the Mass there was a formal dance at the Konzerthaus, with a wonderful red carpet on the stairs leading down to the dance floor. When the dance was over and everyone had left in the wee hours of the morning, we rolled up the carpet, carried it over to the church, and laid it down the main aisle. The next morning we had little flowering plants placed at the end of every pew. Thinking that some singing would be appropriate, we rushed out and persuaded the Vienna Boys' Choir to sing at the Mass. It was amazing that we were able to get them on such short notice, and all the more so considering the condition of my German at the time. We were all set. We had the church, the archbishop, the red carpet, the flowering plants, and the Vienna Boys' Choir. The only question remaining was whether anyone would show up.

When we got to the church at ten minutes before eleven, no one was there. Franz and I, both being born optimists, reasoned that everyone might be a bit sluggish on the morning after the big party. But a few minutes later Ambassador Homi Bhabha, who headed the Indian delegation, arrived. "I understand that even the Russians and the Moslems have been invited," he said. "That will be quite a sight to see, if they come." Next came the Moslem ambassador from Pakistan. All of a sudden delegates arrived in droves and, much to my delight and relief, the Russians walked into the church.

In a matter of five minutes the church was jammed. Just before eleven a big Mercedes pulled up in front, and the archbishop stepped out. I handed him the Russian translation of the Gospel of Christ the King. "The Russians are here," I said. "You lose." Koenig smiled and walked in. As if on cue, the Vienna Boys' Choir started to sing. It was a beautiful Mass. The archbishop read the Gospel in all the languages. As he went through them, the corresponding delegations would stand. By the time he got to the last language, everyone in the church was standing, including the Russians. When he finished he asked everyone to sit down and then proceeded to read my talk, almost word for word.

There were a couple of glitches. In the Gospel of Christ the King, the word "king" was translated into the Russian "czar," and I feared the Soviet Communists might walk out on us. But they must have understood the context, because they didn't react. The other embarrassing moment came during the Offertory, when the church sacristan came in with a great big basket to start taking up a collection. I was so angry, I was ready to throttle him. I reached him before he started and told him to get out of there and that I would sic the archbishop on him if he didn't. Quite a few of the delegates witnessed this little altercation and were having themselves a good chuckle about this attempt of the Catholics to solicit donations from Moslems and Hindus and Russians and nonbelievers. At the time, it hardly struck me as amusing. I had to push the fellow out the door to get rid of him.

The Mass and the sumptuous brunch which followed were not only the high point of that conference, but of every one that followed. We made it an annual tradition, and it was truly marvelous the way it affected the delegates. After our Mass and convivial brunch, everybody would show up Monday morning ready to go to work again, full of optimism and good spirits.

On the Monday after the first Mass and brunch I went over to thank Archbishop Koenig for all his help. I also warned him that he might be hearing from the pastor of Karlskirche because we had cleaned his church without his permission. I explained how I had knelt in Karlskirche before the cleaning to say a prayer and had gotten up with dirt and dust all over my pants. "I've got to tell you, your eminence, that the churches in this town are so dirty you would think the war had never ended." Again, I feared that I had probably overstepped the bounds of propriety with him, but the next week every church in Vienna was cleaned vigorously.

The following year when I went to see Koenig about saying the Mass, he readily consented. In fact, he asked me to write his sermon. Over the years we became good friends. That was very gratifying to me, especially considering the chilly relationship we had had at the beginning. Later we brought Koenig to Notre Dame and gave him an honorary degree.

I said at the beginning of this chapter that offering Mass every day was something I felt was very important for me to do as a priest. I still feel that way. More than that, though, increasingly as the years have gone by, the more Masses I offer, the more evidence

I see that this ancient rite has the power to change people, to change the world.

The only time I have missed offering Mass—and I do not regret it a bit—was when I was when I was chaplain to Vetville, the married students' housing complex built at Notre Dame right after the war. There I met Bill and Helen O'Connor, who were eagerly anticipating their first baby. But it was not to be. When Helen was about six months pregnant, she drove home to Oil City, Pennsylvania, to visit her parents. The road was pretty rough in those days, and it must have shaken her up quite a bit because she lost the baby. I saw her when she returned to Notre Dame, and she was in tears. I tried to reassure her and to advise that she and Bill should have another baby as soon as possible.

Shortly afterward, Helen announced that she was pregnant again. But once again she did not make it to full term. As before, she started having labor pains at six months. Bill rushed her to the hospital and shortly before midnight he telephoned me. We waited out in the hall together. The two of us walked the floor until 3 A.M. Then all of a sudden a nurse raced past us with this tiny bundle. The baby was a boy, and it was very, very small—only three pounds eight ounces. Because of some difficulties that were encountered, the doctors had had to take it by cesarean.

We caught up with the nurse and learned that the baby had a heartbeat but was not breathing. The usual slap on the fanny had not worked. The nurse attempted to give him oxygen as Bill and I stood watching. I remember that part very clearly because the mask went completely over the baby's tiny face. The nurse then turned on the oxygen tank, but nothing came out. I asked her if his heart was still beating. She said, "Yes, but it's not going to be beating long."

So I said, "I'll baptize him."

I went over to the sink and put a glass under the spigot, but there was no faucet to turn on the water. Then I remembered that this was one of those sinks that has the kind of faucet the surgeons turn on with their knees. So I found the thing and gave it a kick and got the water to come out—very cold water, as it happened. When I ran back with the water, the nurse was still trying to get the baby's breathing started, but without success. I said to Bill, "What do you want to call him?"

He replied, "Mark."

With that, I said, "Mark, I baptize you in the name of the Father, and of the Son and of the Holy Spirit." I splashed the water in little Mark's face, and he let out a lusty yowl. "Bill," I said, "your son was born into time and eternity at the same time."

On our way back to the operating room I passed a water fountain and, without thinking, took a drink. Then I realized that I could not offer Mass that day because I had broken my fast. No one was happier than I was when Vatican II changed that rule on fasting before saying Mass. I did attend Mass at Cavanaugh Hall Chapel that morning.

Little Mark, the three-pound preemie, grew up to be a six-foot, two-inch graduate of Notre Dame.

THE CATHOLIC LAITY

FROM 1965 to 1967 I was in the anomalous position of being
president of the University of Notre Dame while leading the
efforts to give away our beloved university, lock, stock, and barrel,
as they say. The university had been founded more than one
hundred years before, in 1842, by a young priest named Edward
F. Sorin of a French missionary order called the Congregation of
Holy Cross. He started the school on the edge of St. Mary's Lake
in the northern Indiana wilderness in three dilapidated log buildings. He had about three hundred dollars in his pocket at the time.
By the 1960s the University of Notre Dame had grown considerably; its net worth was something in excess of half a billion dollars,
and it was still owned, operated, and controlled by the priests of
the Congregation of Holy Cross. It had become, to my mind at
least, the premier Catholic university in the United States. And, to
my mind, the time had come for the priests of Holy Cross to

relinquish ownership and control of the university to a lay board of trustees who would be better equipped to oversee its future well-being.

Only a broad, long view of the future of Notre Dame could bring into focus the benefits of drawing the laity into the decision-making process which would govern this Catholic university. Many protested at the time and many questioned that decision after it was made, more in bewilderment than in protest.

"Why, after more than a century of operation by the priests of Holy Cross, did you turn control of the university over to a lay board of trustees?" That was the question.

The answer was very simple: Vatican II had said that laypeople should be given responsibility in Catholic affairs commensurate with their dedication, their competence, and their intelligence. Many people may not have taken that seriously, but we did. For me, it was the most natural thing in the world. In fact, I had advocated a greater role for the laity ever since I wrote my doctoral dissertation on the subject two decades earlier.

And there were very practical reasons, too, which I believe were part of the thinking of Vatican II. Until that time, both at Notre Dame and throughout the entire Church, clerics had the top positions and the primary responsibility for virtually everything. But times had changed. Running a university, which had once been relatively simple, had now become complex and was getting more so almost by the day. Those three log cabins of Father Sorin's had grown into more than one hundred substantial buildings, a radio and TV station, fire and police departments, a massive food service operation, a highly competitive varsity athletics program, a bookstore, a hotel, seven thousand acres of property in Wisconsin, academic facilities in London, Rome, and Jerusalem, and a program for the future that would require us to raise, invest, and spend hundreds of millions of dollars each and every year. We had reached the point where Notre Dame could no longer be run by a handful of Holy Cross priests.

Some in the Notre Dame family, priests included, or perhaps I should say priests especially, fought the idea. Many of them believed it would be the end of Notre Dame as an inherently Catholic institution. Some of the priests argued that it was sheer folly to give away a half-a-billion-dollar institution when it belonged to us. They could see no reason for doing it; further, they feared the laity would not care about the university as much as they did. A few priests on campus had an extreme sense of propriety about everything connected with the university. It would come out in some fairly ugly incidents. One might see a bush or a branch or something he did not like and tell a groundkeeper to cut it down. If the man said his boss had not instructed him to do that, one of these proprietary types would say something like "Look, I'm your boss. I own this place. Now you do it."

Relatively few members of the community embodied this extreme view. They were against change because it was change. These fellows did not bother me. The toughest opponents I had to face were those who expressed a reasoned, honest opposition. They loved the place, had worked hard for it, and were genuinely concerned about the outcome of what we were trying to do. I respected them, and I felt for them.

The initial discussions on lay governance for the university started in the summer of 1965, when we held preliminary discussions on the front porch of the summerhouse at Land O'Lakes in Wisconsin, where many other important issues concerning the university had been decided. Land O'Lakes is a marvelous retreat close to nature and away from the interruptions and distractions of busy life. It had been bequeathed to Notre Dame after World War II by Martin Gillen, an honorary alumnus. The quiet up there gives one time to think, to reflect, and to make decisions. Gathered there on this occasion were Father General Germaine Lalande, Father Provincial Howard Kenna, all the university vice presidents, several key trustees, and I.

The consensus at the top was decidedly in favor of lay control. Father Lalande believed very deeply in the principle. He had gone through the whole Vatican Council and was undoubtedly influenced by that experience. The provincial of Indiana, Father Howard Kenna, better known as Doc, was another true believer. Kenna, of course, had shouldered more than his share of responsibility for the university over the years as director of studies, and he knew as well as anyone that the university was outgrowing the capabilities of our religious community. And so did I.

But the three of us could not just turn the university over to lay control by executive fiat. We had to observe strict, clearly defined procedures. The first of those was a special provincial council, which was called in January of 1967. Once we agreed as a province to go ahead with it, we had to get the approval of the superior general and his council. We had invited him to the Land O'Lakes meeting, where he had participated in all the discussions, and he was in favor of the idea right from the beginning, so that was no problem.

Next we had to get approval from the Holy See. Under canon law, a religious community owns its property in common, but if it defaults or goes into bankruptcy, the property reverts to the Holy See. In a sense, then, the Holy See had a reversionary interest in this half-a-billion-dollar institution we called Notre Dame. (Today, it is valued at well over one billion dollars.) The logical person in the Holy Cross community to deal with the Vatican was, of course, Father Edward Heston, our procurator general in Rome and a very good friend of mine. He had lived in Rome almost continuously since he had been ordained, spoke all the languages, knew all the right people and where the levers of power were. When the time came, he matter-of-factly went over to the Congregation for Religious and Secular Institutes and dropped our request on the appropriate desk and said, "I need a rescript for this." "Rescript" is a word you don't hear often in the secular world. All it means is a written permission from the Pope.

Our request to transfer our property to a lay board sailed right through, which is highly unusual for the Vatican, a bureaucracy like any other, or maybe I should say, unlike any other. The Vatican obviously did not spend much time studying our request, because it was approved in about two days. That was the first of two surprises. When Father Lalande went to Rome to pick up the rescript, one of the functionaries in the Congregation for Religious and Secular Institutes told him that because of the value of the property, we would have to pay the Congregation a fee of ten thousand dollars. Lalande was not having any of that. "The reason we're doing this," he said, "is because of the Vatican Council, the highest authority in the Church. You cannot penalize us because we are doing something in the spirit of the Council." Lalande took out his wallet. "The normal fee for this is fifteen hundred lira, and that is all you're going to get. If you give me any trouble, I will go to the Holy Father." Lalande's fifteen hundred lira worked out to about three dollars, which is not an exorbitant fee for transferring ownership of assets worth around half a billion dollars.

Some other Catholic colleges were in the process of changing over to lay control about the same time, but to the best of my knowledge, Notre Dame was the first to get it done, and done with the Vatican's approval. The legal work required in this country to make the transfer was handled by our chairman of the board of trustees, Ed Stephan, a prominent Chicago attorney and 1933 graduate of the university and, later, of Howard Law School.

Once the legal transfer of ownership was accomplished, Stephan led the work in setting up a new system of governance for Notre Dame, which was similar to the one governing Harvard, a small board of fellows and a much larger board of trustees. It was not unlike rewriting the constitution, which would govern Notre Dame as far into the future as any of us could see. The work was intricate and delicate because every decision was crucial, not only legally but culturally. We all wanted Notre Dame to continue as it had before, as a premier Catholic university, and also to grow stronger academically and economically. We were particularly careful not to load anything in favor of the clergy. Some of the other religious orders had done this with systems which gave the preponderance of control to the clergy. We established a board of fellows as the central controlling body of the university and we divided its membership right down the middle between lay members and Holy Cross priests, six of each. There was some talk about having eight priests and six laypeople, but we thought that would run counter to the spirit of what we were trying to accomplish. We were dead set against any system that would perpetuate the old system of clerical control. To further ensure that all decisions of the board of fellows would reflect both clerical and lay thinking, we put in a two-thirds requirement for all pronouncements of the fellows.

The board of fellows was a body which had the power to set up the university's bylaws and statutes, and it could also change them with a vote of two thirds of the members. The first fellows chosen were all ex officio members of the board of trustees and they had the power to approve new members of the board of trustees. But their main function was to maintain the Catholicity of the university and its integrity of purpose. One statute, for example, states that the president of the university always must be a priest of the Indiana Province of Holy Cross. That is a very good idea, in my opinion, because it helps to maintain the identity, the continuity, and the strong sense of tradition we have. But the priests did not request that stipulation. Ed Stephan did. He thought as I did on this. He took a lot of heat about that statute from some of the laypeople working with him, but he stood fast.

There were those who feared that turning the university over to a lay board would make us less Catholic, or not Catholic at all. That never worried us. We profess to be a Catholic institution and we operate as a Catholic institution. We keep the Faith. Some have accused Notre Dame of being less Catholic since the transfer. Personally, I think we are more Catholic today than we were in the past—both big *C* and little *c*. One could argue with that, and many do, but I stand by that statement. It is very important that we continue to have *independent* Catholic universities. They are the very places that do the most to advance Catholic thought and influence in this country. We have, and deserve to have, the respect of everyone who values academic freedom and commitment to the principles of reason seeking faith, and faith freely seeking a deeper understanding of all that faith means in our times.

Some people have asked me why we did not just keep the lay advisory board setup that we had before. We had good people on those boards. In fact, most of the members on the old advisory board of trustees just segued right into the first board of lay trustees. Only now they had real power. When I first met with our advisory board, as executive vice president, the board had no real power. Nor did they have much to do. They would come for lunch, and the president would give them a talk about the university. Then the treasurer would get up and present a flowery picture of the finances. After that, their chairman would say, "Any more business? No? Okay, the meeting is adjourned." That is a far cry from the meetings we started having after 1967. The board members really had to scramble to complete all the work on the agenda at those board meetings, and we were constantly adding committees to handle special problems in between meetings. The chairman and the other forty-nine members of the board of trustees are very much involved in all of the basic policies of the university.

One of the first responsibilities of the new board of trustees was the rewriting of the faculty handbook. It was an enormous task. All the procedures for governance and administration, and all the lines of authority in the entire academic order of the university, had to be spelled out anew. With the fundamental governance of the university passing to lay control, everything else had to change, too. It reminded me of the task John Cavanaugh had given me twenty years before, of redoing the articles of administration. But this time the faculty did most of the work. They put basic academic policy under the control of the academic council. The board of trustees reviews everything the academic council does, with the right to approve or veto any of its actions, but the board has never disapproved anything that the council has proposed.

Of course, over the years there have been some disagreements between the academic council and the board, and they have been negotiated privately. Occasionally, when the academic council knew the trustees would not approve something, they just did not bring it up. One such instance involved the way the provost was to be selected. The position is now the second in command at the university, replacing the executive vice presidency. As such, the provost needs to be someone with whom the president is compatible. To make sure of this, the president needs to have the power of approval whenever a provost is selected. When the new rules were being promulgated, the academic council wanted to approve the provost subject only to the approval of the board of trustees. There was no mention of the president's having final approval. Somehow that "little" item escaped the board's attention, even though Ed Stephan had said beforehand that the board would veto such a proposal if it came up. But the academic council's proposal narrowly passed. Some of the board members realized their mistake, but others just as obviously did not. The board asked me to go back to the academic council and persuade them that the president required the right of final approval on the provost. I had to win over the council without letting the faculty members know that if they did not agree, the board would simply change its mind and throw the council's proposal out. That would have set a controversial precedent, with far-reaching consequences. Anyway, I succeeded in doing it, but I am still not sure how.

The board of fellows has an enormous amount of power, and if a crisis came up, they would have to use that power to solve it. For example, if several members of the board of trustees got up and said that they no longer wanted Notre Dame to be a Catholic university, the board of fellows could fire those trustees on the spot. And my guess is that they would.

A word about the way we picked our trustees. I was often accused of picking them all by myself. Not true. Anyone could suggest candidates. As it turned out, for our first new board of trustees, Ed Stephan picked most of them, and I finished second. We sought balance on the board, and that is still the aim today. We wanted a majority of Catholics, but we also wanted Protestants and Jews on our board. We wanted women and members of minority groups, too. At the same time, we looked for people who had the talent or the expertise to help us with special problems. Sometimes there were conflicts between the need for expertise and the need for balance. We might be having a difficult time with our investments, for example, and also needing more Hispanic representation on the board. If a spot opened up on the board and the head of Merrill Lynch was available, I think we would invite him to be on the board before we would invite the head of La Raza. As a matter of fact we did get the head of Merrill Lynch, Roger Birk, to come on the board. That does not mean the Hispanics lost out, because a professional like Birk can make the endowment work better, which in turn enables us to bring more Hispanic students to the university. And, of course, there would be other openings on the board later that an Hispanic could fill. The board probably did not have enough blacks and Hispanics when I was president, and probably still does not. But it continues to make progress in balancing its membership under the leadership of Board Chairman Don Keough, president of Coca-Cola, and our president, Father Ed Malloy.

One of the qualities we always seek is dedication to Catholicism. Notre Dame is a Catholic university and its board members should be dedicated to that proposition—even the ones who are not Catholic. The Jewish and Protestant trustees of Notre Dame understand and respect our Catholic tradition. We have always had great boards at Notre Dame. When I was president, I was the envy of many of my colleagues around the country because of the understanding and cooperation of our board. For many college presidents, the board of trustees is their biggest problem. Politics is often involved both with elected boards and those that are appointed by governors. Many university presidents have to contend with all manner of conflict on their boards. By contrast, I cannot recall a single bad moment with any board I had, and that includes twenty years of lay control. They were always enormously supportive, and generous almost beyond belief. During one of our fund-raising drives, the Campaign for Notre Dame, board members donated nineteen million dollars. They gave almost double that in a recent campaign. And you have to remember that half the people on the board are not wealthy, because they are either priests or academics.

Reflecting on all this more than twenty years later, I would have to say that of all the accomplishments during the thirty-five years of my presidency of Notre Dame—improving the academics, the quality of the students, the endowment, the building program— the greatest change made during my administration was turning the university over to lay control.

Every bit as momentous as changing the governance of Notre Dame, as far as the students were concerned, was the decision to go coed. Coed! Notre Dame? What was the world coming to?

Legal expert Alan Dershowitz (left), *Washington Post* reporter
Robert Kaiser, and Father Hesburgh during a nationally
televised human rights debate with three Soviet
representatives in the 1970s.

Father Hesburgh, with Congressman John Brademas (D., Ind.)
and Speaker of the House Tip O'Neill to his left, discussing
funds for higher education at the Capitol in 1975. (Don Moore)

Colonel Franklin D. Shelton, commander of the 9th Wing at Beale Air Force Base in California, congratulating Father Hesburgh after his February 1979 flight in the SR-71 Blackbird reconnaissance jet. A lifelong aviation buff, Father Hesburgh joined a select few who have experienced speeds in excess of 2,000 miles per hour.

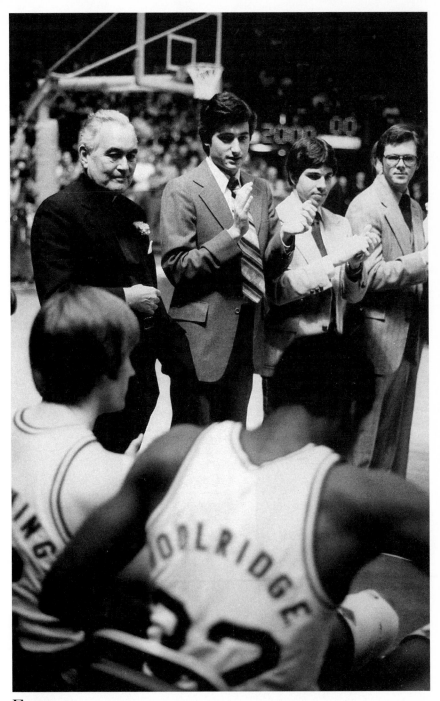

Father Hesburgh in a rare appearance as game chaplain for the Fighting Irish basketball team, February 1980. Notre Dame beat De Paul University 76–74 in double overtime. (Bruce Harlan)

Former Notre Dame football star Rocky Bleier, who was wounded in Vietnam and went on to play for the Pittsburgh Steelers, being introduced by Father Hesburgh at halftime of a 1969 Notre Dame football game. (Bruce Harlan)

Discussing students' concerns on campus in 1976. (Bruce Harlan)

Father Hesburgh dances with a student during a campus picnic celebrating his twenty-fifth anniversary as president. (Bruce Harlan)

With Martin Luther King, Sr., at a 1976 memorial service in Notre Dame's Sacred Heart Church. (Bruce Harlan)

Presenting Canadian Prime Minister Pierre Trudeau with an honorary degree at 1982 Notre Dame commencement exercises. (Bruce Harlan)

Father Hesburgh toasting with Feng Yi, Minister for Science and Technology, during a 1986 summer trip to the People's Republic of China to secure governmental approval for Chinese students to study at Notre Dame's new Institute for International Peace Studies.

José Napoleón Duarte, a former student of Father Hesburgh's who was graduated in 1948 and went on to become president of his native El Salvador—the first civilian to be elected leader of that country in a half century—came back to campus in 1985 to receive an honorary degree. He died of cancer five years later. (Bruce Harlan)

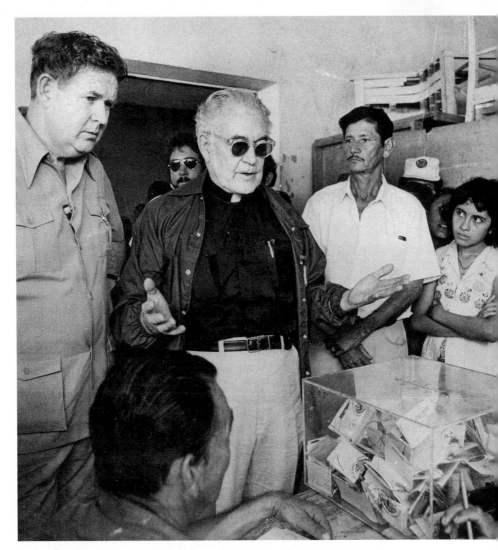

Congressman John Murtha (left) and Father Hesburgh in a polling place in El Salvador as members of the official U.S. observation team for the 1984 election, won by Notre Dame alumnus José Napoleón Duarte's party. (AP/Wide World Photos)

Well, the world of higher education was coming into modern times, a fundamental change in the culture of America. It was the mid-sixties and the sentiment on campus was overwhelmingly in favor of admitting women to Notre Dame. That was a pivotal change from when I became president of the university in 1952. A poll then would have shown, I am certain, that 95 percent of the students were against coeducation. Fifteen years later, 95 percent, perhaps even 99 percent, were decidedly for it. Obviously, the time was ripe to take a historic step.

The most logical step was across the campus lake to Saint Mary's College, a fine, traditional Catholic college with an enrollment of eighteen hundred women, founded two years after Notre Dame by the Sisters of the Holy Cross. It was *the* women's college close by, if not associated legally with the all-male and macho Notre Dame. In the old days, when I first returned to Notre Dame to teach, our young men were allowed to visit the Saint Mary's women only on Sunday afternoons from two to four—in the parlor. At four, a nun would come in and ring a bell and send them back to Notre Dame. Things gradually loosened up, but there was a residue of tension and bad feeling between the two schools for many years. Much of it stemmed, I think, from the perception of the sisters that the Notre Dame men were a bad influence on their women and would lead them astray.

When I switched from teaching to administration, I resolved to do whatever I could to improve the relationship between the two schools. I supported anything that would give the Saint Mary's women a reason to visit our campus—dances, plays, concerts, and so forth. Finally, in 1965, we were able to institute a coexchange program, under which Notre Dame students could take courses at Saint Mary's and Saint Mary's students could take courses at Notre Dame. To make it easy and keep it simple, we did not do any accounting, even though our tuition rates were more than twice per credit hour what theirs were. We knew that more Saint Mary's students would take courses at Notre Dame than the other way around, but we never presented them with a bill for the difference. One year it added up to a cool million dollars.

Because of the success of Co-Ex and of our 125-year association with Saint Mary's and the Sisters of the Holy Cross, we thought that the most logical and correct way to go coed would simply be to merge the two schools. We would have one faculty, one extended campus. Women would continue to be admitted to Saint Mary's, or through Saint Mary's, but they would receive Notre Dame degrees with a notation that the degree had been granted at Saint Mary's College. There would be a common board of trustees, a common budget, a common everything. We would do our best to integrate the two campuses.

The merger would also enable us to realize some economies by combining certain functions. We could have one admissions department instead of two, one public relations department instead of two, one fire department instead of two. Naturally, there would be Sisters of the Holy Cross on the board of trustees and in administrative posts. In fact, we had already made Holy Cross Sister Alma Peter, acting president of Saint Mary's and our liaison, a Notre Dame vice president in anticipation of the merger. Sister Alma was very much in favor of the merger, so much so that she was more like a member of our team than a member of the Saint Mary's team.

We held innumerable meetings with the nuns, primarily Mother Olivet, the superior general, and Sister Gerald, their tough-minded treasurer. On our side the principal negotiators were Ed Stephan, chairman of our board; Jim Burtchaell, our provost; Ned Joyce, executive vice president; and I. We got so close that we signed a letter of intent to merge. There is a picture of that signing, taken in that big lounge at Saint Mary's where our students used to meet theirs on Sunday afternoons.

Although the sisters were in favor of a merger, their concept of a merger was not the same as ours. They wanted to keep on running their own operation—their way. They had their women over there and we had our men over at Notre Dame—and they did not want to change that, either. The main difficulty was tied up with the problem of identity. They did not want to lose their identity. It was very much their own. You could not blame them. For more than a century, talented and heroic Holy Cross women had devoted their lives to achieving that identity.

At one point we talked about the possibility of moving our Law

School to their campus. We thought it would demonstrate that we were really serious about unity and not losing sight of the importance of the Saint Mary's campus. They did not like that idea one bit. There is no question that they would have lost at least a part of their identity, no matter what we tried, in a merger with Notre Dame. When you merge two of anything, something always gets lost, and it's usually the identity of the smaller of the two entities.

There was another factor, too, in the reluctance of Saint Mary's to merge with us. The Sisters of the Holy Cross had already closed two of their colleges, Dunbarton in Washington, D.C., and Cardinal Cushing in Boston. Some at Saint Mary's saw the merger as the Holy Cross Sisters' last stand as a teaching order. If they merged with us, they would be out of the education business altogether, at least as they had known it.

Two weeks after we signed the intent to merge, our negotiations crashed in flames. At a meeting in Palm Beach, Florida, it became apparent that we were not seeing eye-to-eye at all. I thought it was time to bring our differences to a head. "Sisters," I said, "we've been talking about a merger for two years. To me a merger is like a marriage, but I have the impression that a merger means something different to you. You're saying you want to marry us, but that you don't want to take our name and you don't want to live with us."

"That's exactly right," one of them shot back.

"Well, then," I said, "the merger's off." And so it was. It never came up again. We agreed that we would continue with Co-Ex, but with a limit of three thousand credit hours per year on both sides. As long as we both stayed under that number, we would continue to look the other way with regard to financial accounting. There were some hard feelings on both sides, and at least one casualty—Sister Alma. She did not become president of Saint Mary's. We felt bad that she had to suffer because of her support of us. To soften the blow a little, we awarded her an honorary degree from Notre Dame the next year. Recently I attended a party for Sister Alma at Saint Mary's, celebrating the sixtieth anniversary of her profession of vows.

By the time we met in Palm Beach, I must admit, we too were

having some very serious second thoughts about the marriage. Ned Joyce had been working on the financial aspects of the merger with Sister Gerald. The Saint Mary's treasurer wanted us to assume all of the school's debt, plus cover their sisters' retirement needs and some other obligations they had. When Ned analyzed the figures, he discovered that we would have to pay $750,000 a year for twenty years to take care of their indebtedness and another million a year for at least twenty-five years to cover the sisters' retirement and the other obligations. Ned figured we could handle the $750,000 per year, but not the million dollars. In the end, what had looked so easy and logical would have been, if it had come about, a very expensive merger.

We explored the possibility of merging with a number of small Catholic women's colleges, including Barat College in Lake Forest, Illinois; Rosary College in the Chicago area; and one or two others. We thought we might have a cluster of women's colleges on the Notre Dame campus, with their students taking some courses in those colleges but most of them in Notre Dame classrooms. But that did not work out, either.

In the end we simply decided to make Notre Dame coeducational all on its own. Coeducation at Notre Dame began totally without fanfare in the fall of 1972. We simply and quietly admitted fifteen hundred women. Normally those places would have gone to fifteen hundred men, and so there were just that number fewer men around. As I did not want the women living off campus, we put them in several reconditioned residence halls.

Coeducation has had a marvelous effect on Notre Dame. First and foremost, we had always maintained that we were in the business of educating students for leadership, and now we had broadened that commitment to include the other half of the human race. Almost as important, the women brought their great gift of femininity to our campus. During its all-male years Notre Dame tended to be a kind of rough, raunchy, macho place. Our women students brought a good measure of gentility to the campus and enhanced the family feeling of it. With women actually there, the men could stop thinking about them as a breed apart. It soon became clear that the presence of the women created a much more normal and healthier atmosphere on campus. Another facet of coeducation was that with the admission of women we had doubled our source of applicants, and that enabled us to raise our admission standards even higher.

The students and faculty, for the most part, were in favor of coeducation right from the start. The alumni went along with the change much better than most of us thought they would, much better, in fact, than the alumni of Princeton and Yale when those two universities went coed. We had better luck, I think, because our alumni saw it coming because of the publicized merger negotiations with Saint Mary's. But even more important, to my mind, was the fact that a good many of our alumni noticed that while their sons were being turned down for academic qualifications, their daughters were being admitted to Notre Dame.

For several years quite a few of our women students complained that they felt more like visitors than full-fledged students on campus. To a great degree that was to be expected. You cannot take an all-male tradition that is well over a century old and make it disappear overnight. I doubt if that feeling still exists among the women. If it does, it is definitely waning, as you might expect almost twenty years later. For one thing, if you include Saint Mary's in the total community, and we consider them a vital part of it, women now make up almost 50 percent of Notre Dame's and Saint Mary's total enrollment. Considering only Notre Dame, women make up slightly less than 40 percent of all students on campus.

In recent years there has been some sentiment on campus for coed residence halls. But Notre Dame has not gone that far—yet. Coed dormitories, which become overwhelmingly popular on other campuses, were rejected by our administration at the time women were admitted to Notre Dame. I think that was a correct decision then and for now. Over the years, from everything I have heard of other campuses, the disadvantages have outweighed the advantages of men and women living in the same dormitories or on the same floors, or sharing the same bathrooms. Many of the students who have tried coed dorm-living arrangements have found they have given up in the process their privilege of privacy and separateness as single people.

Similarly, I think there is a role for the all-women's colleges in our society. In retrospect I am not all that sorry that our merger efforts failed. Saint Mary's provides a place where women can enjoy the special experience of a very fine women's college, yet still have all the advantages of Notre Dame close by—but not too close. For some women, that is probably a better experience than being at Notre Dame.

I can suggest, however, that the women of Notre Dame make more common cause with the women of Saint Mary's. And naturally I would like to see Notre Dame men continue to get along well with the women at both institutions. Overall, I would like to see cordiality replace the sense of rivalry that seems to exist between the women on the two campuses. If we are all one family in this world, then they are sisters. But perhaps that is the underlying reason for the rivalry. It is beyond me. I know I do feel a certain fondness for Saint Mary's. As for the future relationship between Notre Dame and Saint Mary's, we are like old sweethearts. We did not get married, yes, but we still have a great deal of affection for one another.

With all the changes and modernization which have come about in the Catholic Church, I just wish that priests could have children and grandchildren as I do. Vatican II did not change the obligation of chastity, but there is nothing in the canon law that prohibits priests from adopting, especially on a temporary basis, children who are in need of *parentis locus*.

My foster family started as far back as 1956, when Doc Kenna, our provost, and I were on a talent hunt in South America for professors we could lure back to Notre Dame. When we arrived in Buenos Aires, we made the usual courtesy call on our ambassador at the American embassy, and he invited us to a cocktail party. It was a nice party, as most ambassadorial functions are, but the most memorable thing about it was a couple we met there by the name of O'Grady. Charles O'Grady was one of several brothers who had emigrated from Kansas to Argentina and had risen to prominence in business and social circles there. His wife, Victoria, a vivacious woman who was also an American, had grown up in the Dominican Republic.

About halfway through the party, Victoria came up to me and introduced herself. After the usual pleasantries, she surprised me by saying, "You know, you're the answer to my prayer." I didn't know quite what to make of that, but she went on, "Charles and I have six children. Five girls and a boy. They are all Americans, but they've never seen their own country. We think they ought to have at least a look, so we've decided to send them to Notre Dame and Saint Mary's for college. But they don't know many people in the States and we can't afford to have them flying back and forth all the time, so I give you my children."

The following September the first two, Anne and Virginia, arrived. Then about every other year for the next several years I would get another one. They all had two sets of names, depending upon whether they were up here or down there. They were Anne, Robert and Mary up here, and Anita, Roberto, and Maria down there. The girls all went to Saint Mary's because we did not have coeducation at that time, and Bob was admitted to Notre Dame.

I became very close to all the O'Grady youngsters. Notre Dame and Saint Mary's was their home away from home and I, for all practical purposes, was their father away from home for four years. I grew into the role, and I liked it. When I would introduce one of them to someone on campus, I'd always introduce him or her as one of my kids. I got some very strange looks from time to time, but that was part of the fun. Knowing how important it was for my adopted children to trust me, I never checked up on them through their professors or rectors or housemothers or any number of other sources I could have easily used. Like any other university president, I had as many information sources as did the FBI, maybe more. But I promised each of them that I would not operate that way. I told them that if I found out anything about their grades or their Mass attendance or their boyfriends or girlfriends, or any problems they were having, I was going to have to hear it from them. Then I said that because I was making myself completely dependent on them, I expected them to be completely candid with me, both with the good things and the bad. It worked out very well. We truly loved and trusted each other and we worked out life's problems together.

I introduced them to the Peace Corps during the summers they spent at Notre Dame. Whenever I was going through South America, I would swing over to Buenos Aires and tell Charlie and Victoria how the youngsters were doing. I corresponded with them a fair amount, too. Robert O'Grady became like a son to me, and all the O'Grady girls were like daughters. I shared their joys and sorrows, nurtured and guided them as best I could, and watched them do a lot of growing up.

When the last O'Grady was ready to graduate, Charlie told me he thought I knew his kids better than he did. I could imagine how he felt having them away from home all those years and flying back only once every couple of years or so. "Charlie," I said, "you were with them all the time they were little and growing up. They love you dearly and nothing can ever change that." And I meant that. As much as I like young people, I like them a lot better when they are of college age.

During the time that Anne and Virginia were at Saint Mary's, I received a call from Frank Freimann, a good friend and the chief executive officer of Magnavox, whose avocation was relocating relatives who had been displaced by the war. He had found a young girl named Hely Merle, a distant cousin of his. Originally from Austria, she was living with her parents in Yugoslavia when the war broke out. The Nazis picked up her father and sent him to the Russian front. He was never seen again. Then Hely and her mother were shipped off to a concentration camp, where her mother died. At the age of three, Hely was an orphan. When the war ended, the Russians put her in an orphanage and she stayed there until Frank got her out and brought her to the United States. "I have her in Chicago," Frank told me, "and I want you to come over and get her and see that she gets an education. I'll take care of all her expenses."

When I went to pick up Hely in Chicago, she looked like a plucked chicken who needed a course in makeup. But she had done very well in her classes at the orphanage and she spoke four languages: Serbian, Croatian, German, and Russian. We conversed in German, easily my worst language, but somehow we managed to communicate pretty well.

At Notre Dame, I called up Saint Mary's Academy to see if they could take Hely in. Fortunately for her, that same day a student had dropped out to return to Mexico, and Hely was welcome to the only empty bed they had. As soon as she learned English well—it took her only about three months—I entered her in Saint Mary's College and made arrangements for her to room with Anne and Virginia O'Grady. The two sisters and Hely became the best of friends, and Hely blossomed. She made good grades and developed her considerable natural talents in music, dancing, and sewing. Her skills as a seamstress quickly endeared her to the drama department and soon she was making all the costumes for the school plays.

Hely and I made the same deal that I had made with the O'Gradys. I told her I would never spy on her, but that I expected her to keep me well informed. At the end of her sophomore year she came to me with some important news. "I think I'm in love, and I want to get married." The young man she was in love with was Tony Shork, a Notre Dame senior who had won a Woodrow Wilson scholarship and was headed for medical school. He looked great on paper, but I did not know him personally. I decided that since marriage was such a serious commitment, and Hely was so young, I was going to bend my no-snooping rule a bit. Strictly speaking, I really didn't bend it. I had said that I wouldn't check up on *them*. I never promised anything about people they might marry. I checked out Tony from top to bottom. Much to my delight—and relief—everyone I talked to had nothing but good to say about him. Like any good parent, I still did not want them to rush into a marriage at their tender ages, and so I suggested mildly that they wait a while. They waited from the springtime when Tony graduated until Christmas. Over the Christmas vacation I married them.

Freimann came in from Chicago to give the bride away. Tony's parents were there and, of course, the O'Grady girls. The night of the prenuptial dinner I asked Freimann and Tony's father and mother to talk to each other in German. During the course of the conversation, Tony's parents discovered that they spoke the same Austrian dialect as Frank. They had grown up only nineteen miles away from Hely's parents in southeastern Austria. Hely and Tony's good marriage produced seven children.

All of the O'Gradys went on to successful careers and marriages. Three of the five girls married Notre Dame men, and Robert married a wonderful Saint Mary's woman. None of them went back to Argentina to live. Today, two live in New York, and one each in London; San Francisco; Angers, France; and Naples, Florida. The six of them are parents to twenty-three youngsters of their own, which gives me a current total of thirty "grandchildren." Three of the boys are named Ted. Some of these grandchildren came to Notre Dame and Saint Mary's for study or visits, so after a break of a few years I found myself back in the foster-father business again.

I have learned a great deal from Hely and the O'Grady kids— far more, I am sure, than they learned from me. It was both a wonderful education and a wonderful relationship. Having had it, I just wish there were some way that more priests could have this kind of experience. If there were some way that priests could adopt children, at least in the kind of temporary way that I did, I think they would be better for it, not only as priests but as human beings.

ELEVEN

CIVIL RIGHTS
FOR ALL

I WAS STILL in grade school when I had my first encounter with prejudice. Coming home from school one day and making my usual noisy entrance, dropping my books and calling out that I was home, I got to the door of the living room and stopped short. A neighbor woman was standing there, sobbing, and my mother was trying to comfort her. Embarrassed, I backtracked to the kitchen and busied myself making a peanut butter sandwich. After the woman had left, I asked my mother what had happened.

"Stuck-up neighbors," she said. "The poor woman is broken-hearted, and it's all their fault." She told me the whole story. The woman was Jewish. She had lived in the neighborhood for two or three years and during that entire time, my mother was the only one who had ever spoken to her. The woman finally could not stand it anymore and had decided to move away. She had just come over to say goodbye.

I asked my mother what the woman being Jewish had to do with the neighbors' attitude. My mother sat me down and explained, "Well, you'd better understand one thing. We are living in a segregated neighborhood. It's almost completely Protestant, and there are no other Jews in it, and very few Catholics. The only reason some of them tolerate the few Catholics who live here is because we have a little money. Otherwise, we would not be welcome here, either."

Then I asked my mother why she talked to the woman when no one else did. "I talked to her because I grew up in New York," my mother said. "In our building, we had Jews on the right and Jews on the left, Jews upstairs and Jews downstairs. Both in our apartment house and in our neighborhood, the Jews and the Irish were interspersed. We learned to understand each other, and we supported each other. Otherwise, we would have gone down the drain together. There's no way on earth I could be prejudiced against Jews." That was all she said. No bells and whistles went off, but I never forgot that incident or my mother's reaction to it. I knew then that prejudice was wrong.

While I was growing up in Syracuse, I never knew a black person. There were relatively few to begin with, and none of them lived in our part of town. When I studied at the Gregorian in Rome, I met several black Africans, but our contacts were limited almost exclusively to classes. I was well into my twenties before I had any significant contact with blacks. That was when I was working on my doctorate in Washington. There were blacks in several organizations I was involved with there—the Civilian Conservation Corps camp, the Boys Club, the National Training School for Boys, and a couple of adult study groups. Still, I hardly qualified for membership in the NAACP.

I would qualify today, I think, if only for the fifteen years of intensive work I did as a member of the U.S. Commission on Civil Rights. I was a few months past my fortieth birthday when President Eisenhower appointed me to the newly created commission to study civil rights in America. There were three Democrats, two Republicans, and Father Hesburgh, who proclaimed his independence of all politics. The Democrats on the commission were John Battle, former governor of Virginia; Doyle Carlton, former governor of Florida; and Robert Storey, who was dean of the

Southern Methodist Law School. The Republicans were John Hannah, president of Michigan State University and a former assistant secretary of defense, and J. Ernest Wilkins, undersecretary of labor, the only black on the commission. With three Democrats, two Republicans, and an independent, the potential for conflict along political lines appeared to be fairly high. Eisenhower had further complicated matters by dividing the commission equally between Northerners and Southerners.

When we appeared before the Senate Judiciary Committee for confirmation, the Southerners on the committee voted against everyone they considered too liberal on civil rights, and that included me. I can still remember Mississippi's Senator Eastland sticking that big cigar of his in my face as he challenged me. However, we were all confirmed by a vote of the full Senate, so it did not make any difference what Eastland or his majority on the Judiciary Committee thought about some of us. The Civil Rights Commission was created by Congress in 1957 as a compromise to end a Southern filibuster in the U.S. Senate that had gone on all summer to prevent the passage of any and all legislation concerning civil rights in general and voting rights in particular. It was a highly volatile issue dividing North and South. We had fought a bloody civil war over those issues a hundred years before, and while slavery had been abolished, there was nothing approaching equality of Americans regardless of race, religion, or color of skin.

What we had then in the late 1950s was de jure apartheid, although few would recognize or admit to it, in thirteen of our United States, the thirteen that had practiced slavery a century before. In the North, apartheid was de facto, not sanctioned by law but real all the same. Six million Americans whose skin was black were denied the right to vote; they could not walk in and get served a Coca-Cola in a drugstore of their choice, or go to a toilet of their choice, or take a seat of their choice on public transportation, or swim at any public beach, or get a job reserved for whites, or go to a school with white children, or be buried in a cemetery where white people were buried.

That was America when the members of the Civil Rights Commission were all sworn in at the White House on January 2,

1958. Then we went over to have a look at our office, which was right across from the White House at 726 Jackson Place. You won't find it there today. When Jackie Kennedy was First Lady, she had it torn down as part of a project to rehabilitate the neighborhood. You could not blame her. It was a miserable place. There was only one room big enough for the six of us to hold a meeting. The floor tiles were the kind commonly found in public toilets. The table in the meeting room was dirty and piled three or four feet high with unopened mail, all civil rights complaints sent even before we were sworn in. We had very few staff members and very little money. When Congress had created the commission, they had neglected to establish a budget for it. The couple of hundred thousand dollars that we had to operate with for the year had come from an emergency fund Eisenhower had. In fact, for our first ten years we spent less than a million dollars a year, a ridiculously small amount when you consider that 70 percent of our recommendations—all of which were highly controversial— became federal law.

At our first meeting we decided that since we had only two years of life, we should choose one area of civil rights and bear down hard on it. Because voting was the specific issue which had deadlocked Congress, and brought about the commission, that was the area we decided to zero in on. Our first hearing was scheduled for Montgomery, Alabama, once the seat of the Confederacy, and probably as close to the heart of the civil rights problem as we were ever likely to get. (At least we thought so until we had a later hearing in Jackson, Mississippi.)

We wrote ahead for hotel reservations in Montgomery. With three blacks in our group—Commissioner Wilkins and two black lawyers on the commission staff—we were not surprised to be turned down. From all of the hotels we received very polite letters explaining that it was against the law to have blacks and whites in the same hotel. In those days they used the word "Negro" in the better circles, but most Southerners referred to blacks as "niggers."

We thought we would solve the accommodations problem by staying at the Maxwell Air Force Base in Montgomery. John Hannah knew the commanding officer there and requested accommodations in the Bachelor Officer Quarters for this presidential commission, which would be there on business. The reply came from a major, who was also the public relations officer. He was sorry, but they could not put Negroes and whites in the same BOQ, because the people in Montgomery would never stand for it. Hannah sent a letter to the Secretary of the Air Force, apprising him of the situation. A presidentially appointed federal commission was about to hold hearings in Montgomery and could find no place to stay and was refused even by a federal military base in town. What could he do? The Secretary replied that he did not want to override the decision of the local commander. Hannah read us the letter and said he was going to forget the Secretary and instead write directly to his boss, the Secretary of Defense, Charlie Wilson. Wilson and Hannah were fellow Michiganders and knew each other well from the time when Wilson was president of General Motors and Hannah was president of Michigan State. But Wilson turned Hannah down, too, not wanting to countermand the decision of the Secretary. John was now ready to explode.

There was only one thing left to do, and that was to go to Eisenhower. This time Hannah did not write. He called. "Mr. President," he said, "you gave us a God-awful job to do, and we're trying to get our first hearing going down in Montgomery, but we can't get hotel rooms, and they won't even let us stay on a U.S. Air Force base because we have a black commissioner and two black lawyers." Ike blew a fuse. He was certainly no great liberal, but he was a fair man. He sat down and wrote a scathing executive order to the general at Maxwell, saying that the members of the commission would indeed be accommodated there. My guess is, he probably had a few other things to say, too, because Ike was known to be a man of somewhat salty speech when the occasion demanded. That is what it took—an executive order from the President of the United States to get the black members of our federal commission accommodated in federal housing at a federal military installation. Of course, it should not have been necessary. President Harry Truman had issued an executive order ten years earlier integrating all the armed forces.

We had a very, very difficult time down there after that, too. The only weapon we had was the subpoena. Fortunately, it was a powerful weapon. We could have subpoenaed the Cabinet or the President himself. Some years later as chairman I did, in fact, threaten to subpoena all the members of Nixon's Cabinet, and I once used the threat of subpoena to force John Mitchell, Nixon's Attorney General, to appear at one of our hearings. But that was many years after this first hearing in Montgomery.

In Montgomery the most important person we had to subpoena was a county judge who had refused to let us examine the county voting records. The records would show who had applied to vote, who had been turned down, and why. The judge said he would burn the records before he'd turn them over. His name, by the way, was George Wallace, later elected governor of Alabama on a racist platform.

We forced Wallace to turn over those voting records by going to the federal judge for that district, Frank Johnson. Johnson was not exactly a civil rights advocate himself. He and Wallace had been classmates at the University of Alabama Law School. Johnson said publicly that he did not want to order Wallace to hand over the records, but that as a U.S. judge he had to, and he did. And he told Wallace in no uncertain terms. "Hand over the records," he said, "or go to jail."

The characters who trooped through those hearings could not have been chosen better by a Hollywood casting director. We had some of the reddest-necked rednecks of the species. Many of them were high school dropouts, but in Montgomery they were telling black Ph.D.s from Tuskegee Institute that they could not vote because they, the rednecks, were not yet "ready" to let them vote.

The most telling and infuriating aspect of those hearings was listening to the blacks tell how they had been systematically denied the vote all these years. One common stratagem among the voting registrars was to set one day a month when people could register to vote. The white voters would be registered en masse. The blacks would have to go to some remote place and line up, say between four and five on the third Monday of the month, and then the registrars would flunk them on some minor technicality. The blacks understood the system, but were too scared or too disheartened to fight it. There was not a single black person in all of Montgomery County who was registered to vote!

It did not take us long to amass overwhelming evidence to prove beyond a shadow of a doubt that black people in Montgomery had been denied their constitutional right to vote because of the color of their skin. We presented the evidence to Judge Johnson, the same federal judge who had forced Wallace to turn over the voting records. The records contained the names of sixteen hundred black men and women who had been denied the vote and the reason each had been refused. One had been denied registration because of an error in spelling. In explaining the reason, the registrar had written "spilling," with both i's clearly dotted. When Judge Johnson finished going over the list, he ordered the registrars to register every one of those blacks immediately. He warned that if there were any more "monkey business" regarding voting in Montgomery County, he was going to put every one of them in jail and throw away the key. Overnight, Frank Johnson had become a hanging judge in the cause of civil rights.

From Alabama we moved on and held public hearings in Texas, Georgia, Mississippi, and Louisiana, where it was the same story all over again. The situation was the worst in what was called the Black Belt counties, a wide band of sixteen counties with rich, alluvial soil that was perfect for growing cotton. The population in those counties was between 70 and 80 percent black, but not a single black person was registered to vote in any of them.

During the hearings my fellow commissioner John Battle from Virginia and I became fairly close friends, even though his father had been a Protestant minister and John did not quite know what to think about Catholic priests. John, a former governor of Virginia, was every inch the Southern gentleman. Although not a civil rights advocate per se, he believed very deeply in the fundamental right of all citizens in a democracy to vote. During the hearings in Montgomery, Battle grew increasingly annoyed as many of the voting registration people did their best to stonewall us. During a break in the testimony he leaned over to me and said, "Father Ted, do you think I ought to speak out strongly on this?"

I said, "John, your speaking out strongly would mean a lot more than my speaking out strongly. You're a Southerner, a highly respected Southerner, and they all know that."

Battle really let fly. "I'm a Southerner and I take a dim view of integration of schools and a lot of other things they are talking about up North," Battle said, "but I don't take a dim view of voting. Voting is a central part of a democracy, and if citizens have the basic intelligence they ought to be able to vote. My granddaddy was Colonel Battle of Battle's Brigade of Alabama and fought in the Civil War and was elected to the Senate. But they would not seat him because he fought in the Civil War. I am a deep Southerner, and I'm proud of it, but I am not proud of this city and I am not proud of all the witnesses that have come before this commission. I advise you to examine your consciences tonight and come back tomorrow ready to testify truthfully, instead of making this mockery of democracy."

Some of the stories that came out at these hearings were sad beyond belief. I once asked a black teacher why she wanted to vote. "I have four children, a master's degree in biology, and I'm a teacher at the university, and my husband is a Ph.D.," she explained. "When the last presidental election came up, one of my kids asked me if I were going to vote. I said, 'I can't. I'm black and they won't let me.' My child said, 'That's not right.' That's when I knew I couldn't hope to raise my children in a democracy and teach them about democracy if I could not vote and they knew I could not vote."

At our hearings in New Orleans, witnesses swore that white registrars struck off the voting rolls the names of some two thousand blacks who had been registered to vote in Plaquemines Parish. Those wanting to reregister were required to appear with two registered voters who would testify that they were American citizens and were qualified to vote. There was no way they could qualify. There were no longer any blacks who were registered and could vouch for others. Nor would any registered white voters stand up for a black voter. Somehow, though, the white registrars overlooked a few blacks when purging the voter rolls, and one day a black man came up with two black witnesses and said he wanted to be registered. When the two witnesses pulled out their voter's cards, the registrar just grabbed the cards and said, "Oh, we must have missed you." They disenfranchised them on the spot. That was the kind of story we were hearing in place after place in the Deep South.

The rationalization often was that states had a right to give voters a literacy test as a qualification to vote. In one county a black voter was asked to give his or her age in years, months, and days. Miscalculate by a day and you lost your right to vote. We were appalled at the bizarre stories we heard. In one place the literacy test apparently was not causing enough blacks to fail, and so the voting officials started bringing a Chinese newspaper to the registration place. "What does it say?" they asked a black man who testified for us.

"I guess it says I'm not going to vote," he responded.

One memorable witness who had been wiped off the voting rolls was a dentist who had served as a captain in the U.S. Army in Europe. When he showed up to register, well aware of the difficulties, he presented the registrar with his driver's license with his picture on it, a copy of his federal income tax return, his certification as a dentist, his membership card in the national dental professional society, and his honorable discharge from the Army. One by one he showed these documents to the registrar. When he was finished, he declared, "I am an American citizen as much as you are and I intend to vote."

"Where are the two voters to vouch for you?" the registrar responded.

The dentist told the voting officials that they knew full well he could not produce two witnesses who were voters because blacks were the only ones who would be willing to do it and all the blacks had been stricken from the voter rolls. They told him that if he could not produce two voters to vouch for him, he could not vote. Period.

When he finished his story, I said, "Captain, I believe you, and I am sure that everyone who is watching this on television believes you. I want you to go back to that registration place tomorrow morning and tell them that you testified at this hearing. I am sure they will already know it because they are undoubtedly watching us on television right now. You tell them that you want them to register you forthwith to vote. If they don't register you, I want you to call me immediately and let me know, because I will then call the President of the United States, who was the top general in the U.S. Army, and I will tell him that one of his officers is being prevented from voting in Louisiana. I can promise you that the President will make things so hot for everyone—the governor, the mayor, and the voting registrar, and everybody else—that they will wish they had never heard of you." The next day the dentist went back to register and they put him through, just like that.

We knew that the witnesses who came to testify at these hearings were doing so with a good deal of trepidation. They were risking harassment, possibly even serious injury or death. We felt we had to afford them as much protection as we could, and so we made sure to subpoena them. Normally when you subpoena someone it is because you need to compel him to testify, and we did plenty of that, too. But the other thing a subpoena did was to protect the witness. The law provided that anyone who threatened or injured a person subpoenaed to testify in a federal hearing would get ten years in a federal penitentiary and a ten-thousand-dollar fine. We announced loud and clear that if anyone touched any of our witnesses we would drop everything else and hound them to the ends of the earth until we found them, fined them, and put them in jail for ten years. We took turns making that opening statement. One commission member who did it particularly well, I thought, was Dean Griswold of Harvard Law School, who joined the commission after the Shreveport hearing. Most of the hearings were broadcast on radio and TV, so it did not take long before everyone knew what would happen if they tried to do anything to any of our witnesses. That undoubtedly was the reason that no one ever laid a hand on anyone we interviewed.

As the two-year appointment of our commission approached its end, we scheduled our final public hearing for Shreveport, Louisiana, in July 1959. I came down for it from a fishing trip up in Quebec, arriving at 6 A.M. on the day of the hearing. But we never had that hearing. A federal marshal came up to me and announced, "You are enjoined by Federal Judge Dawkins from holding your hearing because the Civil Rights Commission is unconstitutional." We had spent the last three months and about thirty thousand dollars preparing for that hearing, and now this federal judge declared that we were unconstitutional. All six commissioners and the whole staff were there, but there was nothing we could do. The judge had acted within his powers. We appealed, of course, and a three-judge appeals panel overturned Dawkins's decision by a margin of two to one. The case was appealed to the Supreme Court, which upheld unanimously our right to hold hearings and then went on to issue a strongly worded opinion upholding the constitutionality of what we were doing. For many years after that, we used that Supreme Court opinion as the frontispiece for all our reports.

Our eventual victory in the Supreme Court was sweet but very much in the future. On that hot July day in Shreveport, we were stymied with our scheduled three days of hearings called off and nothing to do. We were staying at an air base there because, as usual, the hotels would not accept us. The food was terrible, the jet noise interrupted our sleep, and it was a hundred degrees in the shade. We were a dejected group of people, commiserating with one another and wondering "What do we do now?" We still had our final report to make to the President and the Congress a month from then. It occurred to me that I had the wherewithal to take all my friends on the commission to a far better place, where we could confer without interruptions and get right down to writing our final report.

Notre Dame had just the place I thought we needed to recoup, reconsider, reflect, and get some serious work done—our summer camp at Land O'Lakes in Wisconsin. We had twenty-seven beautiful little lakes set among seven thousand acres of land up there. It was a wonderful, relaxing hideaway, an ideal place for what the commission now needed. Persuading my fellow commissioners and staff was the easiest bit of persuasion I ever had to do on this commission. In a borrowed private plane, provided by I. A. O'Shaughnessy, Notre Dame's legendary benefactor, we all flew from the sweltering heat and humidity of July in Louisiana to the cool, fresh, sweet-smelling air of northern Wisconsin. I also had the foresight to telephone ahead for all needed supplies and refreshments.

Aboard the plane we settled right down to work on our final report. Hannah and the other commissioners huddled up in the front of the airplane. The staff members and I went to the back and started formulating the final resolutions, which would be the heart of the report. Our preliminary findings and conclusions already had been written in the cities where we had held the hearings.

That first evening at Land O'Lakes was everything I had hoped it would be. The air was crisp and scented with pine, the lakes shimmered cool and inviting, and the steaks and martinis could not have tasted better. The battle-weary commission unwound, relaxed, and made a startling discovery: Every one of the commissioners, it turned out, was an ardent fisherman, and the Lord must have been with us that evening, because we all caught fish—a lot of fish, mostly bass and walleyes.

When it got too dark to continue fishing, we gathered around a big table on the screened porch. Everyone was feeling very mellow because of the great fishing, the driest martinis, and a great dinner. As the moon came up big and bright directly over Tenderfoot Lake, the staff and I trotted out our twelve recommendations and told the commissioners we were ready to have them vote on them. The results of the vote exceeded the expectations of even the hardiest optimists among us. Eleven of the twelve recommendations passed unanimously. The twelfth, on integrating education, passed five-to-one. As I recall, John Battle thought it was a little bit too "sociological" and voted against it.

When we met with President Eisenhower in September, he said he could not understand how a commission with three Democrats who were all Southerners, and two Republicans and an independent who were all Northerners, could possibly vote six-to-zero on eleven recommendations and five-to-one on the other. I told Ike that he had not appointed just Republicans and Democrats or Northerners and Southerners, he had appointed six fishermen. I told him about Land O'Lakes and he commented, "We've got to put more fishermen on commissions and have more reports written at Land O'Lakes, Wisconsin."

I did not tell Eisenhower of how I happened to overhear the three Southerners discussing their vote the morning after. They were having breakfast and I could not help overhear them as I was saying Mass in the adjoining chapel. "What really happened last night?" one of the former governors asked, and the other governor said, "Well, I guess we were really taken in, but everything was so nice, and it was such a welcome change from where we were, that we didn't have the nerve to fight about those recommendations. But we gave our word last night, and we're gentlemen. We're going to keep our word."

Shortly after we submitted our report, Congress voted to renew us for another two years, and we kept going like that for the life of the commission—two years here, three years there, once even for five years. Commission members came and went, naturally. It was very difficult, demanding work, and you could hardly blame a person for wanting to pack it in after a number of years.

The commission, after the first two years, began to enlarge the scope of the hearings to cover not only voting but employment, housing, education, administration of justice, and public accommodations. It may seem hard to believe now, but in the late fifties and early sixties, we were just as bad about public accommodations in this country as they were in South Africa. Practically everything was for whites only—drinking fountains, rest rooms, drugstores, hotels, beaches, churches, cemeteries, barber shops, lunch counters, clothing stores, and schools. Some of the worst abuses showed up in the schools. To cite just one example, the schools attended by black students received only one seventh as much money as the schools for white students.

Where blacks were permitted to tread, they were carefully segregated. They were allowed to travel on city buses, but had to ride in the back. They could go to the movies, but had to sit in the balcony. When federal agricultural subsidies were distributed by all-white county governments, the white farmers got all the federal aid, the black farmers got nothing. There were something like 150 to 200 counties in each of the thirteen Southern states;

only one of those counties had a black official on the agricultural assistance committee which decided the distribution of assistance funds.

The whites had total control of the legal system. If a black man was arrested, it was by a white policeman. He was then put in a cell by a white jailer, arraigned by a white judge, tried by a white jury, and represented by a white lawyer who probably had little, if any, interest in whether or not his black client received a fair trial. Small wonder that blacks rarely, if ever, received justice. There was not a single state university in the entire South, supported by state funds, where a black could study law or medicine, much less enroll as an undergraduate. Every black doctor in the country was a graduate of Meharry in Nashville or Howard in Washington. If you were black and you wanted to be a doctor, that was where you had to go.

When we had our famous hearing in Mississippi, there were only three black lawyers to take depositions from witnesses. Were a lot of black lawyers in Mississippi sitting this one out? No. There was only one other black lawyer in the whole state. He declined to take civil rights cases. The three black lawyers traveled all over the state of Mississippi to take depositions for us. Mississippi had more than two thousand white lawyers at the time, but none would accept a civil rights case.

Lyndon Johnson deserves a great deal of credit for the passage of the Omnibus Civil Rights Act of 1964, a landmark piece of legislation followed by civil rights bills of 1965 and 1968. These seminal laws were based in large part upon the work done by the Civil Rights Commission, and Lyndon Johnson was with us all the way. What we were trying to do was close to his heart. I first met Johnson a few days after he had taken office, following the assassination of John F. Kennedy on that memorable November 22, 1963. It was a customary courtesy call upon a new President by his Civil Rights Commission. Johnson, under tremendous strain during those tumultuous first days, looked exhausted and ashen when we got in to see him in the Oval Office at about 6:30 P.M. He asked our permission to move our meeting into a small room next door, where he could stretch out and rest while we talked, because he had a full night of work ahead of him. We took turns telling him of the problems in civil rights and human rights. At my turn, I suggested he change the name of the government's poverty program because no one likes to be told he is part of a poverty program. I suggested "equal opportunity" program, and Johnson agreed. He then went on to tell us his fundamental aims as President.

His lifelong political hero was Franklin D. Roosevelt, and during his presidency FDR had reduced the number of poor people in the United States from forty million to between twenty and thirty million. That was a real accomplishment which impressed Lyndon Johnson, and he finished that story saying, "When I'm dead and gone, all I want to be said of my presidency is that there were fewer poor people at the end of it than there were at the beginning." There was no doubt in my mind that Johnson was genuinely concerned about the poor, and as the years of his presidency went on I witnessed his commitment to social justice and civil rights.

It took a great deal of courage and commitment for him, the President of the United States and a proud Southerner from Texas, to stand before a joint session of Congress in 1964 and, as the conclusion of his impassioned speech in support of the Omnibus Civil Rights Act, to intone the immortal words of Martin Luther King, Jr., "We shall overcome." Without Lyndon Johnson's courage and vision upon taking office, we would not have come as far as we have today on civil rights and human rights.

I don't think Jack Kennedy, had he lived, could have done it. Jack Kennedy was always very well informed of our activities on the Civil Rights Commission, and I'm sure he knew that what we were doing was right. At the same time, he and his political advisers felt that they had to tread lightly in the civil rights area because to antagonize the South was to virtually abandon any hope of being reelected. Our hearings in Mississippi, for example, were so politically sensitive that once JFK asked us and later his brother Robert, the Attorney General, asked us to delay the start of those hearings. We accommodated them, but we did go ahead with those hearings despite a third request for a delay from a new Attorney General.

In 1968 we had been in business exactly ten years. We had turned out a whole series of reports, dozens of them on housing, employment, education, public accommodations, administration of justice, and voting. We eventually published about a hundred volumes during the fifteen years I was on the commission, plus many shorter reports.

Every time we wrote a report it was a struggle to keep our own emotions out of it. The other commissioners gave me a little freer reign in that regard, because I was the house philosopher and theologian. Even so, they made me confine my more subjective judgments to the back of the reports. But they would often instruct staff members to tone down their prose. "That's a fine statement," John Hannah might say to a staff member. "Just take out all the adjectives and adverbs." On one occasion he went into telling detail. "You don't have to say, 'The oppressive jailer cruelly knocked out the man's eye.' Just say, 'The jailer knocked out the man's eye.' That's just as strong, because those kinds of facts don't need any help to make the desired point." We always made sure we had our facts right. No one ever caught us exaggerating or distorting anything in any of our many reports.

Today the battle over voting is won, but we still need to be concerned with what I call the ineluctable trilogy of education, employment, and housing. In education, for example, right now ghetto schools are turning out four hundred thousand poorly educated black youngsters each year, or four million each decade. These youngsters cannot write, they cannot figure, they simply cannot function in a highly organized, highly complex, technological society. They are not only unemployed, they are unemployable. If we do not provide an adequate education for these young men and women, this country will be in for some very hard times in the near future.

We should not allow ourselves to be distracted by side issues like busing. More than half the students in America normally ride to school on buses, and they always will as long as there are rural areas and suburbs. Whether or not a youngster has to ride a bus is not important. What is important is what kind of an education is waiting for that youngster when the bus arrives at school. Everything in education is interconnected. If a child gets a good education in grade school, that child is likely to succeed in high school, attend college, and go on to a good job, buy a nice house in a good neighborhood, and send his or her children to good schools. If a child does not get that education, he or she travels in the opposite direction toward unemployment, welfare, ghetto housing, drugs, gangs, crime, jail, and probably an early death. That is the choice we make every day with every child attending a public school.

Someone once asked me what I thought the answer was to ghetto schools. I said a bulldozer. It sounds simplistic if you have never seen the insides of one of these schools. Some years ago I visited a ghetto school in Brooklyn. It was a drab, depressing place, covered with graffiti. The windows were barred. The grounds were littered with broken glass. The neighborhood was so unsafe they had to lock the students in. Inside was not so safe, either. Most of the students would not dare to enter a bathroom alone for fear of being abused or beaten up. Absenteeism in that school was 40 percent on any given day. That is why I favor bulldozers for schools like that. Tear them down and start over. That is also why I spent fifteen years of my life on the Civil Rights Commission.

When the Omnibus Civil Rights Act of 1964 went into effect, two young black lawyers on our staff decided to put it to the test. The law said, among other things, that hotels open to the public had to provide equal accommodations for blacks and whites, or they could, for all practical purposes, be put out of business. These two lawyers decided to try to check in at the best motel in Jackson, Mississippi, where on a prior occasion they had not been allowed to pass through the front door. This time, they reported, they were treated courteously and given a nice room. At the best restaurant in town, they were given a good table and courteous service by a white waiter. After that, they went to a movie theater. They bought tickets, sat down in the main auditorium rather than in the balcony without incident, and enjoyed the film. Their experience was typical of what was going on everywhere in the South. One day blacks were barred from a lot of places. The next day they were not. In my opinion, Americans just became fed up with a system that they knew to be morally wrong. The various "wade-ins," "sit-ins," and "pray-ins" all helped the process along and the clincher, undoubtedly, was the persuasive power of the law. The most important factor, however, was the sense of fairness of the American people. Given the facts, they were ready to get rid of apartheid in this country. Obviously, all the problems of racial inequality have not been solved, but apartheid in the United States disappeared forever with the passage of that law in 1964 and it will never come back.

The Civil Rights Commission always made it a practice to pay a courtesy call on the President right after he took office. We had done it with Kennedy and with Johnson, and we paid our courtesy call to Richard Nixon one day in January 1969, shortly after his inauguration. We had a very pleasant chat, and when it was over Nixon asked to have a private word with Bob Rankin, a dean at Duke, where Nixon had gone to law school, and with me. When Rankin came out of the Oval Office, I went in. "What would it take for you to come full-time with the government?" Nixon asked me. "Do I have to see the Pope?"

I assured him he did not have to see anyone but me, and while it was highly unlikely that I would be interested, I was curious to know what he had in mind.

"I'd like you to take over the poverty program," he said. I told him I did not think that was a very good idea. He wanted to know why. So I explained how I thought the poverty program could be made to work, but that my ideas would destroy the patronage system used by the mayors, who were handing out jobs to their pals at thirty thousand dollars a year. However, those political pals knew nothing about poverty. The money would be better spent on training programs that would teach the poor to help themselves.

"Can you imagine," I said, "what would happen in Atlanta, Birmingham, Jacksonville, and the rest of the cities if a Catholic priest came in and wiped out all that patronage? Your name would be mud." Then I told Nixon that the two of us should probably just forget that he ever brought it up.

"Well," he said, "it seemed like a good idea, but I guess you're right."

Being in the Oval Office, which is not the easiest place to be invited to, I thought it would be as good a time as any to bring up some other items. "Mr. President," I said, "as long as I'm here, may I give you some advice that you might find helpful over the next four years?" He said I should go ahead. I started by telling him that if a poll were taken among college students, he would be lucky if 10 percent of them approved of him. With his permission, I recommended that he do four things.

The first thing I advised was to end the war in Vietnam soon. He said he was going to do that. Then I recommended giving the vote to eighteen-year-olds. Third, I said he should abolish the draft, because it was inequitable. Poor blacks and Hispanics were being drafted into the Army while most whites typically had all kinds of ways to beat it. I said we should be moving toward an all-volunteer army. My fourth recommendation was a program whereby any youngster qualified to attend a college or professional school should not be prevented from doing it for lack of money. There should be programs whereby those youngsters could borrow or earn enough money to get a degree. I told him that we needed equality of opportunity in education because it was the best investment we could make. It was, I emphasized, the very future of America. Nixon concurred in all that I said, and indeed during his administration he did all four of these things I recommended that day. He ended the war in Vietnam (although five years later) ended the draft, established a volunteer army, pushed the eighteen-year-old vote, and supported a federal student loan program. But, strangely enough, he never got much credit for any of them because his public relations was so bad the press never publicized his role in these areas.

At that same meeting, I asked the President to accept my resignation from the Civil Rights Commission. After eleven grueling years, I thought I might be running out of ideas, I explained, adding that perhaps the commission needed a whole new look and maybe new leadership. Saying he understood, he promised to get back to me on it. About two weeks later I received a call from someone on his staff asking me if I would accept the chairmanship of the Civil Rights Commission. That made me wonder if Nixon had understood what I had told him. I was not thrilled at the prospect, but I agreed to take on the chairmanship for one year with the understanding that we would talk about it again when the year was up. Two weeks after that, I got another call, this time from Tom Gates, the former Secretary of the Navy and a very dear friend of mine. He did not ask, he ordered me to join his newly created Commission on an All-Volunteer Armed Force. "This was your bright idea," Gates said. "You talked Nixon into it and now I'm the chairman. So because you opened your mouth, I'm putting you on the commission." It looked as though I was going to be pretty busy working for the new Nixon administration.

By the time my year was up as chairman of the Civil Rights Commission, Nixon's people and I were deeply into an adversarial relationship. It was clear by the end of that first year that civil rights had few friends in the Nixon administration. But now I felt I could not resign; it would be like abandoning a sinking ship. So I hung on for three more years, knowing the commission was out of step with at least some members of Nixon's inner circle.

To make matters worse, just as the 1970 midterm elections drew near, our commission completed its report on civil rights within the government. In our findings, the Nixon administration did not look good at all.

It was a yearlong, monumental, thousand-page study of the federal government departments and most of the important agencies, rating their performance in terms of the civil rights laws that were on the books. No subjective criteria were used. All the findings were based strictly on statistics and empirical data that could be easily tabulated and verified, such as the number of blacks employed in each department or agency. The report was in no way an attempt to embarrass the administration. But it did. Rating forty departments and agencies as being either "poor," "fair," "good," or "outstanding" in carrying out the civil rights laws on the books, we found only one, the Department of Health, Education, and Welfare, to rate a "fair." The other thirty-nine departments or agencies all received a score of "poor."

Before the report was supposed to be released, I sent it over to Leonard Garment, who was Nixon's lawyer as well as a good friend of mine. About eight o'clock one morning I received a phone call from Garment. "My God," he said, "what are you trying to do to us?" He told me that the report was devastating and that it would really hurt the administration, coming out right before the midterm elections. I reminded him that he had thought this study a good idea a year ago and that we had publicly announced its due date. The press knew that the report had been completed, and some newsmen had inquired about it. Garment asked me to hold the report until the elections were over, but I said I would not do that because we were not a political commission. The facts spoke for themselves, I said, and that if the facts hurt, then the administration should get busy and do something to correct the causes.

We called a press conference when the report was issued. About forty newsmen and women attended, and it seemed as though they were all determined to get me to condemn Nixon. After ten minutes of provocative questions, I put a stop to it. "If any of you quote what I'm about to say, I'll cut your throats personally," I declared. "You've been trying to get me to say that the President is a bad person, but I am not going to say it. If I do, that will be the headline, and no one will read the report." I reminded them that though Nixon was the ultimate boss, every one of those departments had a cabinet member or a director over it. I then bet them that none of them had bothered to read the forty-page summary of the report, much less the full thousand pages. "Please do read at least the summary and base your stories on the facts you find there," I said, "because the headline of this story is not 'Nixon is a bad man, says head of commission.' The story is that the federal government is not following the civil rights laws that it helped put on the books. That's a pretty good story, and we've provided you with the facts to support it." The press played fair, as they usually did. When the papers came out and the TV news was broadcast, no one said that Hesburgh had refused to call Nixon a bad man.

Shortly after that, Leonard Garment took me to dinner to mend fences, and during the dinner he asked me point-blank to tell him "What's wrong with the President, what's wrong with his administration, and what's wrong with the country."

"In what order?" I asked.

"Any order you want," he said.

When I finished, he leaned back and said, "Would you be willing to tell all that to the President?" I said I would be.

Two weeks later Garment telephoned to admit defeat. He could not get me past "the Katzenjammer Kids" to see the President. The Katzenjammer Kids were Bob Haldeman, chief of staff, and John Ehrlichman, head of the Domestic Council, who guarded the President against unpopular opinions and in so doing insulated him from the outside world. I did not help matters or mend many fences myself with some of my public pronouncements on civil rights matters or by an article I wrote on racial justice in the *New York Times Magazine* in which I spoke out for school busing and alluded to the arrogance of power in government.

By the time the presidential election of 1972 came up, civil rights and the Civil Rights Commission had really been through the meat grinder. The issue of busing had been particularly divisive and bitter, and for all the wrong reasons. I kept saying that if everyone just followed what the Supreme Court had said, there would not be any problems. The Court laid down two very important principles. One, no child should ever be bused from a good education to a bad education. When he or she gets off the bus, it should be at a better school than the one he or she came from. Two, the age of the child must be considered before a decision to bus is made. You have to be much more concerned about busing a kindergartner than you do about busing a child in high school. A very young child might not be able to cope. A high school youngster probably would be.

Nixon, of course, was reelected overwhelmingly in 1972, and a few days after the election, Monday, November 13, to be exact, we were having an executive session—just the six commissioners and

John Buggs, the executive director—in a conference room off Buggs's office. We had just begun the meeting when the phone rang. Buggs picked it up, listened for a few seconds, and then said, "Yes, yes, all right, understood." When he put the phone down, he looked very upset. "The President wants a letter of resignation from all of you, not necessarily to be effective, but he wants a letter of resignation, especially yours," he said, nodding his head at me.

The first thought that leaped to my mind was that the President could not force any one of us to resign. He did not have the power, although the point was not crystal clear. I explained to the other commissioners that the Civil Rights Commission was created by Congress as an independent agency, whose members served for the life of the commission and not at the will of the President. The President could replace me as chairman, but he could not force me, or any of the others, off. In fact, Congress had always set the life of the commission to expire at a time which overlapped an election year. On the other hand, sometimes when the commission's life was renewed by Congress, the new President's letter of appointment to the commissioners read "at the pleasure of the President." But we had never tendered resignations to Kennedy or Johnson when they took office.

Anyway, we went on with our meeting and when it was over, I cornered Buggs and asked him to fill me in on the details. He said the person who called was the secretary of Fred Malek, a White House staff man who worked for Haldeman. The secretary had instructed Buggs to tell me that Malek wanted me out of my office by six o'clock tonight. That got my dander up. I asked John to call the secretary back—not Malek, or Ehrlichman, or Haldeman, but the secretary—and tell her that I had worked for four Presidents and that I understood that the President could dismiss me as chairman, but not as a member of the commission. I told him to tell her that I certainly would move out of the chairmanship if the President really had dismissed me, even though I had heard it only from her, who had it from an assistant who was several steps removed from the President, who had appointed me chairman. I could live with that, I said, but I would not be leaving at six o'clock that night; I would try to be out by the end of the week.

When the media put Ron Ziegler, Nixon's press secretary, on the spot about my being fired, Ziegler tried to make a joke of it. He recalled that someone had asked me during the campaign what would happen if Nixon were reelected, and that I had said I would probably be fired. Ziegler said, "Well, Nixon was reelected, ha, ha, ha." That was not what I had said. I immediately wired Ziegler what I actually said, which was simply that if I were asked to resign by the reelected President, as was his privilege, I would. The next day Ziegler had one of his deputies issue a retraction that included my statement.

By Saturday, I had moved out of the office. I must say that Nixon did replace me as chairman of the commission with a fine man and great civil servant, Arthur Flemming, and not an errand boy as some Nixon critics had predicted. Personally, I had no regrets about leaving the Civil Rights Commission after fifteen years' service. I had fought and won many battles on behalf of racial justice and civil rights, and fifteen years was time enough for one man in that position.

There was a spell of coldness between Nixon and me after I was sacked. But when Watergate happened, I did not rejoice. As President, Nixon had accomplished some good things, too. When David Frost was preparing for the first in-depth interview of Nixon after Watergate, a researcher for Frost called me, wanting some ideas for questions that might embarrass the former President. I declined. Years later I was invited to speak at a National Hall of Fame dinner at the Waldorf-Astoria in New York, to which both former Presidents, Nixon and Ford, had been invited. Ford had many friends and he was a well-liked man. Speaker after speaker began, "President Ford, President Nixon . . ." It did not seem right to me. When I approached the podium, I paused to shake hands, first with Nixon, then with Ford, and when I began my talk, I addressed Nixon first. A minor gesture, yes, but it was not lost on Nixon. Since that night he has sent me a signed copy of almost every book and major article he has written. As one gets older, it becomes more apparent that forgiving and forgetting is much better than holding grudges. Besides, it is more Christian.

My devotion to and my efforts on behalf of civil rights and

human rights have continued unabated through the years. At Notre Dame Law School we now have a Center for Civil and Human Rights, where my commission papers are filed and indexed. It is an active center for the study and implementation of civil rights, and on campus, when it was first established, they called it "The Civil Rights Commission in Exile."

TWELVE

FRIENDSHIP

The BEST safety valve in any truly high-pressure job is a vacation far, far away. To protect oneself against burnout, the best salve on the market is a complete change of scene and activity. For many years, the way I did this was to spend the Christmas holidays with an unlikely pair of men, named Smith and Jones.

Unlikely not because they were different from one another, but because they were very much unlike me. C. R. Smith was the president of American Airlines. Charles Jones was president of the Richfield Oil Corporation.

They were rough and tough Texans, self-made men, highly successful business executives. Both stood six feet six inches tall, and they were raised as Southern Baptists. I met Smith first, in the mid-fifties, during a meeting of the Advisory Council of the College of Business Administration. Why did everyone call him C.R.? If your first names were Cyrus Rufus, you'd want to be called C.R., too. As a member of the council, Smith came to Notre Dame on a fairly regular basis. One evening at a council dinner party Smith maneuvered me into a corner and asked if he knew me well enough to speak frankly. I told him to go ahead.

"You look like hell," he said.

"Thank you very much," I replied, trying not to sound too sarcastic. Inside I knew he was probably right. I was in the middle of my first term as president, which I assumed might be my last, and I was working very long days far into the nights trying to cram in all my work. He was not the first to tell me I was looking haggard. I knew I was not getting much sleep.

"You don't work over Christmas, do you?" he asked. I said I usually didn't. "Fine, I'll send you a ticket to Los Angeles and we'll take off from there and get some fresh air." Smith then proceeded to tell me that he wanted to take me hunting and fishing. I had not had a shotgun in my hands since hunting pheasant as a teenager in Syracuse, and I probably had not held a fishing rod more than a couple of times since then, either. I told Smith I did not want to hunt animals, but that I had no objection to bagging a few birds for the pot. He assured me that we would hunt nothing but ducks and geese. All the fishing would be of the deep-sea variety, something I had never done.

Five days or so before Christmas, I received an airline ticket from Smith, along with a note and some money. I was to buy myself a pair of hunting boots, fly to Los Angeles, and meet him at the Beverly Hills Hotel. I still did not have the slightest idea where we were going or with whom. At breakfast the next morning, Smith told me we were going to the Baja Peninsula with Charlie Jones and his wife, Jenny. Smith was divorced and had never remarried, so it would be just the four of us. We would be flying down to Mexico in Jones's DC-3, from Burbank airport.

Jones and his wife arrived a few minutes after we did, laden down with about forty gifts for the local people they knew. Jenny was affable right from the start. Jones was a little standoffish. Apparently, he had not been around too many Catholic priests, and did not know what to expect.

Our destination was far down the Baja Peninsula, about a five-hour flight in the DC-3. Shortly before noon, Jones turned to me and said, "Well, it's getting toward lunchtime. I don't suppose you'd like a drink, would you, Father."

I said I would.

"Well, I'd like a drink," he said, "but I didn't know if you would."

"Well, I'd like one, too," I said. Jones, who undoubtedly had more experience with abstinent Baptist ministers than with Catholic priests, brightened up considerably.

After lunch he asked, "I don't suppose you play bridge, do you, Father?"

As a matter of fact, I told him, I did play bridge.

Jones then remarked, "Hey, this isn't going to be such a bad trip, after all. You and Jenny will be partners." Jenny obviously did not play much bridge. Jones, I found out later, played every noon at the California Club, and I knew that Smith was a formidable match in any kind of card game. There were stories of poker games where he had acquired cars, boats, and other fairly big-ticket items from his hapless opponents at the card table. Nevertheless, Jenny and I got all the cards and really stomped the two card sharks. Jones did not relish losing, but the mere fact that I knew how to play seemed to buoy his spirits.

When we finished playing, Jones remarked, "I don't suppose you've ever fished or hunted, Father."

I said, "Well, probably not as much as you have, but yes, I've fished and hunted."

With that, he smiled and quipped to Smith, "Things are looking up all the time." His attitude seemed to be: If he had to be stuck with a Catholic priest for a couple of weeks, at least it was a Catholic priest who drank a little, played a pretty good game of bridge, and at least purported to have done some fishing and hunting.

Jones was not done worrying about my being a priest. As we neared La Paz, where we would clear immigration and customs before continuing down the peninsula, he remarked that my Roman collar might cause me trouble in Mexico, where the notion of a secular state was taken very seriously. I told him I thought the typical Mexican in this kind of isolated area would be tickled pink to see a priest. Jones was skeptical. I offered to bet him five dollars that in five minutes a dozen people would ask me for a rosary without my having to say a word. "You're on," Jones said. "I know they're religious, but this is a secular state and I can't imagine any of them asking you for a rosary or even wanting one."

We landed in La Paz and went into the terminal to take care of the customs and immigration formalities. Smith and Jones started filling out forms. I took one of the twelve rosaries I had in my pocket and started twirling it around my index finger. Immediately, a Mexican man standing on line behind us said, "Padre, may I have a rosary?"

I said, "Sure," and gave it to him. I reached in my pocket, pulled out another one, and started twirling it.

"Padre," someone behind me said, "could I have a rosary, too?"

I said, "Sí," and handed it over.

Within a few minutes my pocket was empty. Some of the people put the rosaries over their heads and wore them like necklaces. All Charlie could say was "I can't understand it."

"Just give me my five dollars," I said.

From La Paz we flew for about six minutes to a little pueblo with a population of no more than a hundred. It seemed that half the population was at the strip to greet us when we landed. I still had my Roman collar on, but they had not seen a priest in so long that they did not know what to make of me. "Padre, are you a Father?" one man asked me in Spanish. I said I was. Two or three more questions followed, until they were satisfied that I was, indeed, a Roman Catholic priest. Then they asked me if I would conduct a midnight Mass. I told them I'd do it, but only if they went to confession first. They all laughed at that. "How do you go to confession after forty years?" one man wanted to know. That was how long they had not seen a priest in this remote village. I assured them that I would make it easy on them. Since my Spanish was limited, all they had to tell me were the headline items and all they would get for their penance would be three "Our Fathers."

The place where we stayed was called Rancho Las Cruces. The name came from the three crosses that had been erected on a rocky promontory overlooking the sea. The original three crosses were erected by Cortés in honor of three of his men, whom he had left there to guard the oyster beds in the bay. The three men

were supposed to establish a pearl operation while Cortés continued exploring the Baja. But while he was gone, the three were
killed by Indians; hence the three crosses. During the nineteenth
century a Frenchman started a date plantation there, and much
more recently the small village had been converted into a small,
low-key fishing resort with a little motel, a clean restaurant with
plain but tasty food, and a few small fishing boats. It was, and still
is, a place of great beauty and tranquillity. The gently curving bay
is ringed with sand and backed by mountains covered with pine
trees and cactus. Just beyond the bay lies the Sea of Cortés, teeming
with game fish.

The hunting was like nothing I had ever experienced. It was
utterly fantastic, not only that year but every year after that. The
region is on a major flyway. By Christmastime there are so many
ducks wintering there, the sky is sometimes black with them. We
bagged a lot of ducks and geese over the years, but never more
than we needed for food. The workers at the resort were always
happy to see us hunting, knowing full well they would be feasting
on a lot of nice, plump ducks and geese.

The fishing was equally spectacular. One year I am sure we set
a record for marlin. In three hours we caught thirty-three of those
magnificent game fish. In one period of a little more than two
hours, I caught a total of seven marlin and sailfish myself. It is
truly great sport, at least the way we were doing it. We were using
thirty-pound test lines, and a lot of these fish weighed around 250
pounds. Most of them we tagged and turned loose to breed and be
caught again. We got the tags from the Oceanographic Institution
at Woods Hole, Massachusetts. One of the fish I tagged was later
caught off Tulagi in the Solomon Islands.

It was a great ten days. We caught a lot of fish, bagged a lot of
ducks and geese, played a lot of bridge, drank some margaritas,
smoked cigars, and told stories, some of which, no doubt, grew
better with repeated tellings. When it was time to go back, one of
the Mexican men asked Jones if he was going to bring me back
next year. "Señor Hones," the man said to Jones, "we want you to
bring the priest back so we can have midnight Mass again."

"Well, he behaved better than I expected," Señor Hones said. "I think we probably will bring him back." As I came to know Jones better, he admitted that he had not been terribly pleased to learn that I was coming along that first Christmas. "My God," Jones said. "Here we were going to take vacation and Smith just tells me with no warning that he's bringing a Catholic priest along. I figured you wouldn't drink, wouldn't smoke, wouldn't play cards, wouldn't fish, wouldn't hunt. And I knew you wouldn't cuss like we did. You really surprised me. Except one thing. You never cussed."

Well, nobody's perfect.

At the end of my second Christmas at Las Cruces the villagers told Jones that if he would bring me back there every year, they would build a church. The third year I spent there, the church was done. It was a beautiful little colonial-style building, erected on a commanding cliff about eight or nine hundred feet above the sea. The owner of the ranch, a man named Rodríguez, took me up to see it. When I asked him if they planned to put stained-glass windows in, he explained that they had deliberately left them out because they did not want anything to interfere with the view. "What you see through those windows is better than stained glass," Rodríguez said as he waved toward the green-clad mountains and the sea birds whirling about in the cloud-dappled sky. "It's what God has made."

Smith and Jones took up where God and the builders left off. They bought beautiful mosaics of the Last Supper and the Stations of the Cross. They bought the chalice and donated the money for all the vestments. Jones found an organ that operated on foot power and had it hauled up there. The two of them were responsible for practically everything in that church. Yet neither one of them was what you would call religious. Although raised as Southern Baptists, they had not been to church in many years, I'm sure. That is, until the midnight Mass tradition began in Las Cruces. After that, they went twice a year, once to midnight Mass on Christmas Eve, once again exactly one week later on New Year's Eve. We made a deal after the first year, a simple quid pro quo: They would go to the two Masses if I would play bridge with them afterward. I would have played bridge with them anyway, and I am sure they knew that, but they did like to make deals. It became a ritual: Mass, then bridge. Special words also became part of the ritual. Every year as we walked out of the church together after the New Year's Mass, Jones would turn to Smith and say, "Well, that's it for another year."

We went to Las Cruces every year for fourteen years running. Smith missed once and Jones missed once because of unexpected business problems, but I made it down there every time. Of course, I took my Christmas vacation when Notre Dame did, the same time every year. Those ten-day vacations at Las Cruces were just what I needed, coming as they did just about in the middle of the school year. Returning to Notre Dame, I always felt completely rested and renewed. The fishing and hunting had very little to do with it. What renewed me were the beauty and tranquillity of the place, the fresh air and the slow pace, and, of course, the company of two men who differed so markedly from the clerics, academicians, and government types I associated with the rest of the year. Whenever I would introduce Smith or Jones to people, I would say, "This is the fellow I spend my winter vacation with. Thanks to him, I've been able to keep my sanity all these years."

They would invariably respond, "The only way a Catholic priest can have a decent vacation is to take it with a Texas Baptist."

Those idyllic days ended when Charlie Jones died in 1970. A few years before that, C.R. phoned me. "Better get down to the Presbyterian Hospital pronto, Padre," he said. "Jones is really facing a tough one. They're going to amputate his leg and that will kill him. He needs help."

I arrived at the hospital in New York City just as the doctor told Jones that the operation would be the following morning. Jones, with his customary bravado, quipped, "Well, as we say at Notre Dame, let's get the show on the road."

I told Charlie I would offer Mass for him at St. Patrick's Cathedral and would be with him at 7 A.M., when they came to take him into the operating room. The surgeon came in about 7:05 and said, "Charlie, during the night I had a bright idea: I'm going to cover your leg in tough plastic and pump in oxygen under high pressure to try to open the veins and arteries." The idea worked, and Charlie was able to keep his leg.

The Christmas after Charlie died, a few years after that bout with his leg, C.R. and I went down to Las Cruces, but the carefree joy was gone without Jones. It was particularly hard on Smith. They had been very, very close. "Every time I go around a corner, I see Charlie," Smith said one day. "I just don't want to come down here anymore." And that was the last time we ever did.

Jones had stipulated in his will that he be cremated and buried in Forest Lawn. I was designated to deliver the eulogy. Before that, though, Jenny, C.R., and I offered a quiet Requiem Mass. I think every chief executive officer of every major oil company attended the public service, and most of them probably knew Jones as well as I did, if not better. For that reason I told them right up front that I was there to talk about a man who richly deserved to be eulogized, but not canonized. If I were to do otherwise, I said, Jones would certainly come back to haunt me.

Smith and I continued to spend Christmas vacations together, but at places that were a long way from Las Cruces. We went to Durango, the Yucatán Peninsula, the high Andes of Argentina, Kenya, Spain, the Amazon, and Barbados. We kept this up for another sixteen years. I enjoyed kidding C.R. for being, with the exception of the one year he missed at Las Cruces when he was Secretary of Commerce, the only Baptist on earth who had attended Christmas midnight Mass for thirty years straight.

As Smith got older, we eliminated the fishing and hunting and concentrated on reading. We would each take ten or so books along and read them all. Smith preferred history and biography. He was an expert on Western art and he owned an outstanding collection of bronzes and paintings by Remington and Russell. One day when I was working in my office at Notre Dame he called me up and said, "Padre, would Notre Dame want sixty thousand dollars as a cash gift or a painting?"

Caught completely off guard, I blurted out, "What painting?"

He said, "Russell's *Mountain Men*."

"Well," I said, "we don't have an original Russell and ours is a teaching gallery; I think we'd rather have the painting." I was certainly no expert on the art market; I just had a feeling that the painting would probably go up in value. Not even an art expert could have predicted at the time just how much that painting by Charles Russell would appreciate. The last time someone tried to buy it from us, in the early 1980s, we were offered more than one million dollars, and turned it down.

Nor did Smith's generosity end there. When he retired from American Airlines, he was asked how he wanted his retirement pay and deferred income handled. The one thing Smith did not need any more of was money, and he just said, "Oh, give it to the university for an endowed professorship in business administration." The next question was whether he wanted his alma mater, the University of Texas, to have it then or later on. "Who said anything about Texas?" Smith shot back. "I want you to send it to Notre Dame." And that's how we happen to have the "C.R. Smith professorship" in the College of Business Administration. It is now worth well over one million dollars.

C.R. became increasingly frail in his eighties, but he and I continued to take our Christmas vacations together as long as he was able, in the warm, calm, easy vacation spots in the Caribbean, especially in Barbados. He celebrated his ninetieth birthday in a wheelchair, but feisty as ever, in September 1989. He died in April 1990. I did one of the eulogies at the Arlington National Cemetery, where he was buried as a World War II major general. C. R. Smith was one of a kind. With heavy heart, I had offered a Requiem Mass for him that morning.

I still take those midwinter breaks, but none of them compare to those memorable times with Smith and Jones in Mexico.

THIRTEEN

ACADEMIC FREEDOM

ONE OF the ongoing debates in Catholic higher education concerns the nature and mission of Catholic universities. In other words, what are they doing and what are they supposed to be doing? The issue that most often precipitates and frequently inflames the debate is academic freedom.

Should ecclesiastical authorities have control over universities that call themselves Catholic, and if so, how much control should they have and in what ways should that control be used and not used?

In 1954 we had a classic confrontation over the issue of academic freedom, with Notre Dame on one side and the Vatican on the other. At the center of it was John Courtney Murray, an eminent Jesuit theologian. Murray had been invited to Notre Dame to take part in a symposium on the Catholic Church in world affairs. It was a prestigious gathering that included several other prominent theologians and intellectuals. Murray spoke on church-state relations, an area in which he was an acknowledged expert. His thinking and research led him to the position that persons in a pluralistic society have rights, and that one of those rights is the right to their own opinions. He did not believe Catholic theologians, or anyone else, should be silenced because they happened to disagree with the current noninfallible understanding of Church doctrine. Religious convictions for everyone, Murray contended, were a matter of conscience and faith.

Murray's views were not shared by some powerful conservative theologians in Rome, among them Cardinal Alfredo Ottaviani. Ottaviani's position, to simplify or oversimplify it, was that error had no rights. If you disagreed with Church doctrine, you had no right to promote your view. Nonsense, said Murray. Error is an abstraction and only persons have rights. A person's position, held in good faith, has every right to be heard.

The papers delivered by the participants in the symposium were collected and published by the University of Notre Dame Press as *The Catholic Church and World Affairs*. Review copies had hardly been sent out to editors and reviewers when I received a letter from our Superior General, Father Christopher O'Toole. He said that Ottaviani wanted him, O'Toole, to make sure that the book did not reach the bookstores. Furthermore, Ottaviani did not want anyone to know why the book was being withdrawn. And further, O'Toole was not to tell anyone that Ottaviani had given the order, nor was I to tell anyone that O'Toole had passed the order on to me. O'Toole concluded his letter with this dictum: *Roma locuta est, causa finita est.* Rome has spoken, the cause is finished.

The cause was not finished as far as I was concerned. The tone and content of that letter hit me like a challenge to action. Though head of the "Holy Office," Ottaviani was not the Church. I had no intention of ordering the book withdrawn. Both his letter to O'Toole and O'Toole's to me constituted a frontal assault on academic freedom at Notre Dame.

The first thing I did was gather my university council together, consisting of Holy Cross priests, most of them vice presidents in the university administration. Not only were they all appalled at the idea of censorship, they all agreed that it would be ridiculous even to try to suppress the book. For one thing, Murray's article was about as orthodox a philosophical statement as you could imagine on the subject of church-state relations, despite Ottaviani's opinion. Compared with what emerged from Vatican Council II on the same subject a few years later, it was even rather tame.

With the backing of the council, I telephoned O'Toole in Rome and told him my position: I understood his concern, but I would not suppress the book. If he ordered me to do it, I would resign. There was no way I was going to destroy the freedom and autonomy of the university and, indeed, the university itself, when so many people had devoted their lives to building it. Ottaviani had the right to disagree with the book, but the Church was bigger than Ottaviani. There were practical problems to be reckoned with as well. The reviewers already had the book, and some early critiques were very favorable. It had been selected by the Catholic Book-of-the-Month Club. If we tried to withdraw the book, the press would be all over me wanting to know why, and if all they got from me was a "no comment," we would be finished as a university and I would be finished as its president. Notre Dame would lose all its credibility in the United States, and so would I, if an official in Rome could abrogate our academic freedom with a snap of his fingers.

O'Toole kept insisting that this was a very serious matter and that I was not being cooperative. Even in religious communities, it was understood that its members could hold widely differing opinions. The problem here was that O'Toole was not just any member. He was my highest religious superior. Feeling that I could not appear to be completely intractable on the matter, I suggested a compromise. "Give me a few weeks," I said. "When the book sells out, we just won't print any more copies of it." O'Toole said Ottaviani would not like that. I replied that I was sorry about that, but if he did not accept my offer, his only other option was to fire me.

Still not satisfied, O'Toole finally agreed to allow the book a month or so while he held Ottaviani at bay. When the month was up, the book had sold six thousand copies, our break-even point, and we figured our troubles were over. But they weren't. Joe Fenton, the conservative head of the theology department at

Catholic University in Washington, came upon a copy of the book in a Washington bookstore and immediately called Ottaviani. This time Ottaviani did not bother going through Chris O'Toole. He called the Superior General of the Jesuits, who in turn called Murray. He informed Murray that he, the General, had been ordered by Ottaviani to take Murray's book out of circulation. Nothing could be done about the copies that had already been sold or remained in bookstores, but he told Murray that the only books he was going after were the ones that remained at the University of Notre Dame Press. He ordered Murray to buy them all.

When Murray called with this news, I just told him to consider the five hundred remaining copies of his book paid for. Then I had them squirreled away in an attic somewhere to await the day when we would no longer have to worry about this kind of thing. But then, the books would probably be worth ten times the price.

But this sorry episode still had not played itself out. Apparently, O'Toole felt that he needed to further appease Ottaviani, and so he wrote a letter to all the Holy Cross religious superiors, ordering them to ban Murray from teaching courses or lecturing at any of their institutions. Murray was already scheduled to give the annual retreat for the Holy Cross priests at Notre Dame, and our religious superior had the unpleasant task of breaking the bad news to him. We did, however, let everyone know where we stood. At commencement the following spring we gave Murray an honorary doctorate.

John Courtney Murray was fully vindicated several years later at Vatican Council II, which he attended as a theological expert for Cardinal Spellman. He was chosen to draft the Council's article on religious freedom. It was the one session of Vatican II that I attended and I was delighted when Bishop Mark Hurley came up to me and said, "Here's a historic document for you." He handed me the original draft of the article on religious freedom, written by none other than John Courtney Murray and later ratified by the Council and published as an official document of Vatican II. It was Cardinal Spellman, by the way, who saw to it that Murray received that assignment. The Vatican II article was much stronger on religious freedom than what Murray had written in *The Catholic Church and World Affairs.* If any doubt remained with regard to Murray's standing, Pope Paul VI invited him to concelebrate Mass with him in St. Peter's at the end of the Council.

Also celebrating Mass with the Holy Father that day were other well-known theologians whose writings had been suppressed in the past and whose theological positions were fully vindicated and made part of the Council documents. This is called the Holy Spirit at work.

Many years later Ottaviani visited Notre Dame and I gave him the grand tour. He was well up in years at the time, and I will never forget his words when we finished. "Give me a place like this," he said, "and I'll convert all of Italy." Then he added, "Padre, you probably have difficulties from time to time. Whenever you do, a letter is all I need, and I will take care of them for you." I thought I knew Ottaviani pretty well, but this was a side of him that surprised me. He was much more complex than I had given him credit for. The day we drove him to Chicago he was not feeling well, and he just put his head back on a pillow and told the monsignor who was traveling with him that he was going to say his Breviary. Considering his age and his failing eyesight, he was excused from saying it, but he recited the whole office from memory, and in Latin, which took an hour. I had to admire him for that.

Nine years after the Murray imbroglio, I found myself once again in the middle of a maelstrom over academic freedom. It began at the 1963 triennial meeting of the International Federation of Catholic Universities in Washington. The IFCU was in a shambles. It had no independence, no organization, no treasury or office, not even a decent, workable constitution. Most of the members who cared about it felt that it had to be reformed or revitalized, and they thought I was the one to lead them to the promised land. One by one the various delegations put the pressure on me to run for president—first the Latin Americans, then the Europeans, and finally the Americans. I turned them all down because I was already overworked with my crowded schedule at Notre Dame, the Civil Rights Commission, the National Science

Board, and the Rockefeller Foundation. I even had to leave the meeting early, before the election of new officers, in order to attend a meeting of the Rockefeller Foundation board that Saturday in New York.

Monday I received a call from Gérard Lepoutre, a federation delegate from the University of Lille in France. He greeted me with "Congratulations." I asked him what he was congratulating me about. "Don't you know? You were unanimously elected president of the International Federation of Catholic Universities," he said. They had elected me president in absentia. Well, I thought, somehow I'll manage and we'll make this organization amount to something. The council of the Federation had hardly ever had a meeting, so I scheduled one for a time and a place that I figured they could not resist—April in Paris.

The statutes of the Federation held that all its elections had to be approved by the Sacred Congregation of Seminaries and Universities, which was headed by Cardinal Pizzardo, but was really run by a Vatican archbishop, since Pizzardo was very old. In November I received a letter signed by Pizzardo and the archbishop directing me to come to Rome on November 16 for a very important meeting regarding the Federation. They did not ask, they just told me. When I got there I found Monsignor Georges LeClercq, president of the University of Lille, who had been summoned as the newly elected secretary-general of the International Federation of Catholic Universities.

Two others at the meeting were the officers that LeClercq and I had defeated in the election, the rector of Catholic University, Monsignor McDonald, and Dr. Vito, the rector of Sacro Cuore University in Milan. They had not done a thing in the preceding three years except send a one-sentence telegram in Latin telling everyone where the next triennial meeting would be. Moreover, since our election two months earlier, we had not received a single thing from them—no minutes, no records, no money. Despite all that, we soon found out that they had taken a dim view of being voted out of office after one term. I was certain they had whispered in the right ears in Rome. Two others at the meeting were the rectors of the two main Roman clerical universities, Muñoz Vega, the rector of the Gregorian and now the cardinal archbishop of Quito, and the rector of the Angelicum, Father Sigismundi. That made six of us who had been summoned to the meeting.

Shortly after we arrived at the Vatican for the meeting, Pizzardo came in with the archbishop and had us all sit down like misbehaving choirboys. LeClercq and I had thought we had been summoned to Rome to be sworn in as the new officers of the Federation. Instead, the archbishop declared that the election was invalid because we had not followed canon law. He claimed I could not be president of the Federation because the president had to be president of a Catholic university. How about that?

"That's a laugh," I said. "We've been a member of the Federation as a Catholic university since its inception and no one ever returned our annual dues." He said he knew how to interpret the rules and that was the way it was going to be. Then he said that he had decided to set up a commission to run the Federation and that he was appointing McDonald and Vito, plus the rectors of the Gregorian and the Angelicum, which he happened to control, to join us in a six-member council to run the organization. I said I would not go along with that. LeClercq echoed my sentiments. I declared that I intended to fight what he was doing, adding, as an afterthought, that the Holy Father had already congratulated me on my election. I am sure he thought I was bluffing.

The archbishop countered by saying he would leave the room while the rest of us worked it out. I stopped him in his tracks, saying that I had just come four thousand miles at my own expense and would be traveling another four thousand miles back, also at my own expense, and that I expected him to stay right there and hear everything I had to say and that I wanted to hear everything he had to say. There would be no private deals that he could agree or disagree with later, I insisted. Then I went even further. I told him that we would not stand for his autocratic plan and neither would the people who had elected us, and if he persisted he would just end up being in charge of nothing. I really let the fur fly. My Irish mother would have been very proud of me. After some more inconsequential discussion, he dismissed us. I shook his hand and asked for his blessing, which just about killed him, I'm sure.

The archbishop followed this up with a letter to the rectors of all the universities with pontifical charters, telling them why he was not approving my election as president or LeClercq's as secretary-general. He said he was forming a commission of all the rectors of the pontifical universities in the world to run the Federation until the next election, which, he warned, had better be done according to canon law. It was one of the most arrogant letters I had ever read. He did not bother to inform me; I received a copy from one of the Canadian rectors of a pontifical university. After I read it, I just put it in an envelope and sent it to Paul VI's secretary with a note saying that all of this was being done in the name of the Holy Father and maybe it would be a good idea if he was informed. The next time I saw Paul VI's secretary, he said he had never seen the Pope so angry.

Paul VI called the archbishop and gave him three clear orders. First, he was to write to all those universities again and apologize for waiting from September to January to approve Father Hesburgh and the others who were elected. Second, he would approve Father Hesburgh and the others immediately and give them full power to conduct the affairs of the Federation. Third, he would instruct them to write a new constitution for the Federation in which the Congregation of Seminaries and Universities would not even be mentioned. Then he instructed the archbishop to send an apology to Father Hesburgh, with a copy to all those to whom he had sent his previous letter. I have to give the archbishop credit for one thing: He wrote a fifteen-page letter in excellent Latin and he ate crow on every page.

The next time I saw the Pope, I said to him, "I gather you really want the International Federation of Catholic Universities to be a strong organization." He said he did.

At the Federation's next meeting in Paris, we drafted a new constitution. It required no approvals for actions beyond the Federation's own governing board. It made no mention of canon law in the section on elections. It recognized Catholic universities de facto as well as de jure (that is, those with or without papal charters). Paul VI confirmed the new constitution immediately by his own *motu proprio,* that is, on his own personal authority, much as our president would do in issuing an executive order.

We were now off and running. Though we had inherited no files and no money, we enlarged the membership, instituted regular dues, established our office in Paris (not Rome) with a permanent staff, joined UNESCO with consultative status, initiated the Jerusalem ecumenical project, and published our new constitution.

As important as all these moves were, we decided that our most important task was to clarify the nature and purpose of the Catholic university, its relationship to the Church and the state and to its faculty and students. We decided to write a strong statement, get Pope Paul VI to approve it, and deliver it at our next general meeting, which would be held in Tokyo in 1965. I asked my old writing friend Charlie Sheedy, then our dean of Arts and Letters, to write the statement. "This is probably the only chance you're going to get to write a papal letter," I said to Charlie. "I would like it to be heavy on freedom and autonomy and why Catholic universities are special, and put in some very elegant language." Charlie obliged me with a statement that was a little too heavy on freedom and autonomy, but when toned down a bit it was a beautiful, elegantly written letter. It was even more impressive when written in flowing italic script beneath the Pope's private letterhead.

I presented Charlie's letter to the Pope during an audience at Castel Gandolfo. "You have papal letters on everything from devotion to the rosary to marriage and the family," I said, "but I don't know of a single papal letter on Catholic universities." The Pope agreed that he should write such a letter, but said most of his staff was on summer vacation and he did not know how or when he would be able to do it. That is when I revealed that I just happened to have a draft for such a letter and handed him copies of Sheedy's letter in Italian, French, and English. All he had to do was read it or have someone on his staff read it, make any changes he wanted, and get it to me in Japan the following week so I could read it at a meeting of the International Federation of Catholic Universities, to which I was en route. He looked at the letters I had given him, and then put his hands up like the Italians do and said, "You're doing my work for me."

The morning our Federation meeting opened in Tokyo, a Japanese man walked across the stage where I was sitting and handed me an envelope. It was Charlie's letter, substantially in the form that he had written it. Even in edited form—some of the enthusiasm for freedom and autonomy had been deleted—it was still probably the best statement ever made by a Pope on universities and higher education.

It took a few more years and many more meetings to get the final document hammered out so that it would be acceptable to all the delegates worldwide, but we finally finished the job on November 29, 1972. Called *The Catholic University in the Modern World,* it was unanimously approved by the forty delegates, who represented a total of twenty-three countries. The Plenarium, a group of cardinals who oversee the Congregation for Catholic Education, also accepted it with some minimal reservations. After nine years of hard work and negotiation it seemed, at long last, that everyone was agreed on what Catholic universities were, what we were, what we should be doing, and how we should be doing it.

The opening lines of the document give a good summary of its content:

> Since the objective of a Catholic university, precisely as Catholic, is to assure in an institutional manner a Christian presence in the university world confronting the great problems of contemporary society, the following are its essential characteristics: 1) A Christian inspiration not only of individuals, but of the university as such; 2) a continuing reflection in the light of the Catholic faith upon the growing treasury of human knowledge, to which it seeks to contribute by its own research; 3) fidelity to the Christian message as it comes to us through the Church; 4) an institutional commitment to the service of the people of God and of the human family in the pilgrimage to the transcendent goal which gives meaning to life. *All universities that realize these fundamental conditions are Catholic universities whether canonically erected or not* [italics mine].

We thought that the last sentence would lay to rest, once and for all, the persistent question of what makes a university Catholic. The same thought was elaborated in another passage:

There are various categories into which Catholic institutions of higher learning will fall. While every Catholic university's fidelity to the Christian message as it comes to us through the Church involves a recognition of the teaching authority of the Church in doctrinal matters, nevertheless, different institutions have different relations to ecclesiastical authority, since these relations have been determined and conditioned by many different historical and national situations. On this basis, various categories of Catholic universities can be discerned: some have been directly established or approved by ecclesiastical authority, while others have not; some have a statutory relationship with this authority, while others do not. The latter, provided that they maintain the essential characteristics of every Catholic university which were described above, *are no less Catholic, whether by a formal, explicit commitment on the part of their founder, trustees, or faculty, or by their implicit tradition of fidelity to Catholicism and their corresponding social and cultural influence.*

Another long-standing bone of contention had always been autonomy and academic freedom, and on that our document had this to say:

The academic freedom which is essential if the science of theology is to be pursued and developed on a truly university level, postulates that hierarchical authority intervene only when it judges the truth of the Christian message to be at stake.

Furthermore, the legitimate and necessary autonomy of the university requires that an intervention by ecclesiastical authority should respect the statutes and regulations of the institution, as well as accepted academic procedures. The recognition of Church authority in doctrinal matters does not of itself imply the right of the hierarchy to intervene in university governance or academic administration.

The form which a possible intervention of ecclesiastical authorities may take will vary in accordance with the type of Catholic institution involved. Where the university has a statutory relationship with Church authorities, presumably these will spell out the conditions and modalities to be observed in any hierarchical intervention. If there are no such statutory relationships, the Church authorities will deal with the individual involved only as a member of the Church.

The document concluded with one more statement on the various ways in which the nature and mission of the Catholic university could be achieved:

> To be sure, this ideal [of the Catholic university] even considered as such is not univocal. There is no one type of Catholic university which would be the model to be imitated everywhere in the world. The needs and aspirations of the various countries with their specific cultures and problems require that the idea of the Catholic university be adapted to each particular situation. For the Catholic university truly to fulfill its mission, it is necessary both that its Christian inspiration be real and efficacious and that the university be deeply rooted in its own mileu.

This concluding paragraph illustrates, above all, the difficulty of legislating univocally for Catholic universities across the world. What might be supportive of freedom in the case of a university in a Communist, or highly authoritarian, or anticlerical country, could easily be a denial of freedom in a free country.

We hammered out this document on the role of the Catholic university in the modern world virtually word by word at two ten-day meetings in Rome. And when it had been approved, we thought we had settled academic freedom and independence for Catholic universities. But only a few years later, it cropped up again. In June 1974, Cardinal Garrone, the new head of the Congregation for Catholic Education, invited some colleges and universities to contribute to the formulation of a "new academic law of the Church."

None of us needed to be told what this was: The conservatives in the Vatican were again on the attack against academic freedom in Catholic universities. Following a good deal of discussion, Monsignor John F. Murphy, executive secretary of what is now called the Association of Catholic Colleges and Universities, wrote a national response to Cardinal Garrone's request. Monsignor Murphy's long and thoughtful document was entitled *Relations of American Catholic Colleges and Universities with the Church*. Here is a key part:

> Since the colleges and universities in the United States have received their charters from the respective state governments and have independent legal existence as private, nonprofit, educational institutions, the notion of canonical establishment by the Holy See has never been thought of as typical or standard in the United States. In the spirit of Vatican Council II and with the long history we have had in providing a genuine Catholic educational experience in an American framework, we believe the word "cooperation" or the phrase "mutual support" best characterizes the kind of relationship that should exist between institution and Church.
>
> The language of "juridical relationships" and "canonical establishment" found in recent documents from the Congregation for Catholic Education does not seem to find focus in the vocabulary and the substance—and indeed, the spirit—of Vatican Council II's documents and declarations. The former appears to conceive of the university as "an arm of the Church," rather than the locus for interplay between Church and world, a canonical and juridical concept, rather than the dialogue approach of *Gaudium et Spes* [Vatican Council II's statement on the Church in the modern world].
>
> We do not think a juridical relationship between the Church and Catholic institutions in the exercise of their proper autonomy is desirable or even possible at this stage of American history, given the prominence of church-state issues. Since we have been asked to comment on the forthcoming conference in Rome in 1974 concerning "an academic law of the Church," we do not consider appropriate nor legally feasible the extension of jurisdiction over non-canonically established institutions, at the expense of existing rights of local bishops or the institutions themselves.
>
> It is our collective experience that the Rome 1972 document clearly identifies the essential characteristics of American Catholic colleges and universities. We concur that "all universities [and colleges] that realize these fundamental conditions are Catholic universities whether canonically erected or not."

We cannot speak for Catholic institutions in other lands; their circumstances and cultures differ from ours. We can only say that juridical canonical statutory relationships which would infringe upon proper institutional autonomy are not in keeping with our circumstances, and would make no positive contribution to our efforts to maintain and strengthen Catholic higher education and its service to the American Church.

Monsignor Murphy was being charitable in saying that this proposed legislation would make no positive contribution. What we were all saying was that it would be positively harmful and would jeopardize our freedoms and our reputations as authentic institutions of higher education. Monsignor Murphy concluded his document with a positive note that expressed what all of us in Catholic higher education strongly believe:

We propose to find in close collaboration with our bishops and the American Church, contemporary models of relationships which will serve the Church community effectively in our times. Cooperation in an atmosphere of trust and respect will enable us to respond to the serious problems of secularization which afflict our age and exert pressures on Catholic higher education.

What Monsignor Murphy was saying, of course, was, "If it isn't broken, don't fix it." In Catholic higher education in America, we have enough problems with the outside world without creating new ones within our own world. In an effort to cultivate the cooperation he spoke of, Monsignor Murphy persuaded the American bishops to organize an official joint committee of presidents of Catholic institutions of higher learning and some American bishops to discuss matters of joint concern. We met once or twice annually for many years, and the committee is still functional. One of the most important results of these discussions was a draft document that was eventually published in 1980 by the whole American hierarchy: "Catholic Higher Education and the Pastoral Mission of the Church." This document was concerned with only one aspect of higher education, so the American Catholic bishops added the following broader endorsement of documents already produced elsewhere and cited above:

> The full nature of the Catholic university and its role in the modern world have been carefully described in the benchmark document issued by the Second Congress of Delegates of the Catholic Universities of the World, convened in November of 1972 by the Sacred Congregation for Catholic Education. We are pleased with the careful description for the juridical relations between ourselves and your institutions in the document "Relations of American Catholic Colleges and Universities with the Church," issued in 1976 by the Association of Catholic Colleges and Universities. We believe this document accurately describes how Catholic colleges and universities function in the American context. In this pastoral message, we need not restate the intellectual importance of Catholic colleges and universities in the modern world, since this has been adequately treated in these documents.

This letter of the American bishops, like the letter of Pope Paul VI to Catholic universities, was the first of its kind. The year before the American bishops wrote their letter, Pope John Paul II addressed the university presidents' group at Catholic University in Washington. The date was October 7, 1979. Though rather existential, as is the Pope's style, we found his remarks encouraging. I quote them in part:

> A Catholic university or college must make a specific contribution to the Church and to society through high-quality scientific research, in-depth study of problems, and a just sense of history, together with the concern to show the full meaning of the human person regenerated in Christ, thus favoring the complete development of the person.
>
> Furthermore, the Catholic university must train young men and women of outstanding knowledge who, having made a personal synthesis between faith and culture, will be both capable and willing to assume tasks in the service of the community and of society in general, and to bear witness to their faith before the

world. And finally, to be what it ought to be, a Catholic college or university must set up, among its faculty and students, a real community which bears witness to a living and operative Christianity, a community whose sincere commitment to scientific research and study goes together with a deep commitment to authentic Christian living.

This is your identity. This is your vocation. Every university or college is qualified by a specific mode of being. Yours is the qualification of being Catholic, of affirming God, His revelation, and the Catholic Church as the guardian and interpreter of that revelation. The term "Catholic" will never be a mere label, added or dropped according to the pressures of various factors.

I think we all greeted this statement—nonjuridical and substantive—as a good summary of much that we had been discussing and saying since 1963, when the conversation about Catholic universities was seriously begun. But in our innocence we had not anticipated that the new code of canon law, yet to be elaborated, might nullify all our goodwill and good efforts, as well as our good results.

The code of canon law that we were operating under was published in 1917. It was decided at the Vatican Council that a revised code was needed, and a commission had been appointed to accomplish that revision. Several versions of the revised code were circulated and discussed by bishops and canonists. By early 1981, the proposed canons pertaining to Catholic higher education circulated among the members of the Bishops-Presidents Committee on Catholic Higher Education, the board of directors of the Association of Catholic Colleges and Universities, and the International Federation of Catholic Universities. All these groups found the proposed canons wanting and foresaw serious problems if they were to find their way into the revised code. I agreed with this assessment and voiced my concern in a letter dated July 24, 1981, to all the American bishops. Much of what you have been reading here was taken directly from that letter.

There were three canons that particularly troubled me. In my letter to the bishops I suggested that all three be dropped from the revised code of canon law that was scheduled to be issued in 1983. Here are the three canons. I have cited them by their original numbers and quoted them verbatim. My comments on each of the proposed canons are verbatim from the letter I wrote to the bishops.

Canon 763: "No university may bear the name 'Catholic university' unless it is conceded by the Apostolic See."

In view of the history of the controversy on what constitutes a Catholic university since 1963, university people may be excused for being touchy and gun-shy of a simple law like this. One can think of strict ways of interpreting that canon so that it does not seem to apply to us. One can suggest an alternative version that is less open to misinterpretation. But as a veteran of many years of controversy on this precise subject, with scars to prove it, I would simply say, why open up an old wound, now healed? A problem does not now exist, thanks to years of fair discussion and serious decision. My suggestion for proposed Canon 763 is simple and direct: drop it, and let well enough alone as regards this troublesome controversy now laid to rest.

Canon 765, part 2: "The respective conferences of bishops and diocesan bishops have the right and duty to exercise vigilance that the principles of Catholic doctrine be faithfully observed in these universities; and likewise to require that teachers be removed from office if reasons of faith and morals demand."

This is such a broad invitation to interfere in the internal academic administration of the university, with no reference to all of the cautionary conditions elaborated with such care at the second Rome meeting, that further commentary is not needed if university autonomy means anything. Again, several emendations have been suggested, but the history in this matter makes one wary. Current practice in American academia makes a bald statement like Canon 765, part 2, simply unacceptable, unworkable, and destructive of local custom and law. If forced into this unqualified corner, the best Catholic universities would simply refuse or cease to be universities in the accepted American sense of that word. Due process is also at issue.

Canon 767. "In any kind of institute of higher studies those who give theological courses or courses related to theology require canonical mission."

Again, this canon is so broad and so unqualified—what does not relate to theology?—that it completely destroys academic autonomy giving someone (who?) outside the university, possibly outside the country, full control over who teaches and who does not teach in all institutions of higher studies, presumably Catholic.

From a simple consideration of collegiality and subsidiarity, so carefully elaborated in Vatican Council II, it would seem that the author of this proposed canon simply does not understand what has been happening in the Church since the early '60s. While one can understand that "canonical mission" might have been useful in dealing with Adolf Hitler, the fact is that university professors have been teaching for centuries without this "canonical mission." To simply impose this condition on universities, who alone are traditionally and rightly empowered to decide who teaches and who does not teach within them, is to force the best of them to leave the small and embattled group of Catholic universities. Academic freedom has traditionally been clearly defined by true universities: *Lehrfreiheit* and freedom to decide who shall teach and what shall be taught. Catholic universities are not less free or less faithful to Catholic tradition and Catholic faith which they deeply cherish. Again, my simple advice regarding Canon 767 is: drop it.

I closed my letter to the bishops with these two paragraphs:

Everyone remembers Santayana's famous dictum that those who forget history are condemned to repeat its mistakes. I have given this rather lengthy account of the events since 1963 in the hope that those who carefully study what has been accomplished will not attempt to turn the clock back to where it was in 1963—because even then it indicated the wrong time.

I have spent my whole adult life, since age eighteen, in Catholic universities, here and abroad. For the greater part of my life, I have endeavored to create a great Catholic university. Creating a great university, even after 140 years of existence, is not an easy task. Creating a great *Catholic* university, in service to the People of God who are the Church, and the broader society as well, is an infinitely more difficult task. We in America, that I know best, have made great progress. We are presently beset by enormous external problems, mainly financial, which we must solve by ourselves. We must also cope with an all-pervading secularism which has little regard for our serious Catholic commitment. The distant history of Catholic universities is not reassuring as regards survival. However, we are making a mighty comeback and in this our only request at the present time is understanding, fruitful collaboration, and support. Our own bishops have given us all of these in abundance. If they are heard by the Commission on Canon Law, we will continue to move forward.

Over several years between the time the canons were first formulated and the time when they were incorporated into the 1983 revised code of canon law, many others raised their voice in defense of academic freedom. Most of them were in Catholic higher education, but there was support from many quarters, including some in the Church hierarchy, most particularly the American hierarchy. But when the revised code was published, the three educational canons remained little changed. Canon 763, renumbered as Canon 808, now reads: "Even if it really be Catholic, no university may bear the title or name 'Catholic university' without the consent of the competent ecclesiastical authority." In the revision, the words "competent ecclesiastical authority" have been substituted for "Apostolic See."

The main concern of this canon seems to be to prevent the word "Catholic" from being used by institutions that are not Catholic. The present Pope, however, seemed much less concerned about this when he addressed the presidents of Catholic colleges and universities in the United States, partially quoted above. In any event, the canon is not retroactive, so any college or university that called itself Catholic before the revised code was published—that is, before November 27, 1983—is not subject to this provision.

Would those founded after November 27, 1983, request permission to call themselves Catholic if they were so inclined? Probably not.

Canon 765, part 2, which was renumbered as Canon 810, part 2, reads: "The conference of bishops and the diocesan bishops concerned have the duty and right of being vigilant that in these universities the principles of Catholic doctrine be faithfully observed."

When Canon 765, part 2, was published as Canon 810, part 2, the second part of the last sentence was dropped: "and likewise to require that teachers be removed from office if reasons of faith and morals demand." We welcomed the deletion of that statement. It would have constituted a broad invitation to interfere in the internal affairs of a college or university. We are still not happy with this canon, however, as the matter of vigilance is open to wide interpretation.

Canon 767, renumbered in the revised code as Canon 812, emerged as follows: "It is necessary that those who teach theological disciplines in any institute of higher learning have a mandate from the competent ecclesiastical authority."

Canonists and other careful readers of Canon 812 discern several subtle differences between Canon 812 and the proposed earlier version, Canon 767, but the essence changed very little, in my opinion, and I will let stand my original objections to it.

When the theologian Father Charles Curran was dismissed from his teaching post at Catholic University, it was Canon 812 that was invoked. Bear in mind that Catholic University is a canonical university with a pontifical charter (most American Catholic universities have state charters) and therefore comes under considerably more scrutiny from the Vatican than noncanonical universities do. Still, the Curran case, in my opinion, could have been handled much better than it was, allowing Curran to continue to teach, the university and its theology department to maintain their academic integrity, and the Church to save face while continuing to proclaim its authority. The president of the university or the cardinal could have simply said, "We agree that what Father Curran is teaching is in apparent conflict with Catholic doctrine, but even though we disagree with him, we feel that the right of a respected, bona fide theologian to teach according to his own convictions and the right of the university to permit him to do so are more important than strict fidelity to the prevailing orthodoxy." For his part, I am sure that in his graduate teaching and writing Father Curran would be perfectly willing to specify what was his personal opinion in apparent disagreement with current noninfallible Catholic teaching. This was the way Archbishop Weakland handled a situation at Marquette University in which a professor in the theology department expressed some prochoice views with regard to abortion. Weakland stated publicly that what the professor was teaching about abortion was contrary to Catholic doctrine, but said he would not order Marquette to fire him because he considered the academic freedom of the university to be too important.

Catholic universities can run up against the same problem when they invite speakers to their campuses. At Notre Dame we have always maintained an open speakers policy. That means we do not have hard-and-fast criteria for speakers, other than that they have something intelligent to say and can attract an audience. Most particularly, we do not require speakers to agree with what we stand for as a university or as Catholics.

Back in the 1950s Cardinal Stritch invited me to have dinner with him one evening at his mansion in Chicago. "The reason I wanted to see you," he said, "is that I had an inquiry from headquarters about a talk that Abba Eban gave at Notre Dame." Ah yes, I thought. Eban, who was the Foreign Minister of Israel at the time, had spoken against the internationalization of Jerusalem. The Vatican favored internationalizing Jerusalem and obviously had not liked his speech. I remarked to Stritch that I did not think the Vatican would want to see Rome internationalized and that Jerusalem had been the capital of the Holy Land a lot longer than Rome had been the capital of Italy. What's more, I said, under the Israelis, there was more access to holy places than there had been before, when the city was split in two. Then I told him that our open speakers policy went hand in hand with our belief in academic freedom. The cardinal understood perfectly. He had done his duty in communicating the displeasure of the Vatican and I had done mine in communicating the philosophy of the university. We had a nice dinner and the subject never came up again.

The strongest supporters of independent Catholic universities in America are the American Catholic hierarchy. They appreciate what we do and we appreciate what they do. Basically, we have divided the responsibility for providing quality Catholic education. They, along with a lot of dedicated priests, religious brothers, and nuns (mostly nuns) have performed a wonderful job in educating youngsters from the elementary grades through high school. We have done equally well in providing quality education on the university level. The Church hierarchy in the United States does not want to interfere in our work because they understand that we are running a system that has educated hundreds of thousands of Catholics without costing them a cent. The few times when members of the American hierarchy have tried to interfere with us were times when they were told to do so by Rome. Otherwise, I don't think they would have done it. Together, our two educational systems have civilized, Americanized, and Catholicized millions of people in this country. Our combined Catholic educational system is unique and the best in the world.

Where do we stand now vis-à-vis academic freedom? No one can say for sure. To most of us in Catholic higher education, the three educational canons in the 1983 revised code of canon law were a big disappointment. They nullified or seemed to set back the hard work we did to produce the 1972 document on Catholic higher education, and they raised anew an element of distrust and animosity that we had laid to rest years before. Still, the discussion has continued, despite those new canons. There is now in progress something called an Apostolic Constitution about Catholic Higher Education. Several drafts of it have been circulated, and defenders of academic freedom in Catholic higher education have been part of the process. One of them is my successor at Notre Dame, Father Edward Malloy, who was elected to attend all of the meetings in Rome to discuss and amend the original draft of the proposed constitution. Each subsequent version is an improvement, and so we live in hope.

The debate continues, and that alone augurs well for academic freedom in Catholic colleges and universities in this country. I have no doubt that while the discussion may be tiring at times, it does help us better define the great and inspiring task of Catholic education, what it does, and what is needed to do it, and we are better for that. I continue to be optimistic, which is my nature, and I strongly endorse the motto engraved on our highest university award, the Laetare Medal: *Magna est veritas et prevalebit* (Truth is great and it will prevail).

FOURTEEN

THE HOLY FATHER

THE FIRST time I ever saw a Pope was on the last Sunday of November 1937 in Washington Hall at Notre Dame. He was a cardinal at the time, and I was a student, happy to see him because in halting English he declared a school holiday and we had the day off. I never dreamed at the time, of course, that this lean, somber man would one day become the Pope and that I would be in Rome to see him elected. That was Eugenio Cardinal Pacelli, Roman-born, noble in appearance, an intellectual who had been an important diplomat in Germany, an influential insider in the Vatican. He was the "favorite" among those who speculated upon who would become the next Pope. But as a student I certainly knew nothing about "the fast track" within the Church hierarchy.

When Pius XI died, I was studying at the Gregorian, which closed down and stayed closed until a new Pope was elected. That took a couple of weeks because the election could not proceed until all the cardinals of the Church around the world had to come to Rome to vote. We enjoyed a long holiday at the Gregorian.

The afternoon of the election, I was in St. Peter's Square. I can remember the exact spot where I was standing when the white smoke went up after the third ballot. The dean of the College of Cardinals, Cacciadominione, appeared on the balcony and announced, *"Habemus Papam."* (We have a Pope.)

The new Pope was Pacelli, of course, because few, if any, of the others were in his league, or at least that is what everyone thought at the time, including me. As time passed, though, I grew to like him less. During my three years of study at the Gregorian, I saw him quite a lot. He reminded me of someone pictured on a holy card—hands folded, eyes cast down. He was very formal, stiff, unapproachable, sitting ramrod straight in a chair while receiving visitors. Many years later, when Frank Folsom and I would deliver our report as Vatican representatives on the International Atomic Energy Agency, Frank always had to dress in formal attire. Even for a 9 A.M. appointment, Frank would have to don tails and a white tie. Entering the audience room, we had to go through a whole routine, which included genuflecting three times and kissing the ring. When that silly protocol finally passed into oblivion, I was a happier priest.

Frank and I saw Pius XII at least once a year to deliver our report on the IAEA. His closest confidant was the governor of Vatican City, Enrico Galeazzi, a papal count, and protocol called for Frank and me to submit our report to Count Galeazzi before we presented it to the Pope. Count Galeazzi always found something he wanted us to tone down because it might offend the Pope's sensibilities. We would have our meeting with the Pope the next day, but it was always very stiff and formal and boring. I could not help but feel uneasy before him. But to be fair, he was a scholar, a master of many languages, and, in his own way, a very holy man. He also wrote some very interesting documents that advanced the intellectual life of the Church.

Despite my lack of personal feeling for Pius XII, I always managed to get along with him, which is more than I can say for his Secretary of State, Cardinal Domenico Tardini. During one of our visits to the Vatican, Tardini strongly criticized us for socializing with the Russians on the International Atomic Energy Agency. We both explained that the Pope had given us full power, but no instructions, and that we had given ourselves instructions, one of which was charity. We tried to be pleasant and friendly toward everyone. I told Tardini that we did not go to Vienna to fight. We went there to help make peace in the world. Since we were representing the Vatican, we felt we should set an example by being a moral force for peace, which the record would show we had been.

Tardini was unconvinced. "You shouldn't even talk to the Russians," he said. "They hate us and they would kill us if they could." Folsom chimed in and said that he had just been reading St. Matthew that morning. I knew that was a little white lie, but justified for the point Folsom wanted to make. He quoted St. Matthew to Tardini. "The Lord said, 'Love your enemies. Do good to them that hate you.' What do you say about that?" Folsom asked. Tardini just stood up, stamped his feet, and walked out of the room. That was the last time we ever saw him. The following year when we came to Rome, his assistant was the Secretary of State.

I do not think Pius XII was really functioning as Pope during his last few years in office. After he died, there was a rash of articles about the medical treatment he had been receiving. It was really bizarre. His doctor was actually a dentist.

John XXIII was supposed to be an interim Pope, or so many people thought, because of his advanced age when he was elected. He was not expected to live very long or do very much. He certainly fooled everybody. I met him only once. Frank Folsom and I were there, as usual, to deliver our report on the International Atomic Energy Agency. Technically we could have reported to the Secretary of State and been on our way, but if you were a papal ambassador, as both of us were, it was expected that you would see the Pope, too, if he wanted to see you. He usually did. John XXIII, not much of a world traveler, knew little if anything about America, but he enjoyed hearing about it. The first time I

met him I mentioned that I was from Notre Dame, and he wanted
to know if that was the Catholic university in Washington.

There were many charming stories about John XXIII, all of
which are very believable and in keeping with his character. He
told a friend of mine once that he thought up Vatican Council II
while sitting on the edge of his bed pulling up his socks. He was
wondering what he was going to tell the College of Cardinals that
day and he just said to himself, "Oh, I think I'll call a council.
That will get them all talking." I have no doubt that the story is
true because it was told to me by Joe Buckley, the Superior General
of the Marists, who had it straight from John XXIII.

Many people, myself included, believe that the Holy Spirit
worked through John XXIII in extraordinary ways. Vatican Council II was exactly what the Church needed. In my opinion, John
XXIII did more for the Church, the faith, the cause of reform,
and the acceptance of Catholicism than anyone since the Refor-
mation. With the guidance of the Holy Spirit, John launched
Vatican Council II and prevented the Curia, the hierarchy or
bureaucracy which ran the Vatican, from taking it over. That was
not easy or simple, because of accumulated dust. Having lived
about half my life before Vatican II, I much prefer the half that I
have lived since then. John XXIII made the difference.

Of all the Popes, I knew Paul VI the best. Our relationship went
back to the days when he was Pius XII's Secretary of State and I
was just getting into the swing of things as the president of Notre
Dame. I found him to be a very intelligent, saintly, complex
person. Over a period of several years we became friends.

One of the most extended and pleasant times I spent with him
was when I invited him to come to Notre Dame in 1960 to preach
at our baccalaureate Mass and receive an honorary doctorate. For
years we had always had a cardinal give the baccalaureate sermon.
I must admit that I invited the future Pope, who was then known
as Giovanni Battista Cardinal Montini, only after five other cardinals had declined my invitation. It was not a very good year, 1960,
in that we were having trouble, too, finding a commencement
speaker. Five men already had turned us down.

One day, with less than a month to go before graduation, I walked into my office and Helen said, "You just lost another one." That was Albert Meyer, the cardinal archbishop of Chicago. I was stumped for ideas. "Helen, this is getting serious. Where do we go from here? We need a preacher and we need a speaker." Helen had never failed me at anything, and so I turned her loose on half the problem. "Helen, you suggest the speaker and I'll find the preacher."

"OK," she replied, thought for a moment, and then calmly suggested, "Let's ask President Eisenhower to be the speaker."

"How on earth do you expect to get the President of the United States to speak at a commencement on less than a month's notice?"

"Well," she said, "you'll never know if you don't try."

"All right, you're an Eisenhower fan. You write that letter and I'll write to a cardinal I know in Milan."

We sent both letters out, signed by me, on a wing and a prayer, you might say, and promptly got back two acceptances. So, after failing to attract American cardinals and university presidents, we booked the next Pope to give the baccalaureate sermon and the President of the United States to give the commencement address.

A day or two before graduation, Frank Folsom met Montini in New York and flew him out to Notre Dame. Most European cardinals would have turned up in a cassock and sash and beaver hat, but Montini never tried to impress people with his office. When he got off the plane in South Bend, he looked dapper, wearing a soft Borsolino black fedora, a tailored black clerical suit, and Gucci shoes. His one problem was his English. During his ten years in Milan his English had deteriorated. I enlisted the help of a couple of my adopted O'Grady girls, who were trilingual, and they worked on his sermon with him, then clean-typed it for easy reading.

Because few others could converse with Montini in Italian, I spent a great deal of time with him while he was at Notre Dame, mostly on long walks around the campus. He loved the campus and insisted on seeing all of it. At each residence hall he would go into the chapel to say a quick prayer. From the time he spent in each place, I figured him to be a three-Hail-Marys man. The new main library was just a hole in the ground at the time, and I described our plans for a new three-million-volume library. He remarked that there was a great library in Milan, the Ambrosiana. I told him how much we would like to microfilm the Ambrosiana collection and make it available to America through our new library. He promised to try to arrange it. Shortly after, Canon Astrik Gabriel, director of our Medieval Institute, followed through on Montini's offer, and that is how we happen to have the manuscript treasures of the Ambrosiana on microfilm in our library.

We wanted to make sure that Eisenhower and Montini had some time together during their relatively brief stay on campus, and so we arranged a meeting in a room at the Morris Inn when the commencement ceremonies had ended. We presented both our guests with token gifts of appreciation. Ned Joyce had gathered some souvenirs for Ike, small things like Notre Dame caps and buttons and a few joke items like a putter that broke in half as soon as you swung it and a miniature football for his grandson, David.

When the President had thanked us for our gifts, Montini started speaking softly in Italian. He said that he, too, had something for Eisenhower. Then he produced a beautiful blue box and opened it. Inside was a block of marble with a bronze angel holding several severed chains. Montini said the statuette was symbolic of what Eisenhower had done for Europe. At the base of the statue was a scriptural quote in Latin from the Old Testament: *"Et abstulerit vincula de medio eorum,"* which in English is: "He took the chains from their midst." Montini added his own comment: "You freed us and we are deeply grateful."

Ike was very moved by this. For a moment or so, he choked up and could not speak. Finally, he thanked the Pope, and their visit came to an end. Before leaving Notre Dame, Montini presented several gifts to the university. The ones I remember the best were copies of sketches signed by Leonardo da Vinci and some theological talks signed by himself.

Three years later Montini was elected Pope and within a month he sent me an autographed picture of himself. I think he wanted to show his appreciation for the hospitality he had received at Notre Dame. At any rate, Paul VI and I were good friends well before he became Pope and remained so for many years after. On top of that his Secretary of State was Amleto Cardinal Cicognani, who had blessed my chalice when I was ordained. He was the apostolic delegate in Washington at the time.

I took great care never to presume upon my friendship with Paul VI, but I have to admit that our personal relationship certainly made things easier for me. The next time I went to Rome to report on the International Atomic Energy Agency, for example, I felt more comfortable in conveying to the Pope what was on my mind. I told him rather bluntly that I thought it was time that the Vatican engaged in some degree of détente with the Soviet-bloc nations. Not long after that, the Pope sent Augostino Caseroli, later Cardinal Secretary of State, to patch up differences with the Hungarians and the Czechs. Then he had Archbishop Koenig visit those countries, as well as Poland. Incidentally, the bishop who took Koenig around Poland was none other than Karol Wojtyla, who would later become Pope John Paul II.

A permanent ecumenical institute, to which the different branches of Christianity could send representatives to study together and further the cooperation of all religions of the world, was the brainchild of Paul VI. It was in April 1963, during Vatican Council II, that Paul VI asked me to stop off and see him while on my way to a meeting in Paris of the reconstituted International Federation of Catholic Universities, of which I had just been elected president.

At lunch that April day, the Pope told me that he had long dreamt of a time when all branches of Christianity would be united and that he would play a role in the unification. He had tried to conceive of a place where Christian theologians could study and live together as they had been doing in Rome during Vatican Council II. At first he thought of Assisi, because everyone liked St. Francis, but he dismissed the idea of Assisi as too romantic. Geneva, another possibility, was too Protestant; Canterbury was too Anglican; Istanbul and Moscow were too Orthodox.

Then, after a thousand years of separation between the Roman and Greek Orthodox churches, Paul VI met Patriarch Athenagoras in Jerusalem. It was the only possible neutral place for them to meet. They met again in Rome and in Istanbul. But Jerusalem was in his mind now as the appropriate place for what he envisioned as an ecumenical institute.

Paul VI explained that one of the greatest blessings of Vatican Council II was that it had brought him in close contact with many Protestant theologians and clerics whom he grew to like and respect. The experience further nurtured his dream of Christian unity. As the end of the Council drew near, great Protestant theologians like Oscar Cullmann and K. E. Skysdgaard bemoaned the fact that they would probably never have another opportunity like this one to share their thoughts. They all agreed that there ought to be a place where the dialogue could continue.

As a result of his own thoughts and the discussions he had had with others, the Pope decided what he wanted to do. He would build a permanent ecumenical institute, and he would build it in Jerusalem.

When he finished telling me all this, the Pope smiled benignly at me and said, "Now that you're the head of the Federation of Catholic Universities, it would be nice if you could take on the responsibility for this ecumenical institute for me."

"Holy Father, I've been involved in a lot of things in my life, but never with ecumenism. I hardly know anything about it." I went on to explain that my lack of experience might be the least of the problems. The Federation of Catholic Universities was still a very weak organization. However, the more we discussed it, the better I liked it. It occurred to me that the Pope's ecumenical institute might be just the project and sense of purpose that the Federation needed to raise itself from the dead. I promised to introduce the idea to the new council of the Federation at our meeting in Paris that week.

Next, the Pope and I talked about the building for the ecumenical institute. We agreed that it should be something simple. He had an idea for a chapel. I suggested bringing in some Benedictine monks who would be there all the time, creating an atmosphere of prayer. So I was hooked. The Pope knew he had given me a difficult, time-consuming task, and he was always very good at expressing his gratitude.

After lunch Paul VI asked me to join him in his library. There, he produced an official copy of the first document of Vatican Council II on the liturgy. "I've signed one of these for the Vatican Archives and one for my personal archives," he said. "Now I am going to sign the third copy for my favorite Catholic university, Notre Dame." And so he did, and presented it to me.

With that quiet smile of his, he then asked, "You do have a doctorate in theology, *non è vero?*"

"Yes," I responded. "But that was a long time ago and I would hardly consider myself a professional theologian today."

"But if you have a doctorate in theology, you can a wear a ring."

"I wouldn't be caught dead wearing a ring!" I blurted out.

"Will you just listen? You are a priest and I am the Holy Father, so will you listen?"

"*Si, Santo Padre,*" I said sheepishly.

"When I was your age, I was chaplain of all the Italian university students. When I was appointed archbishop of Milan, they gave me my episcopal ring with my seal on one side and FUCI's [Federation of Catholic University Students] on the other side." Then he signaled to his secretary, who handed him a small green leather ring box. He opened it and inside was a beautiful gold ring with a large central emerald surrounded by diamonds. With that same shy smile, he said, "I give you my ring."

Idiot, though honest idiot, that I am, I admired the ring, but knew that I could never wear it without having to explain how I came by it. I explained this to Paul VI as I put the ring back in the box and the box in my jacket pocket. Thanking him as best I could, I said I would give the ring to Notre Dame.

His secretary, Don Pasquale Macchi, who knew me well, gave me his honest opinion when we were alone: *"Pazzo americano."* (Crazy American.) Nevertheless, somehow I felt that the Holy Father understood. Years later, when Paul VI died, Pasquale Macchi sent me the Holy Father's white cassock and skullcap to go with the ring in Notre Dame's museum.

In taking on Paul VI's assignment, one of the first things I had to do was to find a site for the ecumenical institute somewhere in Jerusalem. The apostolic delegate of Jordan and Jerusalem had spent a year and a half on this and had not yet come up with a site. When I began making inquiries, I received a call from my friend Pierre Duprey, a White Father (now a bishop) whose order worked mainly in Africa and who was vacationing in Jerusalem and also had been working on this project.

In Jerusalem, Pierre drove me to several sites that were under consideration, but neither of us liked them. We then drove around Jerusalem all morning, looking here and there at places with which Pierre was familiar, until we came to a remote hilltop ringed with olive and pine trees. On the hill were some old, deserted buildings, the remains of a hospital and a school. Pierre explained that the site had been developed at least a hundred years before by some Austrian Knights of Malta, led by Count Caboga, who was buried there. The site, covering thirty-five acres, was the highest point between Jerusalem and Bethlehem. From the hilltop you could see both Jerusalem, which was about a ten-minute drive to the north, and Bethlehem, about a five-minute drive to the south. The Mediterranean sparkled off in the distance to the west. To the east you could just make out a scattering of Arab villages. The road that Joseph and Mary took to Bethlehem ran along one side of the property. On the other side was a new road between the two cities. We looked at a few other sites, but we knew that this was going to be the place.

The property, known as Tantur, still belonged to the Knights of Malta, but a small group of Salesian Fathers was living on it, harvesting olives and paying their living expenses by selling the olive oil. The buildings had walls many feet thick, but they were in terrible shape. Only the chapel and the crusader gate were worth preserving. We knew if we bought the place we would have to tear down most of it and start over. Pierre and I examined the property very carefully and talked with the Salesian Fathers. When we had checked everything out as best we could, I reported our findings and recommendation to Paul VI, and was amazed that he knew all about the history of Tantur.

In due course, the Vatican purchased the Tantur property from the Knights of Malta and leased it to Notre Dame for fifty years at a dollar a year. And that was only the beginning. To gain a broad consensus among religious leaders on the way the building would look and function, I established an ecumenical advisory committee of thirty representatives of all Christian churches. Consulting with them and attending planning sessions all over the world, I traveled at least a quarter of a million miles on behalf of this one project. It took seven years in all before the ecumenical institute was opened in Jerusalem in 1970. The result, though, was a very fine building. Today you could not reproduce it for twenty million dollars. More important, since 1970, more than two thousand Protestant, Orthodox, Anglican, and Catholic theologians of all ages, both men and women, have lived, studied, and prayed together at the institute. The dream of Pope Paul VI lives on today at Tantur in Jerusalem, working to achieve Christian unity at a place where Christianity began.

Pope Paul VI was constantly presenting me with gifts, either for the university or for myself. I had a chance to reciprocate his generosity when I found that he shared my fascination with space travel. *Ranger* had landed on the moon some years earlier and the Apollo flights were beginning. I called my friend Jim Webb, administrator of NASA, to see if I could pry some pictures loose for the Pope. As a head of state, the Pope should have received pictures anyway, but I learned that NASA had inadvertently omitted him from the complimentary list. Webb swung into action and came up with a beautiful album of still photographs of *Ranger* and a movie of the Apollo launchings and landings. The next time I needed to go to Rome, I let Webb know. He sent his deputy with me and had his Paris representative meet us there for the presentation.

The Pope was delighted, of course, and gave papal medals to the deputy and the Paris representative and gave me a gold medal to take back for Webb. He also did one other thing that has stayed with me all this time. Webb's deputy in Paris was a scientist I knew, Bob Seaman, and at the last moment I found out that his wife and twelve-year-old daughter had come to Rome with him, and so I invited them to accompany us to the Vatican. It was too late to arrange an audience with the Pope, but I gave them a quick tour of some rooms in the Vatican Palace which the public normally does not see. Dressed for the inclement weather, they were bundled up from head to toe in rain gear, complete with plastic babushkas. They waited for us downstairs while we presented the NASA photos and films to the Pope in his library.

When we finished watching the movies and the Pope was getting ready to hand out the medals, I asked his secretary if he could give me a couple of rosaries for Seaman's wife and daughter, who were downstairs. No problem, he said, and handed two rosaries to the Pope for his blessing. As he took them, the Pope asked, "Now who are these for?" When I explained the situation, the Pope said, "Go get them." The secretary excused himself, disappeared for a few minutes, and came back with Seaman's wife and daughter, who, of course, were still in their plastic babushkas and rain gear. He shook their hands, welcomed them in his halting English, and presented each of them with a rosary. The family was Episcopalian, but they were thrilled. After that, whenever I traveled to Rome I would check with Webb for any available space films for the Pope. Invariably when I called the papal secretary and offered the new space films, the Pope would invite me to dinner.

Over the years I spent many a pleasant evening having dinner with Paul VI and watching space movies afterward. My feeling of closeness to him came out occasionally when, if we were talking in French, I would forget protocol and call him *Mon Père,* instead of the proper *Très Saint Père* (Very Holy Father). One day it occurred to me that I was out of line with my familiarity and I apologized profusely. He merely waved me off, saying, "*Mon Père* is just fine."

One private dinner was particularly memorable for me. I had three 16 mm films with me, each of them twenty-eight minutes long. Before the showing, we had a simple meal of meat, potatoes, salad, bread, cheese, and red wine. When we had finished eating, the waiter came back with a big cake. "Wow, that's some cake," I exclaimed. "I've studied and eaten here for three years and never have seen a cake like that." The Pope smiled and replied, "It's for your birthday. Happy birthday." I never suspected that the Pope knew the date of my birthday. I bowed to him and made a big show of cutting the cake. Then the waiter appeared with champagne. About the time I thought the surprise party was over, in came the waiter again, this time with a bottle of I. W. Harper bourbon. The Pope grabbed an empty tumbler and then proceeded to fill it almost to the top with bourbon. He handed it to me and said, "Now we're going to have an American drink."

"Holy Father," I said, "it's easy to see you do not know about bourbon. It is not like wine. If I were to drink this, someone would have to carry me out of here."

He laughed and said, "Put some ice in it."

After celebrating my birthday, we went into another room to watch the movies. One of them showed an astronaut bouncing along on the moon toward the spacecraft to the tune of "Yellow Submarine." The Pope watched the movies with the innocent delight of a little boy. He was enchanted. Afterward his secretary remarked that the only time the Pope thoroughly relaxed was when he was watching those space movies. He was a man who worried easily and people gave him much to worry about, his secretary told me. I am sure he did not have many carefree moments like this.

Pope Paul was also fascinated with books. On one occasion, I brought over all the books in print from the University of Notre Dame Press. The books covered a whole table, and the Pope picked them up, one by one, and read the titles, and fondled them. He was oohing and aahing, as though it was Christmas morning. In return he gave me several very valuable books for Notre Dame, including a reproduction of the *Codex Sinaiticus*, which is the oldest and most beautiful Greek text from the ancient monastery in the Sinai. It was a very faithful copy, right down to the imperfections in the parchment. When I brought it through customs, the U.S. agent looked at it bug-eyed and asked me what it was worth. "It's priceless," I said. There was no duty to pay, though, because it was written in a foreign language.

I saw Paul VI often in those days at the Vatican, either on behalf of the International Atomic Energy Agency or as president of the

International Federation of Catholic Universities or in connection with the Jerusalem Institute. After one of our meetings I brought up a personal matter that was troubling me. It concerned Mark McGrath, a Holy Cross priest and Panamanian bishop who had run afoul of a powerful Vatican bureaucrat, a cardinal who was then head of the Vatican Council's Theological Commission. Mark was a brilliant theologian and had served on the Theological Commission. But at the moment he was in virtual exile in a brand-new diocese in Santiago de Veraguas in the blackwater-fever country of northern Panama. He had twelve priests working for him, but no money. Paul VI knew all this, of course. What he did not know was why Mark had been sent there.

I asked Paul VI if I could bring Mark, a member of our congregation, back to Notre Dame to be dean of the theology department. He had been a dean before at the University of Santiago in Chile and was the founding editor of *Teología y Vida*. I thought he deserved a much more important office than the backcountry of Panama, but only the Pope can change a bishop's appointments.

When I had made my pitch, the Pope just shook his head sadly. "But they say he's too progressive," he said. In the Vatican "progressive" is a dirty word, tantamount to "ultra-liberal" in the United States, perhaps just a shade above being a "Communist."

I asked the Pope who had said that about Mark. He said the cardinals. "You mean this cardinal, don't you?" I asked, naming the man. He did not answer, but he didn't deny it, which meant I was right. As head of the Theological Commission, the cardinal had tried on many occasions to impose his own will on the members of the Theological Commission. Mark's sin was that he did not let Cardinal Ottaviani get away with it. I told this to Paul VI, but he still just sat there and shook his head. Finally I said, "Let me suggest that I send you everything that Bishop McGrath has written in the last five years and you have one of your theologians read it all; I am sure he will report to you that Bishop McGrath is as orthodox as you and I are." Paul VI assented to that.

The next time I was in Rome, the Vatican Secretary of State, Archbishop Angelo Dell'Acqua, called me into his office and said that the Pope's theologian had reviewed Bishop McGrath's writings and had concluded that he was a very fine theologian. The Pope also wanted me to know that he was sorry about what had been said about him. Subsequently, Paul VI, gentleman that he was, invited Mark to come to Rome and receive his apology. Paul VI then said, "You will learn something about the church of the poor in Santiago de Veraguas, but you won't be there forever." Later some other machinations that had given the Pope the wrong idea about Mark came to light. They involved the archbishop of Panama, and subsequently led to his resignation. When the archbishop resigned, Mark McGrath was named the new archbishop of Panama. He has held that assignment ever since, and helped hold things together down there during the brutal dictatorship of Manuel Noriega and afterward.

In 1969, Pope Paul VI and I were reported to have had a "falling-out." I do not think we did, but I do think I know how that story got around. At the time there was a controversy over an article written by Cardinal Suenens of Belgium in which he took a critical view of the way the Vatican Curia operated in attempting to thwart some of the reforms of Vatican II. He was careful not to criticize Pope Paul. My guess is that there were two reasons for that. One, he and Paul were close personal friends, and two, I do not believe he really felt that the Pope always was aware of what his staff in the Curia was up to.

Suenens and I were reasonably well acquainted since he had received an honorary degree from Notre Dame, and he apprised me of what he had said in his article and also sent me a news story on his views carried by the Catholic news service in Europe, Information Catholique. When I read the news story, it was very clear that he was not aiming his criticism at the Pope, but rather at the Curia. "This is going to cook my goose with the Curia," he said, "but I think it is my duty as a cardinal to speak out when I can see that the Church is not going the way it is supposed to in light of what happened at Vatican II."

Not long after that, I myself was interviewed and asked by a New Zealand reporter what I thought of Cardinal Suenens's views as reported in the various articles. At the time I was on an around-the-world trip with Doc Kenna, our provincial. Anyway, in the midst of questions about all kinds of Catholic matters, I was asked my opinion of Cardinal Suenens and his views. I responded candidly that I thought Suenens was a kind of prophet and a very courageous man, because what he was saying was going to make him very unpopular in certain circles. The reporter then wanted to know if I thought Suenens was critical of the Holy Father. I said no, he was critical of the Vatican bureaucracy. Before we got off the ship, the reporter showed me his story. Everything he had written, everything he had quoted me on, was perfectly accurate, and I thought no more about it. I imagined it would probably appear in a Catholic paper in New Zealand, but it went out on the international religious news service and was picked up by most of the Catholic papers in the United States. The little old ladies in tennis shoes and the ultra-right-wingers sent it off to Rome, of course, with nasty letters saying that Hesburgh was picking on the Church again.

A few months after that, I got a call from a very dear friend of mine, Ed Heston, who had been my spiritual director in the seminary and had spent most of his adult life in Rome. He was an archbishop and head of the Vatican press service. For some reason he was passing through on his way to the western United States, and he phoned me to say, "I'm calling you because just before I left Rome I got a call from the number two man in the Vatican State Department and he told me that they had seen a lot of copies of the interview you gave to that New Zealand reporter and that you had gravely offended the Pope by taking Suenens's side against him."

I tried to correct him. "Ed, the report didn't say that. It said very clearly that Suenens was not criticizing the Pope. He was criticizing that body to which you belong, the Curia."

Heston said that the Pope's number two man wanted me to write him a note saying I had been misquoted so that he could show it to the Holy Father. I could not do that because I had not been misquoted, I told him. He urged me to write to Rome and say that I did not mean it or that I had thought it over and that I had probably made a mistake and would not say it again. "Ed," I replied, "if I'm asked that question by a reporter tomorrow morning, I'll say exactly the same thing again, because I mean it."

"They are accusing you of ingratitude," Heston said.

"They've done some nice things for me and I, in turn, have done some nice things for them."

"Well, they think you are disloyal, too."

"They're confusing disloyalty with honesty," I said. "The most loyal thing I can do for the Pope is to be honest with him, as I always have been."

"You're being stubborn," he retorted. "You better get used to being in the doghouse."

"I can take that, but I am not going to retract something that I believe to be the truth." I was being stubborn. Maybe I should have gone directly to the Holy Father. At the time, however, I did not see that alternative. I thought his man was speaking for him. Incidentally, I should also say that there are many highly intelligent and totally dedicated people in the Curia. Pierre Duprey, now a bishop and under secretary of the Secretariat for Christian Unity, is one of the best, and there are many others.

Not long after that flap, Frank Folsom died, and I thought it would be a good time to resign as the Vatican's representative to the International Atomic Energy Agency. Frank and I had worked so closely together for those fifteen years that I could not see myself breaking in a new person. My heart would not have been in it. In resigning, I recommended appointing a European to the job. While I was at it, I also suggested that the Pope needed an international advisory group, not just Italians, and not just men. I got a nice letter back saying the Curia appreciated my long service, but they made no serious attempt to talk me out of resigning.

I then decided to resign as president of the International Federation of Catholic Universities. The Federation now had an office in Paris, a workable constitution, a good-sized budget, and enough dues-paying members. Three terms as president was enough. I proposed Hervé Carrier, a Canadian rector of the Gregorian, as my replacement, and the members of the Federation elected him at their next meeting. That left me with only the Jerusalem Institute and its work on ecumenism. I just could not give that up, even though I was plenty miffed at the disloyalty charge.

Some time later I was in Rome for a meeting, which ended with an audience with the Pope. I went in with the sixty or seventy others in the community and sat down in the back of the room. I was taken unawares when the head usher from the Vatican came up to me and said, "You're supposed to sit up front. You know that."

"No, I don't know that," I replied.

"Well, I'm telling you to sit up front."

With that, he grabbed me and hauled me up to the front row. The Pope came in shortly after that and gave a very gracious talk. When he finished he walked over to me and said, "Where have you been?" I said I had been working.

"But I've heard you've been in Rome," he said, "and you haven't come to see me."

"Holy Father, you are very busy and you know that I would come to see you if I had something to talk to you about, but I don't want to just come in and waste your time."

"Well, I'm telling you that when you are in Rome, you come to see me. I want to see you."

After this conversation I was more convinced than ever that it was only the Curia that was upset by what I had said in that interview, not the Pope. I began to wonder if he even knew about it. Some time later Cardinal Gerald Emmet Carter, the primate of Canada, told me of a somewhat similar incident that had happened to him, which made me fairly certain that Paul VI knew nothing of my interview.

Cardinal Carter had been an auxiliary bishop when he was asked to draft the Canadian Bishops Commission's response to Paul VI's encyclical *Humanae Vitae*, which took a very conservative line on artificial birth control. Basically, the Canadian response was that Catholics ought to read and seriously consider what the Holy Father had to say, but if after reading the encyclical they felt they could not, in conscience, follow it, they should not feel that they were less Christian or that they could not receive the sacraments. That was a far-out position for many bishops outside of Canada.

Carter told me that not long after that he went to Rome to see the Pope on some other business and he was really expecting to be called down on his outspoken article. When he and the pontiff were alone, he decided to broach the subject rather than sit there wondering when the Pope would. "Holy Father, I suppose you were rather upset by that statement on *Humanae Vitae* that I prepared for the Canadian hierarchy."

"No, I was not upset at all," Paul VI responded. "I said what I had to say as Pope and you said what you felt you had to say as pastors to your own people. I take it that you respect me and are not upset by what I had to say as Pope and I respect you and am not upset at what you had to say as pastors to your people."

That may illustrate better than anything else what a truly extraordinary man Pope Paul VI was. Ever since he died in 1978, whenever I'm in Rome I always try to visit St. Peter's to say a prayer at his tomb. He had said that he wanted to see me whenever I was in Rome, and so in a way I am still honoring his wish.

FIFTEEN

FORGIVENESS

About five weeks after Gerald R. Ford became President, he offered conditional clemency to the 113,337 civilians and servicemen who had evaded the draft or had received dishonorable discharges from the armed forces during the Vietnam War. He also appointed a Presidential Clemency Board, of which I was a member, to review and make recommendations to him on all applications for presidential pardons or clemency.

The country was deeply divided at the time over what should be done with the young servicemen who had been in trouble during a time of war and with those who had fled to Canada to avoid the draft. With the country so divided on the issue, it was courageous of the new President to offer clemency or pardons to those who might have been wrongfully convicted or been given punishments that may have been too harsh. It was politically risky, too, because most of those least sympathetic to these young men were members of Ford's own Republican Party. On the other hand, Gerald Ford, personally a man of great goodwill, saw as his

primary task as President the need to put an end to the acrimonious divisions in the United States. He had pardoned former
President Nixon over Watergate and he offered conditional clemency to this nation's draft dodgers and deserters. His purpose, he
said, was to end the ideological conflicts of the past, to pull the
nation together, and to get on with the work ahead of us.

The President's offer of clemency was extended to the known
100,115 fugitives or discharged offenders who had gone "absent
without leave" during wartime, and 13,222 draft offenders, convicted and unconvicted.

The most formidable aspect of the Clemency Board's work was
the sheer quantity of the applications. Of the 21,729 persons who
applied for clemency in response to Ford's offer, 15,468 applied to
the Clemency Board. At the start, the board consisted of only nine
members to review all the cases. Even when the number of
members was doubled to eighteen, the assignment seemed almost
impossible. We had only a year to get it done.

The most efficient way to review all the cases, we decided,
would be to split the Clemency Board into six groups of three,
with each group being as representative as possible of the political
and philosophical spectrum on the board as a whole. Theoretically
this meant that each group of three would have a conservative, a
liberal, and a moderate. In my group, for example, the counselor
for the Air Force was the conservative, a Vietnam paraplegic was
the moderate, and I was the liberal.

In fact, I was considered to be the most liberal of the eighteen
members of the board. That designation came about because
before we could make up the groups of three, we had to assign a
ranking to each of us. The second most liberal person on the
board was another priest, Father Frank Lalley of Boston. At the
other end of the spectrum was General Lew Walt of the Marine
Corps, the commanding general of I Corps in Vietnam.

Walt and I had several interesting exchanges. One of the most
significant, which revealed clearly where we stood, took place right
at the beginning of our meetings. "I'm against amnesty," Walt
declared, "and if one person out of a hundred gets amnesty, I will
think we're doing badly."

"Well, if ninety-nine out of a hundred do *not* get amnesty," I retorted, "I'm going to think we're doing badly, because I'm in the forgiving business and amnesty means forgiving."

"If ninety-nine out of a hundred get clemency, what do you think the American people are going to call this board?" Walt demanded.

"They'll probably call it the Presidential Clemency Board," I said, "which is what we are." I also thought, though I did not say so on this occasion, that if Nixon and Agnew got off for the things they had done, why not these young soldiers and men who had refused to serve? How many of them had done anything as serious as had the former President and former Vice President?

One of the first things I did on the board was to apprise my fellow members of what I had learned as a member of the U.S. Civil Rights Commission. The plain truth was that, in the South at least, black offenders were meted out far harsher penalties than were given to whites who had committed the same offense. I wanted each case folder marked W or B so that we would know if the person was white or black, because that did make a difference in the South. Some members of the board objected strongly, saying, "This is racist." To make my point I let the other members of the board know what I knew about U.S. Judge William Harold Cox of Jackson, Mississippi. He was the same judge I had tangled with when I was on the Civil Rights Commission. On the basis of that experience, I knew that no black who had come before him on a Vietnam-related case could possibly have received a fair trial. Judge Cox had handled a lot of cases of young men who had not registered with their draft boards or showed up to be inducted.

Before we began our job of determining whether amnesty was in order, I urged the others to review ten cases handled by Cox and mark each folder with a W or a B to identify the defendant as either white or black and then compare the sentences. Again some board members opposed this as prejudicial. I promised them that it would not be and that they would soon find out why. When we reviewed the ten folders, they had no trouble discerning the wide discrepancy in the severity of sentences imposed by Cox, strictly along racial lines. For the same kinds of offenses, Cox had sentenced the whites to three months in jail, suspended, and the blacks to four years at hard labor. That shocking discovery made a big impact on the Clemency Board. After that, they automatically granted amnesty to any black who had been sentenced by Cox.

Though the life of the Clemency Board was for one year, we could not realistically work full-time on this alone; most, if not all, of us had other jobs to do. We decided, instead, to devote the better part of that summer to the task, when we could all be in Washington at the same time. This meant that each of the six groups would have to decide a hundred cases per day. With many of them it was not simply a matter of deciding whether or not to grant amnesty. We also had to decide on a full pardon or conditional amnesty and the length and form that alternative service would take, or no clemency at all, and finally whether or not medical treatment should be allowed. Each three-member team tried mightily to agree on each individual case, because if we could not agree, the case had to be reviewed by the entire board— all eighteen members.

Keeping up with the caseload was brutal. In order to dispose of a hundred appeals every day, we had to stay up half the night reading documents, then start the next meeting at eight o'clock the next morning. Many of the files on these cases, especially those involving military courts-martial, were an inch or two thick.

By the time our demanding summer session was over, we had worked our way through all 15,468 cases, which I thought was a spectacular feat. We gave outright pardons to 4,620 military deserters and 1,432 draft evaders. We pardoned another 7,252 deserters and 299 evaders on the condition that they perform some sort of alternative service. Only 911 applicants received no clemency. Of these, 885 were deserters and 26 were draft evaders.

The trouble was, those 15,468 who had applied to the Clemency Board represented only a small percentage of the total number of cases. There were nearly 100,000 cases in which men had entered the military and then deserted. McGeorge Bundy, who was president of the Ford Foundation, asked me if there was anything he and his staff could do to help. I suggested that the Ford Foundation finance a small task force to research and devise a plan for disposing of the rest of these cases involving deserters and draft dodgers. Mac Bundy came up with $250,000 and I chose the staff director and the research director of the Clemency Board, and the three of us cranked out a program, which was published as a three-volume set of books. The first volume dealt exclusively with what we thought the new President of the United States should do when he took office. At the time we did not know if we were writing the program for Gerald Ford or Jimmy Carter.

When Carter was elected President, I called him up right away and said I had something very important for him to look at. He was at home in Plains, Georgia, resting up after the November election, but he was scheduled to fly to Washington to meet with the congressional leadership the next morning at Blair House. He agreed to see Bundy and me at 7:30 A.M. before his meeting with the congressional leaders. At that hour of the morning I can always use a lift to jolt me into full wakefulness, and I got one when an aide announced us to Carter as "Father Bundy and Mr. Hesburgh."

I reviewed with the new President the first of the three books prepared by the Clemency Board and several large charts which summarized our findings and recommendations, and observed the President nodding his head in agreement.

Our three books and charts undoubtedly influenced Carter's subsequent actions, but a story I told him that morning may have accomplished even more. One good, illustrative, down-to-earth, true story could demonstrate better than any report or chart how some of these young men had been victims of a war they did not start and should not have had to fight. The story I told Jimmy Carter was about a young white farmhand from Georgia. I never knew his name, because the files carried only serial numbers. I'll call him GI Joe.

Joe was having some problems at home, and he probably thought he could solve them by joining the Army and going to Vietnam. He took his eight weeks of basic training and another eight weeks of advanced training. At the end of those sixteen weeks he was sent to Vietnam as a forward observer. Sometime during training or shortly after he started as a forward observer in Vietnam, Joe developed a detached retina in one eye. That is certainly a disabling condition for anyone, and far more so for a soldier who is supposed to pinpoint the location of the enemy for an artillery bombardment.

Joe knew he had a serious problem with his vision, and so the first time he qualified for twenty-four hours of R and R, he reported to the medical section. Instead of getting treatment, he got the bureaucratic run-around. The desk sergeant told him he would have to wait two weeks to get a doctor's appointment. Joe told him he could not wait that long, because he had to be back at the front in twenty-four hours. With his eyesight impaired, there was a very real possibility he could misjudge the enemy fire or make an error that would direct fire on his own troops. Joe explained that. The sergeant's answer was: "Tell your troubles to the chaplain."

Instead, Joe walked to the airstrip, boarded a helicopter with a group of departing GIs, and flew to Saigon. No one challenged him. No one stopped him from boarding a plane in Saigon and flying to Travis Air Force Base near San Francisco. At Travis, however, they asked for his orders. He did not have any. So they nailed him for desertion; even worse, abandoning a combat zone. He was court-martialed, given a dishonorable discharge, and sentenced to nine months at hard labor.

That was not the end of Joe's troubles. In the brig he had to sleep on a mattress so thin that he developed a chronic back problem. When a doctor finally got around to looking at his eye, he discovered that Joe's retina was practically gone. They had to operate. Then they botched the operation. Meanwhile, his other eye began to deteriorate.

After serving nine months in the brig, Joe went back to Georgia and got married. But now he could not get a job because he had been dishonorably discharged and was practically blind. Not only that, but the government cut off his medical benefits, even though there was no question that his eye problems were a direct result of his military service. He could not afford to buy a pair of glasses. Then his wife became pregnant. So there he was back in Georgia having volunteered and served in combat in Vietnam—unemployed, practically blind, and about to be a father. I told Carter that this young man was not the primary cause of the problems he was having; the government was. Carter nodded his head in agreement and asked what he could do. I handed him the book and said, "It's all in here."

I had met Jimmy Carter in 1976 when he was campaigning for the presidency and I was, according to him, of some help. Actually, we met on the telephone. It was a Sunday night after I had returned from an extensive trip to Latin America and I was in my office catching up on some work. At about nine-thirty the phone rang, and when I picked it up, a man with a Southern drawl said, "I'd like to speak to Father Hesburgh."

"You're talking to him. Who's this?"

"This is Jimmy Carter," he drawled. "I'm talking to you from my kitchen in Plains, Georgia, and I'm calling you because I need some help."

"Why do you need help?"

"I think I'm in trouble with the Catholics."

I realized the trouble he was talking about because he had recently come out against a constitutional amendment on abortion. But before getting into that, I complimented him on his acceptance speech at the Democratic convention and said I thought he was right about what America needed. But, I said, I made myself an inviolate rule never to endorse anyone for any political office. Nevertheless, I felt free to advise him that his trouble with Catholics was of his own making.

From a purely political standpoint, I told him, he never should have declared himself on the abortion issue because the President has no control over constitutional amendments. For a constitutional amendment to be adopted, it must first get a two-thirds vote in Congress, then be ratified by three fourths of the states. The President is not part of the process. I advised Carter not to put himself in the middle of that debate when there was no reason for him to be there. He thanked me and said I had helped him already. Then he gave me a telephone number that rang in the kitchen of his home in Plains, saying I could call that number any

Sunday night whenever I wanted to give him any more advice. Anything I wanted to send him, he said, should be sent to Rosalynn's mother at an address he gave me. That would prevent it from getting confused with the mass of stuff that was addressed to him at home.

I also passed on a message I had been given by General Torrijos, the strong man running Panama, who wanted the next President, whether it was Carter or Ford, to know of the need for a Panama treaty giving control of the canal to that country in order to avoid civil war and bloodshed. I talked with Carter from time to time during the campaign and after the election, and he asked me and some others to prepare lists of people we would recommend for positions in his administration if he was elected.

About a week after I talked with Carter about the amnesty problem, I was in New York on some other business and decided to check my list of potential candidates for positions in the Carter administration with Cyrus Vance, a former Secretary of the Army who was then chairman of the Rockefeller Foundation. He was at the top of my list, and in time he became Carter's Secretary of State (and I succeeded him as chairman of the Rockefeller Foundation). About fifty of the hundred men and women I recommended were selected for positions in the Carter administration.

After sounding out Vance about the future, I told him the story about the young Southerner whom the Army had treated so badly. "That's really awful," he commented. "We've got to do something about it." As it happened, the next person on Vance's schedule was an ophthalmologist who headed a famous eye clinic at the Baylor School of Medicine. After I returned to Notre Dame, I received a call from Vance. He said he had told the story of my GI Joe to the Baylor doctor, and the ophthalmologist had been so moved that he offered to treat the young man free of charge. Vance gave me the doctor's number in Houston and told me to get him the name of the Georgia veteran and the rest would be taken care of.

Finding Joe's name and identity in the mass of material was not all that simple. I phoned Larry Baskir and Bill Strauss, who had been our two right hands on the Clemency Board. They remembered Joe's case vividly because I had raised quite a ruckus when it was referred to the whole board and clemency was denied. Larry and Bill did not hold much hope that the file could be found. They thought it was probably buried in one of those thousands of boxes at the National Archives, with no way of telling which one it was in.

"Unless you've got a copy of the file among your own papers," they said, "there's no way you're ever going to find it."

"Pray, then, that it's in with the stuff I took with me." The next call I made was to the Civil Rights Center at Notre Dame, where I had put all my amnesty files. Describing the case in detail to a librarian there, I asked him to look for my notes at the top of the file, which would be handwritten in red ink. "It will say 'complete amnesty, plus medical benefits,'" I told him, "and it'll probably include some nasty remarks." I said that I thought the file number would be somewhere between 213 and 230. That was just a wild guess.

About fifteen minutes later the librarian called me back. "You weren't far off," he said. "His file number was 219."

Everything I needed to know about Joe was in the file, including the most important thing of all, his Army serial number. I called it in immediately to Cy Vance. As a former Secretary of the Army, he had a lot of clout at the Pentagon and would have no trouble getting that number matched to the name of the soldier. Vance called the doctor at Baylor with the former soldier's name and address. The doctor said he would take care of the young man as soon as he could. A couple of months later I received a letter from the young man saying that the Baylor doctor had restored his eyesight and he would be able to get a job and, with some luck, amnesty. A day after he took office in January 1977, Carter issued a presidential proclamation granting "full, complete, and unconditional pardon" to draft evaders of the Vietnam era. That was the civilian portion of our program. Carter turned the military part of the program over to the military, which, by the way, handled it very well. Everything seemed to be going smoothly until Congress jumped in and said all those remaining cases had to be decided individually, which was exactly what we had been trying to avoid.

It was estimated that 500,000 servicemen went AWOL during

the Vietnam War, and another 175,000 received undesirable discharges. These statistics inspired a further grant of $225,000 from the Ford Foundation to Notre Dame to study the problems of those who evaded the draft or deserted, as well as veterans who served out their tours of duty. In view of the result, this has to rank high among the many wonderful initiatives of the Ford Foundation. They also gave our Civil Rights Center another large grant to facilitate our work.

In 1979, President Carter appointed me chairman of the Select Commission on Immigration and Refugee Policy, replacing Governor Reubin Askew of Florida. It was a select commission indeed, with four public members chosen by the President; four U.S. senators, two from each party, came from the Senate Judiciary Committee, including the chairman, Senator Ted Kennedy; and four congressmen, two from each party, from the House Judiciary Committee, including its chairman, Representative Peter Rodino, of New Jersey. Also serving on this commission were Secretary of State Cyrus Vance, Secretary of Labor Ray Marshall, Secretary of Health and Human Services Patricia Roberts Harris, and Attorney General Benjamin Civiletti.

Equally formidable was the assignment of this commission: to devise a national policy that would with fairness control the millions of illegal aliens who were crossing our borders every year and playing havoc with the labor supply and economics of the country. What made this task doubly difficult, if not near impossible, was that the various economic and political segments in our own pluralistic society had diametrically divergent views on the subject.

Immigration policy had never been one of the bright spots in our democracy, at least not after 1880. The amazing thing I learned when I joined this commission, which came to be known as the Hesburgh Commission, was that it was only the second such commission on immigration in the nation's history. In other words, the United States did not ever have much of an effective national policy on immigration. Until the 1880s this country had no immigration law at all. But after Leland Stanford had imported hundreds of thousands of cheap "coolie" laborers from China to build his railroad out West, people in the United States were

Father Hesburgh and his right-hand man, Father Edmund P. Joyce, C.S.C., executive vice president of Notre Dame, are honored at a 1977 dinner observing their twenty-fifth anniversary in office. (Bruce Harlan)

A frequent flier before the airlines had programs for them, the author is pictured arriving at Michiana Regional Airport in South Bend in the 1980s. (Bruce Harlan)

Father Hesburgh in cold-weather gear while visiting the South Pole in 1963 as chairman of the National Science Board's International Science Activities Committee.

President Dwight D. Eisenhower hands out appointments to the charter members of the U.S. Commission on Civil Rights in 1958. Father Hesburgh served on the commission until 1972, the last three years as chairman. (Associated Press)

President John F. Kennedy receiving Notre Dame's highest honor, the Laetare Medal, from Father Hesburgh at the White House in November 1961. (Associated Press)

President Lyndon Johnson congratulates Father Hesburgh after presenting him with the Presidential Freedom Medal in a White House ceremony on September 14, 1964. (AP/Wide World Photos)

President Jimmy Carter meeting with Father Hesburgh prior to the 1979 UN Conference on Science and Technology for Development, to which he was U.S. ambassador—the first time in history a priest held that formal diplomatic status. (White House photograph)

Reporting to Pope Pius XII in the Vatican
in 1957 with Frank Folsom, fellow Holy
See delegate to the International Atomic
Energy Agency. (Vatican photograph)

Pope Paul VI giving Father Hesburgh a facsimile of the *Codex
Sinaiticus*, a rare Greek version of the Scriptures housed in
the Vatican Library. (Vatican photograph)

Father Hesburgh and Folsom again reporting on the annual meeting of the International Atomic Energy Agency to the Pope—this time Pope John XXIII. (Vatican photograph)

Meeting Pope John Paul II in the mid-1980s during the annual meeting in the Vatican of the Pontifical Council on Culture. Cardinal Paul Poupard, head of the Secretariat for Non-Believers, is in the background. (Vatican photograph)

Father Hesburgh with some of his academic hoods on the occasion of being cited in the *Guinness Book of World Records* as having received more honorary degrees (90 at the time of this 1983 photograph) than any other person. Through the 1990 commencement season, Father Hesburgh's total of 121 honorary degrees retains the Guinness record. (Bruce Harlan)

Before the east door of Sacred Heart Church with its famous inscription GOD, COUNTRY, NOTRE DAME, honoring alumni who died in World War I. (Bruce Harlan)

A Hemingwayesque photograph of the author taken by a fellow fisherman on one of the many lakes dotting Notre Dame's remote conference center near Land O'Lakes, Wisconsin.

alerted to what was euphemistically called "the Yellow Peril," and they tried to have the coolies shipped back to China. Severe limitations were enacted against the immigration of Orientals into the United States.

The first official policy-making body to study immigration was the Pendleton Commission, appointed by President Theodore Roosevelt in 1907. That commission studied the problem for three years and issued a thirteen-volume report, which, in essence, said that the human race was divided into inferior and superior races, and that the United States should allow in only superior people like the Northern Europeans and not the inferior ones like the Slavs, Greeks, Turks, Orientals, and blacks. The Pendleton Commission's recommendations became law in 1921 and remained the law of the land until the Communist scare of the 1950s. Then Senator Pat McCarran of Nevada pushed through a new, special immigration law that barred all Communists from entering our land and required all immigrants, whether or not they could read or write our language, to sign an oath of loyalty to the United States. Finally, in 1965, this country got its first immigration law that, at least, attempted to administer immigration without regard to race, color, or national origin. This 1965 law put limits on immigration: Only 20,000 would be allowed in per country, with a total limitation of 230,000 per year.

However, the reality of the situation in 1979 was that no one really knew how many illegal aliens reached this country each year and how many permanent residents here were actually illegal aliens. While the law said we could admit a total of 230,000 each year, somewhere between 800,000 and 900,000 were being allowed in as political refugees and anywhere up to 2 million more were coming in illegally each year. Not all of them were staying, of course; most of them were illegal migrant farm workers crossing the border from Mexico and points south, working on our farms in the South, and then returning home. But then there were hundreds of thousands who came here as visitors and then just simply stayed on, undetected. No one really knew their numbers or where they were all coming from. But the fact was that we had between 6 and 12 million illegal aliens living in the United States.

All of which meant, in short, that immigration into the United States, legal or not, was massively out of control.

Regaining control of immigration was an enormously complex and complicated problem. Our fundamental presumption was that all these people were flocking into the United States to find a better life than the one they had in their native countries, just as your grandparents and mine did years ago. They came here for jobs that paid better than did jobs at home and they were willing to work for wages that were considered low here but high in their own homelands. These new workers were needed by employers hiring unskilled and semiskilled labor. Of course, while employers welcomed these low-pay workers, the unions and native workers resented the competition.

Over an eighteen-month period, we held public hearings in twelve major points of entry in the United States, including New York, Boston, New Orleans, Los Angeles, San Francisco, and San Antonio. We heard from hundreds of expert witnesses and read through volumes of reports and surveys. In the end we produced thirteen thick volumes of testimony, findings, and recommendations, just like the Pendleton Commission before us. Our one-volume summary of findings and recommendations was as thick as the New York telephone directory.

In setting policy, the commission came to the conclusion that the best way of dissuading excess immigration was to make it difficult, if not impossible for these people to get jobs here without legal entry papers. In other words, we recommended widening the front door to immigration—allowing 550,000 legal aliens to enter the United States each year, or about double the 230,000 quota—and closing the back door to illegal aliens.

We also recommended making an exception for our close neighbors Canada and Mexico. They would each be allowed 40,000 immigrants each year. That was further amended so that if fewer than 20,000 Canadians chose to make their homes in the United States, the leftover quota could be applied to Mexico. We estimated that would work out to about 79,000 Mexicans allowed to enter this country legally every year.

The price for opening the front door to more people was to

close the back door by prohibiting companies from hiring people without proper working or immigration papers.

In the end, after much debate, hassling, and compromising, the commission made these major recommendations, which we considered moderate, doable, and effective:

We would increase the overall number of aliens permitted to enter this country and work here legally to about 500,000. We would offer amnesty to all illegal aliens who had lived in the United States for five years or more. If they had not been convicted of a felony, they would receive permanent residence and in another five years could apply for U.S. citizenship. No longer would they have to live in fear of deportation, and they could begin to pay taxes without fear of discovery.

In closing the back door, we recommended a law that would require employers to check on the working papers of each of their workers and the employer would be held legally responsible, with penalties of fines and jail if he or she were convicted of knowingly hiring illegal aliens. People might be able to slip into our wide-open borders, but if they could not get jobs without legal papers, it would do them little good to sneak in.

The catch in this was that millions of illegal aliens were working with forged papers, either a phony social security card or a false driver's license. These cards were made of paper and easily duplicated and sold on the black market.

My solution to this dilemma, which I could not persuade the commission to adopt, was to pass a law requiring all American citizens and legal residents to carry an upgraded social security card in the form of a plastic credit card in which was embedded a microchip carrying essential information. The card could be made so that it could not be counterfeited—not easily at least—and that would put an end to most of the illegal hiring of aliens.

That proposal raised the hackles of the American Civil Liberties Union and similar libertarians who argued vociferously that such identity cards were an invasion of privacy and the first step toward a totalitarian state. I could not convince these opponents that all hope of citizen privacy had gone out the window with the advent of computers, computer data banks, and credit-checking organizations. American workers already carried social security cards, registered in Washington, and presented them for identification for a whole host of reasons. An up-to-date, plastic, microchip card would serve the same purpose and would have the advantage of being difficult and expensive to counterfeit. But I lost that argument. The feeling was that our citizens would resent even the idea of carrying identity cards, which are common in Europe. Our position was that the cards need not be carried, would only be used to obtain employment, and could not be demanded or used in any way by the police. We still lost.

We thought our recommendations were moderate, and with the backing of President Carter and the active support of Vice President Mondale, our report would face little trouble in Congress in becoming the law of the land. But Carter lost the election. In the final three days of his administration, our staff, led ably by Larry Fuchs, a former dean of Brandeis University, worked virtually around the clock to complete our report to the President and Congress as mandated in the law which created the commission. We managed to submit our report officially on the last day of the Carter administration in January 1981. But once Ronald Reagan was sworn in, the new Republican administration decided to reinvent the wheel. President Reagan set up his own fact-finding commission and that commission spent another two years going over the same material, the same issues, the same difficulties as we did, and in the end adopted the same recommendations as we had.

A bill setting up this new immigration policy was sponsored by Senator Alan Simpson of Wyoming and Representative Romano L. Mazzoli of Kentucky, a Notre Dame alumnus. It passed the Senate and was defeated in the House in 1982 and in 1983. Hispanic leaders and various liberals thought it discriminated against Latin Americans. Business leaders criticized the proposed penalties against employers who knowingly hired illegal aliens. Some liberals opposed a plan to set up a government hot line so that employers could check on the status of people who applied for work. Some conservatives opposed on principle any form of amnesty for aliens who had violated our laws for five years. Giving them legal status would make a mockery of our laws and the whole concept of U.S. citizenship, the conservatives argued.

So there were elements of our citizenry who opposed one or more aspects of the proposed immigration law, and yet, overall, I think the majority of the American people wanted some practical solution to the chaos at our borders. It took five years in all for the Simpson-Mazzoli bill to become the Immigration Reform and Control Act of 1986 (IRCA). During those five years, I had set up and operated a very small watchdog shadow commission to act as a sort of lobbying group for the recommendations of our original commission. We kept the pressure on Congress, or at least tried to, so that the Simpson-Mazzoli bill would not slip through the cracks and be lost. By and large, the 1986 immigration law did incorporate most, if not all, of our original recommendations.

And what has been the result? To my mind, it is still, in 1990, too early to tell. For the first three years, illegal entry into the United States had slowed perceptibly, but in 1990 there was a resurgence of undocumented immigrants crossing the Mexican border. Forged documents are still being used in great numbers, enabling employers to hire, even knowingly, illegal immigrants. I still like my microchip identity card as a way of curbing illegal working papers. Best of all, though, three million illegal aliens who had lived in the shadows for many years obtained amnesty and may, in time, become American citizens.

Illegal immigration is a big, complex problem; it will not be solved simply. But I do believe that the new immigration law is a giant step in the right direction. As I wrote in my letter of transmittal for the commission report: "We will continue to be a nation which welcomes immigrants, but we must enforce our laws consistently and fairly, even when that means not letting some people in and deporting others."

SIXTEEN

PEACE IN OUR TIME

THE INTERNATIONAL Atomic Energy Agency, the forerunner of all nuclear disarmament talks, was conceived in a splendid, farsighted speech that President Eisenhower delivered at the United Nations on December 8, 1953. In the midst of a scary Cold War, when many feared a nuclear showdown that could annihilate the world as we know it, Eisenhower urged the delegates from all the civilized nations to turn their attention from building bombs and do something about harnessing atomic energy for peaceful uses, such as for power and in medicine and agriculture. He painted a vivid picture of the two great, colossal powers of the world—the Soviet Union and the United States—glaring at one another across an abyss of mutual nuclear destruction, and he urged the UN to do something about it. That speech moved nations to action.

It took three years of negotiations, again a harbinger of nuclear disarmament talks to come, for the nations of the East and the West to hammer out their philosophical and technical differences in writing a charter for this new, independent agency of the United Nations, through which nations could begin talking to one another about how to harness the awesome power of the atom and put it to peaceful purposes. The most divisive issue, a veritable stumbling block, was how distrustful nations on either side of the Iron Curtain could come to trust one another. The United States and most of its allies favored on-site inspections and a system of controls against cheating. The Soviets and their satellites vigorously opposed controls or anything that allowed foreigners to inspect their atomic facilities.

When the issue was coming up for a vote at the UN in 1956, John Foster Dulles, our Secretary of State at the time, thought the vote on inspection and control would be very close, and so he went looking for support. The Vatican was one place he thought he could pick up a favorable vote. Pius XII had earlier declined an invitation to join the charter conference to establish the International Atomic Energy Agency, saying that the Vatican had no one who knew anything about atomic energy. But he agreed with Dulles on the need for such an agency and for inspections and control to assure compliance. He promised to consider the matter. Dulles telephoned Cardinal Spellman of New York and urged him to try to persuade the Pope to send a delegation. The Pope, again saying that he did not have anyone who knew about atomic energy, told Spellman that he would be willing to appoint a couple of representatives if the cardinal would select them for him.

Spellman called me at eight o'clock the following morning. I had just returned from an extended trip to Latin America for the start of the fall term at Notre Dame. The last thing I wanted to do was pack up and fly to New York and argue with Russians for the next several weeks. But I was in a tough spot with Spellman. The year before, I had turned him down on a bowl game he wanted us to play against Maryland in New York for the benefit of an orphanage in his diocese. I was staunchly opposed to postseason bowl games in those days because they were held when our students were supposed to be preparing for semester exams. To soften the blow, I had promised that if he ever had to ask me to do something else for him, I would do it. So he really had me when he called about the International Atomic Energy Agency

Conference. I told him that if it was very important to him for me to represent the Vatican at the conference, I would do it. He said it was. Then he assured me that it would not take that much of my time because even though the conference was scheduled for seven weeks, I would not have to be there the entire time. When he had me pledged, Cardinal Spellman asked me to recommend someone for the other slot. After a moment's thought, I suggested Marston Morse, a world-class mathematician who at that time was teaching half a year at Princeton and half a year at the University of Paris. He possessed valuable scientific skills, spoke French fluently, and could get to the conference in New York very easily from Princeton.

I let Spellman know that if I was going to do this for the Vatican because they had no one who knew about atomic energy, I expected to be able to vote according to my own conscience and my own knowledge of atomic energy. I did not want to get to the conference only to find some Vatican monsignor whispering in my ear every time a vote came up. Spellman said he would pass the word.

In short order I received a cable from the Vatican Secretary of State saying that Marston Morse and I had full power to discuss, approve, and sign any document of the conference in the name of the Vatican without prior instructions. When I presented the cable to the credentials officer at the UN conference, he could not believe what it said. His exact words were: "Nobody has that kind of power."

The first week or two at the conference I took Spellman at his word and spent as little time as possible there. I would attend the first couple of days of meetings, then hurry back to Notre Dame and read the UN papers and documents while catching up with the university work. My seat was empty most of the week and that did not go unnoticed by some of the Catholic UN observers and activists who were closely monitoring the conference. When they confronted me, I told them what Spellman had said. They said Spellman did not fully understand how this kind of conference worked. They proceeded to explain that my absence would lead the other delegates to conclude that I was not interested in what they were trying to do and that as a result I would have no influence at these sessions. I had to admit that they were right. I rearranged my schedule. From then on, for the weeks that the meetings lasted, I spent Monday through Friday at the conference and did my university work on the weekends.

The conference went well, and I made several good friends, some of whom I would work with again on Atoms for Peace. This group included Gus Lindt, the ambassador from Switzerland; a man by the name of Michaels, representing England; Bertrand Goldschmidt, a French scientist who had worked with the Canadians on atomic studies during the war; Homi Bhabha, the head of the Atomic Energy Commission in India; and last, but certainly not least, Vasily Emelyanov from the Soviet Union, who was third or fourth man down in the Soviet pecking order but who was destined for greater things.

I came to know Emelyanov simply because I asked to meet a Russian delegate. Troubled by the high level of animosity that existed between our two countries at the time, I felt I could do a better job as a delegate if I could establish a personal relationship with at least one of the Russians at the conference. Taking the direct approach, I asked Ambassador Munoz from Brazil, who was the president of the conference, if he would introduce me to someone on the Russian delegation. He took out his list of delegates and, going through the names, he eliminated almost everyone on it for one reason or another. One fellow, I remember, he referred to as an NKVD butcher. Finally he got to Emelyanov and he said, "Here's someone who is a lot like you. He's a university professor, a metallurgist, and a corresponding member of the National Academy of Sciences in the Soviet Union." I asked Munoz if he would arrange a meeting.

The next day during our morning break I was introduced to Emelyanov in the Delegates Lounge, and we hit it off immediately. His translator, Andrei Galagan, was indispensable because neither of us spoke the other's language. After that initial meeting, Emelyanov and I saw each other often. Every time there was a cocktail party—and there were a great many of them—we would get together and talk, with Andrei's help. Quite often other

Americans would join in. Wherever a knot of people formed, the photographers would follow. Emelyanov began to notice that whenever a photographer approached, all the Americans would scatter, except me. One day Emelyanov asked me why they ran and I didn't. I told him about our Senator Joe McCarthy and his anti-Communist witch hunt. I explained that the Americans were worried that if a photograph appeared in the *New York Times* showing them talking to a Russian, McCarthy would get up in front of the Senate and accuse them of being Communists. I told him that, unlike them, I did not have to worry about that because I did not work for the State Department or the President: I worked for the Pope in the Vatican. Emelyanov roared with laughter and my candor helped solidify our friendship.

John Foster Dulles turned out to be right about inspection and control being a sticking point at the conference. As the day for voting approached, a number of Third World countries joined the Russians and Eastern European countries in opposing on-site inspections to verify compliance in nuclear arms limitations. India, for one, had only recently broken free of England and was overprotective of its newly acquired sovereignty. The vote was scheduled for a Monday, which was the worst possible day for me. I had to attend a meeting of the National Science Board in Washington that same day. That would pose enough of a problem by itself, but another one arose besides. On the Friday before the Monday scheduled for the vote, Gus Lindt, the Swiss ambassador, took me aside and told me the European delegates had held a meeting and decided that I should deliver the final talk before the vote on the charter article regarding inspection and control. I was truly surprised because I had been keeping a low profile at these sessions, listening and learning, instead of talking. "We're counting on you to lift the discussion to a philosophical and theological plane. You write a good talk and give it just before the vote, and maybe it will help us win."

We agreed that he would telephone me at my National Science Board meeting in Washington on Monday if it appeared that my vote and my talk would be needed. Sure enough, around noon on Monday I got a call telling me that the UN vote would be taken in the late afternoon and that it looked like it was going to be a squeaker. I excused myself from the meeting, grabbed a cab to National Airport, and jumped on the shuttle up to New York. I was confident that I would make it on time. But that was before we lost an engine. The captain came on and told us we would have to turn back. We were put on another plane, but the delay consumed at least an hour, and now I did not have a second to lose.

Fortunately, I had sketched out a talk in longhand on the flight from South Bend to Washington that morning. I was not quite satisfied with it, but I just did not have the time to give it what it deserved. As I was pondering all this, I glanced at my seatmate, who turned out to be, of all people, Harold Stassen, the U.S. representative for disarmament. If you doubt the existence of God, think about that one for a while. Once we were airborne, I read my talk to Stassen and he was kind enough to offer several helpful suggestions. He showed me where I could strengthen the talk so that my argument for inspection and control would come through loud and clear to the Russians.

By the time we arrived at La Guardia Airport, I had my talk in good shape, but I was afraid I would not reach the UN in time to deliver it before the vote was called. I jumped in a cab, and the driver believed I was in a big hurry and roared off toward Manhattan. At the UN I ran right past the guards without even flashing my ID. Fortunately, they recognized me. When I plopped into my chair in the assembly hall, I was completely out of breath. And I was still puffing when a voice came over the public-address system announcing "the delegate for the Vatican."

Still breathing hard, I began my speech. I told the delegates that while no one likes controls from a political standpoint, they are something we have to live with in an age when nuclear annihilation is an ever-present danger. As a homily on the need for controls in all phases of life, I told this august UN body to consider the delegate who wanted to go from the thirty-sixth floor of the UN to the first floor as quickly as possible. The quickest way to get there, I said, was to step out the window. But if he wanted to make sure he would be able to do business after he arrived, the delegate would do better to take an elevator, a controlled but much safer way of reaching his destination. I made a lot of other obvious points in that talk, using anecdotes, and it seemed to go over well. When the vote was taken, our side won, and by a fairly substantial margin at that. I certainly would not give all the credit to my speech, but if it had anything to do with winning approval for inspection and control, that's good enough for me.

Having done my part in bringing it about, I was shocked when I was stopped from signing the treaty establishing the charter for the International Atomic Energy Agency. Once again a UN credentials officer challenged my right to sign for the Vatican. "Where is your authorization to sign this treaty?" he demanded. I showed him the cable from the Vatican Secretary of State and pointed to where it said I was empowered to act in behalf of the Vatican. "No, no, no," he cried. "You can't possibly have a blank check like that. You have to get a special cable from the Vatican saying that you are specifically authorized to sign the treaty for them."

When I told Spellman about this, he could not believe it. "Your authorization is crystal clear. I ought to know, because I wrote it myself—'full authority to discuss, approve, and sign any text without prior instruction.' " But rather than quibble about it, Spellman cabled the Vatican and I received special authorization. I signed the treaty, shook hands all around, and went home to Notre Dame.

I was pleased with the way things had turned out and happy to be done with it. Except I wasn't. A little while afterward Cardinal Spellman called again. The Vatican wanted me to be its permanent delegate to the International Atomic Energy Agency and to represent the Vatican at an upcoming general conference in Vienna. Once again Spellman promised me it would be no big deal. I would only have to show up in Vienna for a couple of weeks once a year. Little did he know. Little did I know. Spellman was a very persuasive man. He pointed out that the International Atomic Energy Agency would be dealing with important moral issues and that he thought it vital that I follow through with my work because I knew the ropes now better than anyone in the Vatican. I accepted the assignment. Marston Morse opted out, however, because he could not spare the time. As his replacement, I suggested Frank Folsom, the recently retired president of the Radio Corporation of America. Spellman and I both knew Frank very well and were delighted when he accepted.

When Folsom and I reached Vienna, our first problem was a familiar one. Yes, we were confronted by another ubiquitous credentials checker, who declared that we could not both be delegates. One of us had to be the delgate and the other had to be the alternate. That was Saturday. The meeting was to start on Monday. I thought the easiest way to get the problem straightened out would be to go see the apostolic delegate in Vienna, Archbishop Dellepiane. We reached him on Sunday and explained our problem. He said he would not dare call the Vatican Secretary of State on Sunday. It just was not done. I reminded him that the world did not stop just because it was Sunday and that this conference would open the next day. Nothing less than world peace was at stake, I insisted. The Vatican would want us to be there, and for that we needed proper credentials.

Dellepiane became annoyed with me for pushing him, but he consented to make the call. The Secretary of State, the future Cardinal Tardini, apparently was not impressed with my view of the gravity of the matter. He told Dellepiane to write out our credentials himself. The apostolic delegate, now just wanting to get rid of me, asked what I wanted him to type for the authorization. I told him to put Frank down as the delegate and me down as the alternate. That further annoyed him. "That isn't the way it is done by the Holy See," he said. "It is always the cleric first, the layman second."

"I know," I replied, "but we are writing history here. This time you have to put the layman first because we are dealing with a lay organization and it will sit much better with them." After some bickering I convinced Dellepiane to do it my way. When he had finished I said, "Now put your official seal on it and a couple of red ribbons to make it look nice."

Early Monday morning Frank and I presented our ribbon-festooned authorization to the credentials officer. He was suitably impressed, as I thought he would be. As I had said to Dellepiane, only half facetiously, we had, indeed, made history. The Vatican did have a long tradition of putting clerics first and laypersons second. This was one of the first times, if not the first, that a layperson had ever represented the Vatican in an international conference. That pleased me inordinately. It represented a kind of validation of the doctoral dissertation I had written so many years before on the role of the lay apostolate in Church affairs.

Once we got the credentials business straightened out, we had to set up shop, so to speak. I had already negotiated the loan of a new car from Studebaker, which was headquartered in South Bend. Next we needed a driver, a secretary, and a place to stay. We hired a Viennese teenager by the name of Rudi Klein as our driver and a young Viennese girl of Czech descent, Lisa Nechutney, as our secretary. We booked our rooms at the Sacher, probably Vienna's best-known hotel. Unlikely as it may seem, that was our complete setup for the fifteen years that Frank Folsom and I represented the Vatican on the International Atomic Energy Agency. Rudi drove, Lisa typed, and the Sacher provided a home away from home for Frank and me. Every September Frank, Rudi, Lisa, and I were a familiar foursome around Vienna. We went everywhere together—to dinner, to the opera, out to Grinzing for the wine tasting. Every headwaiter in town recognized us on sight. When there was work to be done, we functioned as a team. Otherwise, we behaved more like a family. Frank and I became very devoted to Lisa and Rudi, and they to us.

When Frank and I moved on to other things, so did they. Lisa went on to supervise a department of sixty staff people for the International Atomic Energy Agency. Rudi got married, had a son, and established a very successful travel agency. But he still to this day meets me at the airport when I come to Vienna, or if he can't make it, he sends his son.

Looking back on those years, I think the agency has made some very important strides on behalf of humanity. We helped many Third World countries make use of radioisotopes in agriculture, in medicine, and in other ways that improved their standards of living. As the technology spread, the issue of nuclear proliferation arose. Any country that could build a reactor could also build a bomb. That unhappy fact gave rise to the need to stop countries that had the capability from building nuclear warheads. The International Atomic Energy Agency laid the groundwork for the landmark Nuclear Proliferation Treaty that we eventually produced and more than one hundred nations signed. South Africa and Israel were two countries that did not sign, thereby fueling suspicion that they already had the bomb.

In the course of those fifteen Septembers in Vienna, Folsom and I became extremely close to Emelyanov, my old Russian pal from the agency's earliest beginnings at the UN in New York. He now had the title Glavatom for the U.S.S.R., which in Russian means atom chief. To cite just one example of the familiarity that developed, Folsom started something he called the International Grandfathers Club. He named himself president and appointed Emelyanov as his vice president. They had a lot of fun with that running gag. Folsom had more than twenty grandchildren. Emelyanov, as I recall, had only one or two.

In the midst of the Cold War, Emelyanov was not afraid to let it be known, even to his Russian colleagues, that Frank and I were his friends. At a University of Vienna meeting of agency delegates connected with universities, Emelyanov got up and declared that the Vatican delegation was the only one he really trusted. He said that we always told the truth, we were always ready to work for peace, and we were always friendly and courteous. That was a very courageous statement for Emelyanov to make during the Cold War, because there were several other Russians in the room and everyone there knew the Vatican delegates came from the United States. The room was still abuzz when he sat down. The three of us also had a lot of fun together at those interminable cocktail parties that went with any kind of international agency. There was at least one cocktail party every night during the session, and sometimes as many as three or four, all held in the resplendent foreign embassies with their crystal chandeliers, marble floors, and plush furnishings. It was one part of the job that few people complained about.

One of the most tense moments in all those fifteen years came during a round of speeches in the Hofburg Palace by the delegates of all the major countries in 1958. Just before Emelyanov was scheduled to speak, a dumb, boorish American got up and announced—bragged, really—that the United States had just given two mobile radioisotope units to the agency. They were parked right outside, he declared, but they were going to be taken away pretty soon and anyone who wanted to see them had better do so right away. He might as well have yelled "fire!" A stampede ensued, and by the time the hall was quiet again and Emelyanov began speaking, the place was half empty. He was truly irked by that, and he really took off in denouncing the United States for everything imaginable, including original sin. Unfortunately, among those in the room at the time was John McCone, a good friend of mine, who was attending the conference as the head of the U.S. Atomic Energy Commission.

By the time Emelyanov finished speaking, McCone was plenty irked himself. In fact, he was boiling. Such insults apparently were new to him. He had not had much experience with international conferences, where it was commonplace to denounce your adversaries during the day and socialize with them at night. When the speeches were over, I walked down the palace steps with McCone. He told me that he was ordering the American delegation not to attend the party the Russians were giving that night and that he would ask the French and the British delegation to stay away. I told him he was wrong to do that. It was important, I said, not to let a little petulance shut down the lines of communication between the major nuclear powers. I told him I would have more to say about it later, but for the present I fully intended to go to the Russian party. He gave me a curious look and said, "Well, I guess I have no control over you."

The Russian party was a bust. McCone had obviously prevailed on our allies; not one of them was there. The Russians were embarrassed. All of this struck me as the sort of thing that made other countries think of the United States as overbearing. We had precipitated the crisis. The implication was: Do what we tell you or you won't get your allowance. As I was going through the receiving line, Emelyanov asked to talk to me privately. He escorted me up to the second floor and we walked past tables groaning under the weight of the caviar, delicacies, and vodka that the Russians had flown in for the occasion. Only a relative handful of people were there to enjoy it all. In a far corner of the room, Emelyanov finally spoke. "It's a very sad party, isn't it?"

"Well, you asked for it," I retorted.

That seemed to surprise him. "My people told me it was a very good speech," he said.

"Your people *have* to tell you that because they work for you. But I am your friend and I am telling you it was a very bad speech." Then I gave him a little lecture about how the Americans were to blame for some things, but not everything, as he had charged, and that hurling insults and exaggerations served only to defeat the very purpose that we were all striving for at these meetings. I went on to say, a bit dramatically, I confess, that the same kind of stupid little incident that had given rise to his vituperative speech against the United States could just as easily start a nuclear war, given the climate of suspicion that already existed and the escalation of bad feelings that his speech had caused. I even went further. I told him that a continuation of this verbal abuse could cause a lot of people to end up vaporized, including his grandson.

Emelyanov knew that I personally liked him and would not mislead him. "OK," he sighed, "you tell me what to do and I'll do it." I advised him to sit down with McCone before the conference ended and put the incident to rest, or the bad feelings would continue to rankle until the next conference, which was a full year away.

The next day I related to McCone what I had said to Emelyanov. "I don't want to talk to him," McCone declared. I told him he *had* to talk to Emelyanov. If he refused, the two of them could just as well resign from the agency, I said, because they could not possibly do the cause of world peace any good if they did not talk to each other. "All right," McCone said. "If you think I ought to do it, I'll do it."

I caught up with Emelyanov at a cocktail party that night and whispered in his ear, "It's all arranged." He wanted to hear more, but privately, and he led me over to a big pair of double casement windows, opened them up, and leaned out. Bending out of these big windows as though we were talking to the statue of the man on horseback below, I engaged in what was probably my first try at secret diplomacy. Because they obviously could not meet at either embassy, Folsom and I set up the private meeting in the parlor of our suite at the Sacher Hotel. Frank had Room 52 and I had 54. The parlor, Room 53, was between them. I told him that McCone would bring a young woman from the American embassy to handle the translation chores for him. Emelyanov said he would bring a fellow whom I knew to be a hard-liner and a very tough character. "No way you're going with him," I said, "and you know why." I advised him to find someone with a more balanced outlook, and suggested an Armenian who was too young to be involved in any intrigues or to try to insert his opinions. We set the time of the meeting for 9 A.M., because we had our annual delegates' Mass scheduled for eleven at the Cathedral of St. Stephen and McCone was leaving for Washington that afternoon.

I phoned McCone later that evening. "It's all set," I said. "Nine A.M., Room 53, Sacher Hotel." Once again he reminded me that he was going along with this reluctantly—only because I wanted him to. Considering the alternative, no meeting at all, that was good enough for me.

There were no kept secrets in Vienna. Before the day was over, all the delegates knew that there would be a private meeting between McCone and Emelyanov, the chairmen of the U.S. and U.S.S.R. delegations, and that the Vatican delegates were behind it. Lisa called me up at 8 A.M. and said she was so worried about the meeting and the Mass that she couldn't keep her breakfast down. I said, "Lisa, if it makes you feel any better, I've been having the same trouble."

Shortly before nine I went into our parlor to wait for Emelyanov and McCone to arrive. The parlor was typically Viennese, lots of white and gold woodwork and red velour on the walls. All of a sudden there was a loud bang, bang, bang on the door. It was

McCone with his translator. Two minutes later another bang, bang, bang, and in walked Emelyanov with the young Armenian. The two men glared at each other like a couple of bellicose bulldogs. In order to break the tension, I motioned them over to a corner of the room where a red Viennese screen was standing.

"Gentlemen, I have something behind this screen that you might find interesting." They both approached cautiously, as though they suspected a booby trap, but it was only the little table I used as an altar to say Mass. It was covered with a cloth called an antimensium, which had Russian writing all over it, and some small relics embedded in wax. I explained that an antimensium, or a kind of portable altar in the form of a cloth, had been developed during World War II as a safety measure for the paratrooper chaplains. It had replaced the conventional altar stones because the latter were whacking too many chaplains in the head during jumps.

Saying I did not know much Russian, I asked Emelyanov to translate the characters on the cloth for me. Both he and McCone bent over the cloth with their heads almost touching and Emelyanov began to examine the old Russian script. He started to read. "Matthew, Mark, Luke, and John. Right?" I said right. He continued: "In the name of the Father and the Son and the Holy Spirit. Right?" I said right again. And finally: "This is the crucifixion and these are Mary, John, and Jesus and this antimensium was consecrated for Father Hesburgh by Bishop Elko. Right?" He had it all right because he could read the old Russian, which he said he had studied as a boy. I knew he was right, not because I could read old Russian, but because the cloth belonged to me and I had had it deciphered a long time ago. "Aren't you surprised," I said to Emelyanov, "that I say Mass every day over a Russian cloth?" With that, they both grinned, and I knew there was a chance that their meeting would be a success.

I assured them of their privacy. The doors at either end of the parlor led to the bedrooms, mine and Folsom's, and they would be locked as I left. The telephone would be taken off the hook so they would not be bothered by calls, and there were pads, pencils, and pitchers of water on the table. As I started to leave, McCone said, "Father Ted, I'll see you at Mass at eleven o'clock."

Not to be outdone, Emelyanov chimed in: "I, too, will see you at Mass at eleven o'clock."

I made my exit and went down to the lobby to await the outcome. I forced myself to read the German-language newspaper in order to relax, but I was still fidgeting an hour after the two old war horses had sat down to work out their differences. Ten-thirty came and went and there was still no sign of them. I knew they were still up there. I was sitting near the elevator and there was no way they could get out of that hotel without my seeing them. At ten forty-five they still had not appeared, and the delegates' Mass we had planned was due to start in fifteen minutes. I had to leave.

When I got to the cathedral, Lisa was giving the Vienna Boys' Choir their final instructions, and Frank was overseeing everything else. Frank and I had worked out a seating arrangement whereby I would meet the delegates at the door and walk them about halfway down the aisle and Frank would escort them from that point to their seats. It all went very smoothly except that at three minutes to eleven, neither McCone nor Emelyanov had arrived. For a fleeting moment I pictured them settling their differences with dueling pistols, the walls of our Viennese parlor were already red, and neither man would appear at the Mass.

At eleven o'clock I hurried back to the sacristy to stall Cardinal Koenig's entrance. He was already vested and ready to process to the altar. "Look, Your Eminence," I said, "we're expecting an American ambassador and a Russian ambassador to be here, and we want to put them up in the sanctuary because it is a very special day, and I'll tell you all about that later, but could you hold up the start of Mass until I give you the signal?" He had been through this sort of thing with me before. Very relaxed about it, he simply said, "No problem." I hurried back to the front entrance of the cathedral and waited. And waited.

A few eternal minutes later, in walked John McCone and his wife, Rosemary. As I walked him up the aisle, now half relieved, he turned to me and murmured, "You were right. He is a good person. We buried all the nonsense, and not only that, we made some important plans for the future, which I'll tell you about later." I escorted him halfway up the aisle and Frank took

Rosemary to a front pew seat and John to a chair in front of the altar. As I walked back, in came Emelyanov. I took him up the aisle, as I had McCone, and he told me the same thing that McCone had said, only in German. I thanked him and turned him over to Frank, who put him right next to McCone. The cardinal gave the usual three-minute homily, very much like the one I had written for him some years before. While he was talking, Emelyanov leaned over to McCone and said, "Very good speech by the cardinal. Nothing political."

The delegates there, observing the two representatives of the nuclear superpowers, could sense that peace had come and we could get back to the important work of the conference on Monday morning.

There were many, many human-interest events that affected those meetings of the International Atomic Energy Agency. One year Emelyanov asked me if he could bring a university colleague to our brunch. I invited him on the spot. The man's name was Alexandrov, and he was a prominent mathematician and a member of the Soviet Academy of Sciences. At the brunch I seated him next to Cardinal Koenig, who obliged Alexandrov by speaking Russian with him. At one point, when the Russian felt more at ease, he asked "a big favor" of the cardinal. "My mother lives in a little village on the Siberian border," Alexandrov began, "and she's a deep believer and churchgoer. They use a great deal of incense at her church, constantly swinging the censers, filling the place with smoke, and now they've run out of incense. They cannot possibly get any more of it in Russia, so I was wondering if you could send some over to the embassy. I'll pick it up there and get it to my mother and she will love you forever." The cardinal sent four pounds, enough at least for a long-term relationship if not for eternal love.

At the meetings one year I met Vyacheslav Molotov, who had once been the Foreign Minister of the Soviet Union. Having fallen from grace when I met him, he was on Emelyanov's atomic energy delegation, about three or four notches down from the top. I would run into Molotov every once in a while and greet him with

the German *Grüss' Gott,* which, of course, means God's greetings.
It is the customary Austrian expression for hello. But Molotov was
always a bit taken aback by that, although his wife was not fazed
at all. She would always say *Grüss' Gott* to me without missing a
step.

One Saturday afternoon Molotov called me up and said, "This
is Molotov."

"This is Hesburgh," I answered. "Molotov, what can I do for
you?"

"I called to apologize for being unable to come to your Mass
and brunch tomorrow," he said. "It was nice of you to invite me,
but something has come up that requires my presence."

"That's fine," I politely replied. "It was very nice of you to let
me know." He thanked me and hung up, and I laughed. It tickled
my fancy that a top Russian Communist, Molotov no less, called
me up to apologize for not coming to a Catholic Mass.

The rapprochement between McCone and Emelyanov paid off
when Khrushchev came to the United States in 1959 and took a
fairly extensive tour across our country, including a jaunt through
an Iowa corn field. The climax of his visit was a sit-down with
Eisenhower at Camp David. The top aides to each man on this
occasion were none other than McCone and Emelyanov. It was a
year after they had made peace with each other in Vienna.

Most international agreements take months, even years to complete, especially when they involve world powers who don't trust
each other. This one, though, probably set a record for speed,
because McCone and Emelyanov had grown to know and like
each other. They had agreed to work on some cooperative ventures
during the talk I had set up between them, and by the time they
met at Camp David the accords were pretty well along. They
involved delegations from each country visiting sites in the other
country to inspect the peaceful uses of atomic energy in action.
These included such places as power plants and uranium mines.

They were paired off for the discussions—Eisenhower and
Khrushchev in one room, McCone and Emelyanov in the other.
After a short time McCone and Emelyanov came out with two
copies of the cooperative program they had worked out, one in

English, the other in Russian. McCone handed the English version to Eisenhower and said, "I think you ought to sign this. It is for peace." Emelyanov handed the Russian version to Khrushchev and said the same thing to Khrushchev in Russian. Both Eisenhower and Khrushchev signed. Had it not been for the friendship that had developed between McCone and Emelyanov in Vienna, that program might never have materialized. But it held up all during the Cold War. Each year after that, the U.S. and U.S.S.R. delegations exchanged visits.

I developed another interesting relationship, strange as it may seem, with Leonid Zamyatin, a hard-liner who was an important member of the Russian delegation. For several years he had never spoken to me. He refused even to acknowledge me when I said hello. Perhaps he believed I posed a danger to the Party because I was friendly with Emelyanov. But somewhere along the line his wife became ill and I did a few nice things for her while she was recovering. I sent her flowers, a get-well card, and a promise of prayer. With those minor acts of kindness, Zamyatin's attitude toward me changed completely. After his wife recovered, he showered me with gifts—caviar, vodka, recordings of Russian music. Not only did he speak to me from then on; we became good friends. He later became director of Tass and spokesman of the Foreign Ministry. At present he is the Soviet ambassador to England.

These atomic energy meetings in Vienna also strengthened my own friendship with John McCone. Not long after the visit of the American scientists to Russia, McCone called me at Notre Dame. He said the Russians had treated the American group with exceptional courtesy and in an extraordinary gesture of cooperation had even revealed the production figures for their uranium mines. We obtained the uranium figures as the result of Emelyanov's direct intervention with Khrushchev, McCone said, and now Emelyanov was going to visit the Argonne National Laboratory outside Chicago, and he, McCone, wanted to make sure the Soviet was treated with utmost courtesy here. He was afraid that because Emelyanov was a Communist, the American press might try to embarrass or mistreat him in some way.

John asked me to go to Argonne, where I was a member of their advisory board, and do what I could to see that Emelyanov received good treatment. My primary job was to introduce Emelyanov, which for me was a pleasant task. Basically, I simply introduced him as a good friend of mine and a great man of peace. Then I sat down while the press asked Emelyanov their questions. Much to my relief and satisfaction, they didn't lay a glove on him.

There was always something to worry about or smooth over when you had Russians around during the Cold War era. A while after Emelyanov's visit, two Soviet scientists who worked with him came to the Argonne National Laboratory when I happened to be there for another meeting. I took the occasion to invite them to see Notre Dame. While they were taking their tour of Argonne, a State Department functionary with them informed me that I could not take them back to Notre Dame with me. When I asked him why, he said it was because they would have to go by the steel mills in Gary, Indiana. I couldn't believe it. The whole world knew those steel mills were there. What's more, there was nothing out of the ordinary about them. They were plain, old-fashioned, ugly steel mills. Even if there had been something special about them inside, the Russians certainly were not going to find out about it as they sped by in a car. I conveyed all this to the State Department official. "Well," he said, "you still can't take them to Notre Dame."

"Look," I said, "I have already invited them and they have accepted, and they're coming. If you want to lock me up in jail, go ahead and try." I took the two Russians back to Notre Dame with me, right past those steel mills, and I did not go to jail, nor did I ever hear anything more about it.

During the drive one of the Russians told me that he had just lost his wife. When we got to Notre Dame, I said I would offer a Mass for her in the basement chapel of Sacred Heart Church. He came to the Mass and afterward gave me a big hug, saying, *"Spasibo, spasibo,"* which in Russian means thank you, thank you.

I saw Zamyatin again in about 1970 when I was in Moscow for a meeting of the International Association of Universities. With nothing scheduled for Sunday, I decided to try to visit Zagorsk, which is about sixty miles outside of Moscow. A significant city in terms of history and religion, Zagorsk is considered the birthplace of Russia, and was, and still is, an important center of Russian Christianity. I had always wanted to go there when I was in Moscow, but could never find the time. I had also been warned that the standard tour was a great disappointment because the Russians would not allow tourists to leave their tour bus. I did not want to see Zagorsk that way. I decided to appeal to my old friend Zamyatin, now the head man at Tass. I also had another project in mind with which I thought Zamyatin could help. I just walked into the Tass building, and after arguing with some Soviet functionaries, my card was taken up and Zamyatin came bounding out to see me, with a big smile on his face.

In his private office he ordered tea and asked me why I was in Moscow. I told him about the university group meeting in Moscow. When he asked the polite question, "Is there anything I can do for you?" I seized the opportunity and said, "As a matter of fact there is." I said that I wanted to go to Zagorsk and that I did not want to see it from a tourist bus. He asked me when I wanted to go. I said Sunday.

"We don't like to take people there on Sunday," he said.

"I know that," I replied. "You don't want us to see twenty thousand people going to church."

"You always were difficult," he said, but with a smile. I explained that Sunday was the only day I could go and that I would like, if possible, to take two friends with me, John Ryan, the president of Indiana University, and Herman Wells, the former president. Zamyatin said he would send two young men from his department with us, because they needed to practice their English.

I then broached the more important favor without revealing too much beforehand. Could he set up a luncheon for me so that two of my friends who were important educators in the United States could meet Yeluchin, the Soviet Minister of Higher Education? My friends were Kingman Brewster, president of Yale; Richard Lyman, president of Stanford; and Mrs. Lyman. To round out the luncheon guest list, I said I would like my American friends also to meet my good Russian friends Emelyanov and Zamyatin himself.

Zamyatin at first gave me a hard time about the luncheon. First, he said Emelyanov was retired and out of touch. I replied that I had Emelyanov's phone number and would be happy to invite him myself. Then he said Yeluchin was on vacation. I smiled and said he could not be very far away because he had spoken to our university group just yesterday. Why couldn't he simply find out where Yeluchin was and ask him to come? Zamyatin shrugged his shoulders and picked up the phone on his desk. Two quick calls and both Emelyanov and Yeluchin agreed to lunch with us. At heart, Zamyatin was a good friend.

Sunday morning at nine o'clock two big black limousines all decked out with flags pulled up in front of our hotel and whisked us off toward Zagorsk. Our guides were the two young men from Tass and their wives. As we neared the town, we encountered a lot of traffic, but the drivers just leaned on their horns and everyone moved over to let us by. In Russia I guess they knew when to get out of the way. When we arrived at the church, there was a Mass going on and it was crowded with worshippers. We walked around as discreetly as we could, and I paused at the tomb of the Russian saint Sergei to say a prayer. A monk in a black stovepipe hat filled us in on the history of the place. At the monastery we toured the quarters of the patriarch and saw an extraordinary collection of icons which filled a large room. We had lunch and a nice chat with the archbishop, then returned to Moscow.

"That was one of the greatest days of my life," the wife of one of the fellows from Tass said. "Thanks for making it possible." Well, I was not a big man in Russia by any means, but I was as big as I needed to be with Zamyatin, and it was all because I had done a couple of small things when his wife was sick in Vienna.

The day of the luncheon we were picked up in big black limousines again and taken to a place called the Restaurant Praga. A private dining room on the second floor was set up for us when we arrived. Kingman Brewster, the Lymans, and I went in together and the first person we saw was this pudgy little fellow with two Hero of the State medals pinned to his suit. It was Emelyanov. He came right over and gave me a big bear hug. Then he planted a trinitarian kiss on me—left cheek, right cheek, forehead. Brewster and the Lymans were taken aback by this show of affection. Here was the former head of the Russian Atomic Energy Agency, his chest covered with stars and ribbons, and he was planting kisses all over an American priest.

The lunch was wonderful and the conversation never flagged. I sat between Emelyanov and Yeluchin and traded light barbs with both of them. At one point Emelyanov leaned over and said, "If this fellow gives you any trouble, just let me know, because I was his professor when he wrote his thesis and he had to babysit my daughter while I read it." Yeluchin actually blushed.

Once the eating and pleasantries were over, Brewster, Lyman, and I got down to business with the Soviet Minister of Higher Education. We told him that the best long-range course for avoiding war between our two countries was to help the Russian and American people get to know each other better. And the best way to accomplish this, we said, would be to take ten thousand 18- to 24-year-olds from each country each year and send them to the other country to study, learn the language, and live with families. In ten years, I pointed out, we would have one hundred thousand American students who knew the Russian culture and spoke the Russian language and one hundred thousand young Soviets who would know America. Living with a family for a year would allow these young people to develop close relationships in the other country; they would find surrogate mothers and fathers, sisters and brothers, and those close feelings would bring our nations closer together and wipe away so much of the misinformation, ignorance, and fear that existed.

Brewster, Lyman, and I were really wound up about this. We genuinely believed that such a program would make a war between the two countries virtually impossible. When we had finished, we said to Yeluchin, "Well, what do you say?"

Yeluchin's reply was: "We don't want your hippies." He was completely out of date, of course, because hippies were a thing of the past, and I told him that.

Neither Yeluchin nor anyone else in power ever took us up on the idea. They sent a few hundred older people at various times, but never any big numbers of young people. I have always been disappointed by that, because I think it could work. Maybe the idea will come of age under Gorbachev's plan to open up the Soviet Union to the Western world. Actually, in a small way we already have begun. Since 1988 we have had a few young Russians study at Notre Dame's Institute for International Peace Studies and they have recently formed a Notre Dame alumni club in Moscow.

The astounding recent changes in the Soviet Union under Gorbachev, affecting its domestic and foreign policy, its new outlook on human rights, its new view of political democracy, its new overtures of friendship toward the United States, all had their roots, I firmly believe, in the open communications and exchanges of ideas that developed through the few international agencies in which both the Soviets and the Americans took part. The International Atomic Energy Agency was only one of those groups in which Americans and Soviets came to know one another on a personal, human basis. Frank Folsom's silly little International Grandfathers Club in the IAEA made the subtle point that Soviet and American scientists and diplomats also were grandfathers who did not want ever to fear that their grandchildren might one day be incinerated by hydrogen bombs.

The cooperative plans and proposals being negotiated between President Gorbachev and President Bush in the 1990s had their origins in international conferences held over these past thirty years. Those were dark, icy days back then during the Cold War. Now, I believe, we are beginning to see the light at the end of the tunnel, and that light comes from the bright sunshine of truth, faith, trust, and friendship. Especially friendship.

SEVENTEEN

STARTING THE FUTURE

On JUNE 11, 1987, at nine o'clock in the morning, which was a month and two days after I delivered the President's Valedictory beamed from campus via satellite television to some fifty thousand alumni across the country and around the world, Ned Joyce and I left Notre Dame by the back entrance. A hundred or so well-wishers gathered for the occasion to see us pull out in a Skyline recreational vehicle for a long, unaccustomed vacation together. Since neither Ned nor I had ever been in such a home-on-wheels and neither of us knew how to cook, the betting in South Bend, Indiana, was that we would not get past Gary, eighty miles away. As we waved back to our friends and colleagues, I held up a sign in the window: "GARY OR BUST."

We had a year of great adventures ahead of us, all around the world. That will be the subject of another book.

Behind us, Ned and I left the work of thirty-five years together. The student body had doubled, while the faculty had tripled. The annual operating budget had grown from $6 million to $230 million; the endowment from $6 million to more than a half billion. Since 1952 we had tripled or quadrupled the space available in classrooms, libraries, laboratories, offices, and public spaces. Almost everything that existed on the campus in 1952 had either been renewed or demolished. Faculty salaries had grown from among the worst to the among the very best in the nation. Endowed and other scholarships had risen from $100,000 to more than $60 million annually. Just before we left, a new $300 million fund-raising campaign had been announced, and $247 million of that had already been pledged or given.

These are interesting, significant figures denoting growth and progress. But as Ned and I drove west, the reality of the Notre Dame that we had left was that of a great university, a warm, good place, getting better each year, thanks to the dedicated lives of thousands of people intimately involved. We had no doubt that we were leaving Notre Dame in the hands of great new leadership, too, in the persons of Father Edward Malloy, the new president; Father Bill Beauchamp, the new executive vice president; and all of the other officers of the university. I remembered the only advice on parting that I gave Monk Malloy: "Be yourself."

Ned and I both believed that the best gift we could give to the new administrative team was to disappear for a year, and then to slip back quietly and undertake some unobtrusive, nonadministrative tasks that might be useful to the university.

Now, having slipped quietly back on campus two years ago, as we had planned, I am prepared to advise my age peers that retirement is not as bad as many fear. Actually, it can be and has been exciting, fulfilling, productive, and not dull or boring at all. On my return, I found my old office desk, my books, and, best of all, my secretary of almost forty years, Helen Hosinski, moved to the thirteenth floor of the newly named (I tried to avoid it) Theodore M. Hesburgh Library. Ned Joyce occupied the office adjacent to and similar to mine. My new office fulfilled all my desires, with bookshelves from floor to ceiling and a window giving the best possible panoramic view of the Notre Dame campus with the gold dome and the Sacred Heart Church spire in the center.

STARTING THE FUTURE

When I was asked what I wanted to do in retirement, I replied (humbly) that I wanted to work on five ideas that I believed could change the world and profoundly affect all of humanity:

Peace in a nuclear age.

Human rights and justice worldwide.

Human development in terms of new economic, social, and political structures in the Third World.

Ecology, the next great threat to the survival and development of humanity.

Ecumenism, the bringing together in peace of all Christians, as well as all the Sons of Abraham—Jews, Christians, and Muslims who call Jerusalem a holy shrine to the one true God.

The first three ideas—peace, human rights, and human development—are intimately interrelated, since there can be no peace in the world without human rights and equitable development of the resources we all have to live with. As the old Latin adage goes, *opus justitiae pax*, peace is the work of justice. I am well aware that many sophisticated people have thought that all those commissions and committees working on peace, justice, and human rights were in fact toying with unrealistic, pie-in-the-sky dreams. But the Iron Curtain has been torn down, the Berlin Wall has been knocked down, the supposedly invulnerable dictators of Eastern Europe have been overthrown. Free elections, democratic reforms, and human rights are ideas that have never died and are now sweeping across the world we know.

The great, fearsome arsenals of nuclear warheads and the intricate systems of chemical and biological warfare are in the process of being eliminated for all time in the sweep of new enlightenment across our globe, led at this time by Mikhail Gorbachev. The fear of annihilation beyond our control is being abated. We have, indeed, started down this new road of peace, trust, and cooperation between East and West, which can only benefit men, women, and children everywhere in the world.

When the fear of mutual nuclear destruction is corralled and controlled, we will then turn the full force of our attention and ingenuity to the even broader task of preserving our own habitat, our own environment. At this time, which is only the beginning, we have begun to recognize the problems affecting our ecology. "We have met the enemy, and he is us." Pogo was right. Bad grammar but good sense.

It is we who have made our air unbreathable, our water undrinkable, our land sterile. It is we who have blithely turned a beautiful habitat into a garbage heap. We have polluted our rivers, lakes, and seas. We have even risked absolutely irreversible disaster by creating a greenhouse effect which threatens to destroy the earth's temperature balance and to eliminate the ozone layer that protects us from dangerous ultraviolet rays. We have chopped down and destroyed the forests that absorb noxious carbon dioxide and produce in return the very oxygen we breathe. Correcting these man-made threats to our planet is the role of ecology in our future. Recognizing the problems, of course, is not enough. We must now study what is best to do to reverse our ignorant foolishness of the past. And, most difficult of all, once we agree, we must actually take bold action and *do* what must be done.

The last great idea which has absorbed much of my life and will continue to do so is Pope Paul VI's dream of ecumenism, the bringing together of all Christians in a meaningful study of the facets of religion that bind us all together, rather than the differences that separate us. Like all great ideas, this, too, is an ongoing process in improving the quality of our lives. Ecumenism addresses the deepest desires in the soul of man in recognizing and accepting the fundamental truths and meaning of our existence on this earth.

Fortunately, upon my return to Notre Dame I did not have to start from scratch. During the latter years of my presidency, I had founded an institute or a center for study and action in each of these five areas. Each institute has a good executive director, which relieves me of administrative work and allows me, as chairman, to discuss the development of programs with the staff and a board of directors consisting of some of the best national and international advisers in each area. My primary responsibility with each of the institutes is to look after their survival and growth by raising needed funds for their development. Fortunately, I have a good head start, having already raised the money for their endowments. That runs into the millions, but is never enough.

During the last ten years or so of my presidency at Notre Dame, I was either involved or in contact with a wide variety of other institutes or centers devoted to international peace, human rights, Third World development, ecology, and ecumenism. In fact, upon my retirement I took a count and found that I am on the board or advisory council of about fifty of these centers and institutes around the world. This has helped me keep our own centers and institutes well informed on what is being done elsewhere, so that we will not waste time in duplicating other programs or reinventing the wheel.

In 1987 we had a pivotal breakthrough in the development of these independent study institutes. Mrs. Joan Kroc, the widow of the founder of the McDonald's restaurant chain, who had endowed our Institute for International Peace Studies, visited Notre Dame to meet with our faculty and scholars of the Peace and Kellogg institutes. At the end of her visit, she asked me, "What do you really need now to consolidate these programs?"

I said that we needed to pull them all together in one place because that would give them and the international dimensions of Notre Dame visibility and impact.

Being a very bright lady, Mrs. Kroc said, "You mean a building, don't you?"

"Yes," I admitted.

"But I don't believe in giving money for buildings."

"That's your decision," I said. "After all, it is your money and you already have been very generous in supporting our peace program, which we could not have done alone." Mrs. Kroc knew of my long-held belief that universities should support special institutes from specific endowments only, and not from tuition income. We let it go at that and I drove her to the airport for her flight home to San Diego.

The next morning Mrs. Kroc phoned me. "I thought about your building all the way home," she said. "You really do need it, so start planning it. The day you break ground, I will send you six million dollars."

When I thanked her, she added, "But there's one condition. You have to call it the Hesburgh Center for International Studies."

I reminded her that the university's trustees had just renamed the main campus library in my honor upon my retirement. "I really do not want my name on another building," I said. "Why don't we call it the Kroc Center for International Studies?"

"I don't want my name on a building either," she said.

"Then we're even."

"Not quite," she retorted. "I have the money: no Hesburgh Center, no building."

I agreed because I did want that building, even if it had to have my name on it. She was very convincing and enormously generous as well. Someday, I keep hoping, we will put the Joan Kroc name on the peace program she made possible.

A wonderful complex of buildings is now taking shape, and sometime next year we will have a unique International Center, with flags of many nations flying there, at the entrance to the campus. It will signify that Notre Dame is fully engaged in promoting peace and justice all over the world.

These five purpose-directed institutes will remain at the top of my "to do" list of work as long as I am able to carry on. But they have not and will not consume all my time in retirement. I have other long-standing commitments that, happily, I am able to continue. This past year I gave five guest lectures to classes at Notre Dame and met with ten alumni groups around the country and abroad. I was in Europe for meetings several times, in Moscow twice, in Latin America twice, and I have lectured at a dozen or so other colleges and universities. I offered Sunday-night Mass in most of our twenty-nine residence hall chapels on request, and I have had individual meetings with hundreds of graduate and undergraduate students on a wide variety of subjects, most of them personal. Mail pours into my office every day from all over the world, and it all gets answered. The phone continues to ring, connecting me to colleagues and friends on both coasts. Articles are requested just about every month and they are written. I am finishing one book and about to begin another. And who knows what will come in tomorrow?

Retirement is wonderful!

Yes, I am overcommitted. But that has always been the pattern of my life. I cannot remember a time when I did not have a dozen jobs to do at the same time. As the years went on and my commitments to worthy causes grew, I learned how to cope with this supercharged style of life. When it became plain that I had to cut back and give up some of my activities, I began by giving up golf and then bridge. They consumed too much time.

The next rule in coping with an excess of personal commitments is to do what you are doing flat out, giving it your full, undivided attention. Don't worry about what you just did. When you leave it, leave it. Don't worry about what you have to do tomorrow; time enough for that tomorrow. Give the present task full attention, with no concern for what is coming up next in line or what has just been passed.

The real secret to handling the demands upon you is possessing inner peace. No matter what the problems, the tensions, the pressures, one can only help oneself by thinking clearly and acting calmly and resolutely. This cannot be done without inner peace, born of prayer, especially to the Holy Spirit, in search of light, inspiration, and courage. I have a simple three-word prayer that has served me well for many, many years: "Come, Holy Spirit." It has never failed me.

Operating widely outside of the university for so many years, as I have, requires talented and dependable help inside. That support has always been there for me at Notre Dame from Ned Joyce, Provost Tim O'Meara, all of our other vice presidents, and, of course, the center rock for the fulcrum of my activities, my ever-faithful, astute personal secretary, Helen Hosinski. Of course, I have always done my best to be faithful to each and every one of them, for fidelity begets fidelity, and we have all worked in tandem for the same purpose—for the greater good and benefit of Notre Dame and her students. God bless them all.

So, even in retirement, the pattern of activity continues. I am always amused when someone asks me, "How are you enjoying your retirement?" The honest answer is that I am enjoying it very much. I do often bite off more than I can reasonably chew. So I chew a bit longer and harder. Somehow, some way, everything eventually gets done, but often not as quickly as I would prefer. It is not, I assure you, that I am slowing down. It is that the work is piling up faster and faster. The mail pile is a bit too high, the phone messages back up too far, my 2 A.M. bedtime comes too quickly every night. Then there is that talk to give in Washington and the meeting in New York and . . .

In the midst of all this last year, Creed Black, president of the Knight Foundation, cajoled me into being cochairman of the Knight Commission on Intercollegiate Athletics with my old friend Bill Friday, president emeritus of the University of North Carolina at Chapel Hill. Our task: to clean up the current moral mess in so-called big-time football and basketball. Between us, Bill Friday and I have sixty-five years of experience in integrity on the playing fields of a public and a private university. We both know we have our work cut out for us. Big-time football and big-time basketball, with television rights and box-office receipts reaching into the millions of dollars of profit, are replete with temptations to win and become "Number One" at any cost. There have been reform movements going back to President Theodore Roosevelt, and they have all failed. Knowing this, or despite knowing all this, Bill Friday and I have such reverence for universities that we agreed to try. Wish us luck.

Then Derek Bok, president of Harvard University for almost twenty years, called. He asked me to "stand for election to Harvard's Board of Overseers," which is its board of directors. I admired Derek and owed him a favor, and, yes, knowing the time and travel involved, I agreed, and, yes, I was elected by a resounding vote, and I will serve there. And when a small, wonderful Lutheran school, St. Olaf College in Northfield, Minnesota, celebrates its one hundredth birthday and asks a Catholic priest to give its commencement address to the graduating class of 1990, what can you say? "I'm too busy"? Never.

So that's what I am doing today—what needs to be done as best as I can do it. At seventy-three, I don't feel a year older than I did at thirty-nine. But the joints are beginning to creak.

All of which brings me back to where I began. Beneath it all, or perhaps above it all, I am what I am: a Catholic priest. I enjoy being a Catholic priest. I enjoy offering Mass each day for the whole world. I relish praying the daily Breviary, especially now that it is shorter than before, a mere half hour, and in English. After forty-seven years of priesthood, I still appreciate belonging to everyone, not just Catholics, and doing what I can to respond to human needs. And those needs include the spiritual longing for freedom, human dignity, and basic human rights, as well as the physical necessities of adequate food, housing, education, medicine, and employment, especially in the developing countries of the Third World.

One of the greatest modern heresies that I hear from time to time is that in our modern world one person cannot make a difference. I do not believe that for one moment. I know it is factually inaccurate. And I never hesitate to say so, especially to our students at Notre Dame. One person or group of persons can make an enormous difference in our lives and our way of living. Dr. Albert Schweitzer did, Rachel Carson did, Mother Teresa did, Tom Dooley did, and Jim Grant did. History is replete with heroic people who realized that they could make a difference, and did—despite the conventional wisdom of the day.

I have lived long enough to see real, significant changes made for the good in our lives, and I have been fortunate enough to have participated in some of them. I have seen apartheid in our country, woven into the law of our land for more than two hundred years, eliminated virtually overnight by the passage of one law, the great Omnibus Civil Rights Act of 1964. I have seen six million black Americans unable to vote suddenly franchised by the Civil Rights Voting Act of 1965. We went in this country from six elected black officials to more than six thousand, including the governor of Virginia and many prominent mayors of our major cities.

I have seen a million Cambodian refugees, many of them children without parents, destined to die in a war zone at the Thai border, without food, medicine, or shelter. A group of dedicated religious leaders of all faiths raised half a billion dollars, provided volunteers to render service in Cambodia, and delivered some sixty thousand tons of seed, enabling those refugees and a whole nation to survive. Jim Grant, the talented director of UNICEF, initiated a program called Child Survival, based on five inexpensive, lifesaving treatments, and has saved two and a half million endangered children a year, mostly in the Third World, who otherwise would have died.

We are all seeing in amazement the vast changes now sweeping the Soviet Union and the Eastern European bloc of nations. For years Andrei Gromyko walked out of meetings every time the problem of human rights was raised with the Soviets. Now it is a top-priority item on the agenda of reform in the Soviet Union. Last year the top legal establishment in Moscow asked me, a Catholic priest, to give them a lecture in the conference room of the Soviet Central Committee on the provision for religious freedom in the First Amendment to our constitution. As a result of the new era of cooperation between East and West, the Soviet legal establishment is revising its own constitution. So far, more than eight hundred political prisoners have been released unconditionally from Soviet prisons. There is real change in the air, and it is spreading all over the world.

And so it goes. The challenge today is having enough imagination and creativity to guide these changes toward democracy, freedom, and justice.

Looking back over the years of my life, I can see clearly what we needed most, and need now: faith, vision, courage, imagination, and ingenuity. Education should lift personal expectations, not debase them. There are great social problems everywhere, but that should not discourage people. Our universities can and should help in the search for solutions to these problems. They can and should inspire students to participate in the great causes of our day. One person can make a difference. And no one knows what he or she is capable of until he or she tries.

I cannot encapsulate here all that the University of Notre Dame has meant to me and to my life. I can only try by repeating one sentence I spoke from the heart in my valedictory address: *"To have been president of such a company of valiant searching souls, to have shared with you the peace, the mystery, the optimism, the joie de vivre, the ongoing challenge, the ever-youthful ebullient vitality, and, most of all, the deep and abiding caring that characterize this special place and all of its people, young and old, this is a blessing that I hope to carry with me into eternity, when that time comes."*

These are the thoughts and ideas that have driven me through life. We all suffer doses of discouragement and disillusionment, but those are distractions for the most part, not driving forces. I believe that with faith in God and in our fellow humans, we can aim for the heights of human endeavor, and that we can reach them, too. Optimism is often thwarted, hopes dashed, and faith threatened, but we will never know what heights we can achieve unless we try.

I guess that I would like my life to say, to the young people especially: He believed, he hoped, he tried, he failed often enough, but with God's grace, he often accomplished more than he rationally could have dreamed. Remember for me those wonderful words of Scripture: "God has chosen the weak of this world to confound the strong." So we are weak. No matter.

ACKNOWLEDGMENTS

I would like to thank several persons without whose help this book would never have been born.

Patricia Kossmann, formerly of Doubleday, urged me every year for a decade to write my memoirs. I was always too busy.

Dick Conklin, assistant vice president for university relations at Notre Dame, did, however, persuade me to do some oral history, and several interviews with him in 1982 and an update in 1989 resulted in more than a thousand pages transcribed from audiotape. This gave us the core of an autobiography.

When I finally succumbed to Pat's blandishments, a 1958 Notre Dame alumnus and professional writer, Jerry Reedy, was enlisted to organize the oral history material into book form, which he did after some interviewing of me on his own. At this point we called upon Alvin Moscow, a noted biographer, whose experienced hand helped compress the text and focus the message of the book.

Throughout the process, Dick Conklin and I carefully reviewed and edited the evolving book, to the point where I for one became weary of reading about myself.

Lastly, I am deeply grateful to Doubleday deputy publisher Bill Barry and his colleagues for their steadfast encouragement of, and commitment to, the book.

This is essentially a memory book. I am conscious of the fact that memory tends to be benign when one is recalling one's own life. I have accumulated a small mountain of archival material, but I did not relish the thought of spending most of whatever years the Good Lord may still grant me buried in the footnotes of the past. Hence my memory book. Whatever mistakes it may contain are attributable only to me. One last thought: I tried to tell a true story without consciously hurting anyone. If I failed in any particular case, my apology is sincere beforehand.

Again, thanks to one and all who so generously and capably helped this book to see the light of day. We now all hope it will have a good life, which for a book means it will enter into other's lives.

Theodore M. Hesburgh, C.S.C.
Notre Dame, Indiana
July 11, 1990

INDEX

INDEX